POL MARTIN

—

A GUIDE TO

MODERN COOKING

OVER 620 PHOTOGRAPHS IN FULL COLOR
EASY STEP-BY-STEP TECHNIQUES
A SPECIAL MICROWAVE SECTION
SMART AND SIMPLE RECIPES
NUTRITIONAL DATA FOR EACH RECIPE
CALORIE, CARBOHYDRATE, PROTEIN, FAT AND FIBER CONTENT

B R I M A R

*The author wishes to thank
Melissa du Fretay for her invaluable
assistance.*

Cover Design
Zapp Studio

Graphic Design
Barsalo & Associés

Photographs by
Pol Martin (Ontario) Ltd Studio

BRIMAR PUBLISHING INC.
338 Saint Antoine St. East
Montreal, Canada H2Y 1A3
Tel.: (514) 954-1441
Fax: (514) 954-1443

Legal deposit: Second Quarter 1989
Bibliothèque nationale du Québec
National Library of Canada

The information in this book is true and complete
to the best of our knowledge. All recommendations
are made without any guarantees on the part of the
author and the publisher. They disclaim all liability
in connection with the use of this information.

ISBN: 2-920845-53-5

Printed and bound in Canada

CONTENTS

INDEX

†: Microwave Recipe

KEBAB IT !

KEBAB IT!

It seems to me that shish kebabs have been getting the short end of the stick because the rare time you do come across a kebab dinner is usually in a restaurant and with only a selection of two on the menu! Now don't you agree that it would be far more interesting (and less expensive) to experience the delight of scallop kebabs nestled on a bed of fried parsley? I thought you would and that is the reason for this book which is just brimming with innovative and exciting kebab recipes for the home. For those of you who have yet to make kebabs before, be assured that it is easy and little effort is needed for success especially if you have these utensils: a selection of skewers in metal and wood, a large ovenproof platter and a very sharp knife for accurate trimming and shaping. I urge you to be creative with these recipes and by all means serve them for lunch as well as dinner. Besides fantastic meat and fish kebabs you will find some super vegetable kebabs that are ideal for spicing up an otherwise routine meal and a selection of fun desserts that can add the finishing touch. So with your skewers in hand, off we go to the kitchen — let's prepare something different tonight!

Mustard Marinade for Meat or Fish

1 SERVING	207 CALORIES	0g CARBOHYDRATE
0g PROTEIN	23g FAT	0g FIBER

1 ¼ cups	(300 ml) olive oil
5 tbsp	(75 ml) Dijon mustard
2	garlic cloves, smashed and chopped
1 tsp	(5 ml) tarragon
	juice 1 lemon
	few drops Tabasco sauce
	salt and pepper

Mix all ingredients together in small bowl. Pour marinade over chosen meat or fish and refrigerate 30 minutes.

In preparation for cooking, drain marinade and reserve for basting.

This marinade is strong enough to use just as flavouring without marinating 30 minutes. Keep this in mind if you are short of time.

Marinade for Lamb or Fish

1 SERVING	175 CALORIES	1g CARBOHYDRATE
0g PROTEIN	19g FAT	0g FIBER

1 cup	(250 ml) olive oil
3	garlic cloves, smashed and chopped
3	shallots, finely chopped
½ cup	(125 ml) lemon juice
½ tsp	(2 ml) crushed rosemary
½ tsp	(2 ml) oregano
	salt and pepper

Mix all ingredients together in small bowl. Pour marinade over chosen lamb or fish and refrigerate overnight.

In preparation for cooking, drain marinade and reserve for basting.

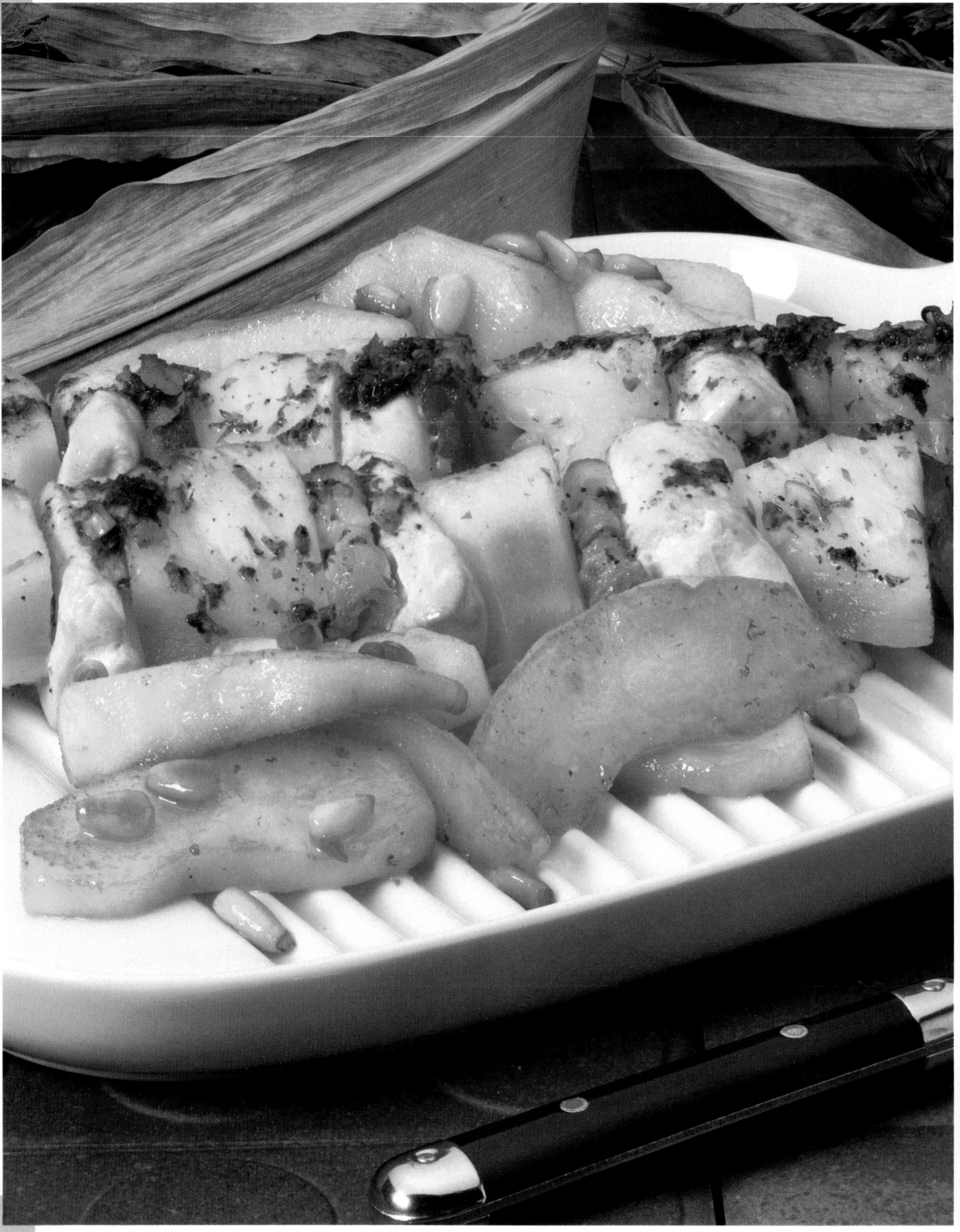

Pineapple Chicken Kebabs

(serves 4)

1 SERVING	321 CALORIES	12g CARBOHYDRATE
21g PROTEIN	21g FAT	0.4g FIBER

2	chicken breasts, skinned, halved and boned
½	pineapple, cut in 1 in (2.5 cm) pieces
5	slices cooked bacon, cut in half
3 tbsp	(45 ml) butter
2	garlic cloves, smashed and chopped
2 tbsp	(30 ml) chopped parsley
	few drops Worcestershire sauce
	salt and pepper

Preheat oven to 450°F (240°C).

Cut chicken in 1 in (2.5 cm) pieces. Alternate along with pineapple and bacon on skewers; set aside.

Melt butter in small saucepan over medium heat. Stir in garlic, parsley and Worcestershire sauce.

Set skewers on ovenproof platter and baste with melted butter mixture. Season well with pepper.

Cook 12 minutes in oven, turning skewers over once or twice. Baste again if desired.

These kebabs serve well with sautéed apples and pine nuts.

The first step in making kebabs is to prepare the ingredients as directed in the recipe.

Alternate chicken, pineapple and bacon on skewers.

A simple mixture of butter, garlic, parsley and Worcestershire sauce will give a delicious flavour to kebabs.

It is important to baste the ingredients evenly before cooking.

Marinated Drumsticks

(serves 4)

1 SERVING	277 CALORIES	13g CARBOHYDRATE
27g PROTEIN	13g FAT	1.4g FIBER

2 lb	(900 g) chicken drumsticks
1 tbsp	(15 ml) Trinidad-style hot sauce
1 tsp	(5 ml) Worcestershire sauce
2 tbsp	(30 ml) oil
1	green pepper, in bite-size pieces
2	bananas (not too ripe) peeled and sliced thick
	salt and pepper

Preheat oven to 450°F (240°C).

Score drumsticks with knife and place on plate.

Sprinkle hot sauce, Worcestershire, oil, salt and pepper over chicken.

Place chicken on skewers and cook 10 minutes in oven. Turn skewers over and cook another 10 minutes.

Remove drumsticks from skewers and let cool.

Alternate chicken, green pepper and banana on skewers; place on ovenproof platter. Cook 8 minutes in oven.

Serve with a spicy sauce.

Score drumsticks with knife and place on plate.

Place chicken on skewers and cook 20 minutes in oven.

Sprinkle hot sauce, Worcestershire, oil, salt and pepper over chicken.

Add green pepper and banana to skewers with chicken; finish cooking 8 minutes.

Indonesian Chicken

(serves 4)

1 SERVING	381 CALORIES	7g CARBOHYDRATE
23g PROTEIN	29g FAT	1.0g FIBER

2	chicken breasts, skinned, halved and boned
½ cup	(125 ml) chopped walnuts
½ cup	(125 ml) lime juice
1 cup	(250 ml) hot chicken stock
2	garlic cloves, smashed and chopped
1 tbsp	(15 ml) olive oil
1 cup	(250 ml) sour cream
2 tbsp	(30 ml) chopped chives
	salt and pepper

Cut chicken into ½ in (1.2 cm) pieces. Place in bowl along with walnuts, lime juice, chicken stock, garlic, salt and pepper; marinate 2 hours in refrigerator.

Thread chicken on skewers and place on ovenproof platter. Reserve ⅓ of marinade.

Baste skewers with oil and broil 6 to 7 minutes each side in oven 6 in (15 cm) from top element.

Before kebabs are done, mix reserved marinade with sour cream and chives. Serve with chicken.

Spicy Chicken Breasts

(serves 4)

1 SERVING	290 CALORIES	23g CARBOHYDRATE
27g PROTEIN	10g FAT	1.2g FIBER

¾ lb	(375 g) mushroom caps, cleaned
¼ tsp	(1 ml) lemon juice
1 lb	(500 g) chicken breasts, skinned, halved and boned
1 tbsp	(15 ml) Worcestershire sauce
2	beaten eggs
1 cup	(250 ml) breadcrumbs
1	red pepper, in bite-size pieces
	Mexican hot sauce to taste
	few drops melted butter

Preheat oven to 450°F (240°C).

Place mushroom caps in bowl and sprinkle with lemon juice; set aside.

Cut chicken in 1 in (2.5 cm) pieces and place in another bowl; add Worcestershire sauce and hot sauce. Marinate 15 minutes on countertop.

Pour beaten eggs into large bowl. Using tongs add chicken pieces; mix until coated.

Roll chicken in breadcrumbs and alternate along with mushroom caps and red pepper on skewers.

Place skewers on ovenproof platter and sprinkle with melted butter. Cook 15 minutes in oven, turning skewers over once or twice.

Marinate chicken pieces in Worcestershire and hot sauces. Place bowl on counter for 15 minutes.

Roll chicken in breadcrumbs.

Coat marinated chicken in beaten eggs.

Alternate chicken, mushroom caps and red pepper on skewers.

Garlic Wing Kebabs

(serves 4)

1 SERVING	251 CALORIES	14g CARBOHYDRATE
15g PROTEIN	15g FAT	0.9g FIBER

32	chicken wings, middle section only
3	garlic cloves, smashed and chopped
½ cup	(125 ml) barbecue sauce
2 tbsp	(30 ml) honey
1 tbsp	(15 ml) lemon juice
2 tbsp	(30 ml) oil
1 tbsp	(15 ml) wine vinegar
½ tsp	(2 ml) brown sugar
16	green onion sticks, 1½ in (4 cm) long
16	zucchini sticks, 1½ in (4 cm) long
	salt and pepper

Place wings, garlic, barbecue sauce, honey, lemon juice, oil, vinegar and brown sugar in bowl; marinate 30 minutes in refrigerator.

Drain and reserve marinade.

Alternate onion, chicken and zucchini on skewers; place in ovenproof dish. Baste with marinade and season well. Broil 12 minutes 6 in (15 cm) from top element; turn over twice.

Change oven setting to 450°F (240°C) and finish cooking 7 minutes close to bottom of oven. Season during cooking.

Serve kebabs in baskets if available.

Note that the middle section of the wings should be used for the kebabs. Use remaining wing parts for other recipes.

Marinate wings in garlic, barbecue sauce, honey, lemon juice, oil, vinegar and brown sugar.

Mid-Wing Skewers

(serves 4)

1 SERVING	153 CALORIES	4g CARBOHYDRATE
14g PROTEIN	9g FAT	0g FIBER

32	chicken wings, middle section only
12 oz	(355 ml) can beer
2	green onions, thinly sliced
½ cup	(125 ml) catsup
2 tbsp	(30 ml) HP sauce
1 tbsp	(15 ml) soya sauce
1 tbsp	(15 ml) finely chopped fresh ginger
1 tbsp	(15 ml) wine vinegar
¼ tsp	(1 ml) Tabasco sauce
1 tbsp	(15 ml) honey
1 tbsp	(15 ml) oil
	salt and pepper

Preheat oven to 450°F (240°C).

Reserve leftover parts of wings for other recipes. Place the middle sections in bowl; add beer and green onions. Marinate 1 hour in refrigerator.

Meanwhile, mix catsup, HP sauce, soya sauce, ginger, vinegar, Tabasco and honey together; set aside.

Drain chicken and discard marinade. Fill skewers with chicken and place in ovenproof dish; season well and baste with oil.

Cook skewers 18 minutes in middle of oven; turn over twice.

Remove from oven and baste with catsup mixture. Change oven setting to Grill (Broil) and place dish on rack 4 in (10 cm) from top element; broil 5 to 6 minutes.

Turn skewers over, baste again and finish broiling 5 to 6 minutes.

Remove chicken from skewers and accompany with baked potatoes.

Marinate chicken in beer and onions for 1 hour in refrigerator.

Mix catsup, HP sauce, soya sauce, ginger, vinegar, Tabasco and honey together; set aside. This mixture will give chicken lots of flavour.

Chicken, Onions and Zucchini

(serves 4)

1 SERVING	166 CALORIES	8g CARBOHYDRATE
20g PROTEIN	6g FAT	1.4g FIBER

1 lb	(500 g) chicken breasts, skinned, halved and boned
1 tbsp	(15 ml) chopped fresh ginger
3 tbsp	(45 ml) soya sauce
1	garlic clove, smashed and chopped
8	pearl onions, blanched
1	yellow pepper, in bite-size pieces
8	small pieces zucchini
1	red pepper, in bite-size pieces
4	lemon wedges
1 tbsp	(15 ml) oil
	salt and pepper

Cut chicken into ½ in (1.2 cm) cubes. Place in bowl along with ginger, soya sauce and garlic; marinate 30 minutes in refrigerator.

Drain chicken and reserve marinade.

Alternate chicken, vegetables and lemon wedges on skewers. Place in ovenproof dish and season well. Baste with marinade and sprinkle with oil.

Broil 8 minutes in oven 6 in (15 cm) from top element. Turn skewers over once and baste with marinade twice.

Marinate chicken in ginger, soya sauce and garlic for 30 minutes in refrigerator.

Alternate chicken, vegetables and lemon wedges on skewers. The lemon will give a special flavour.

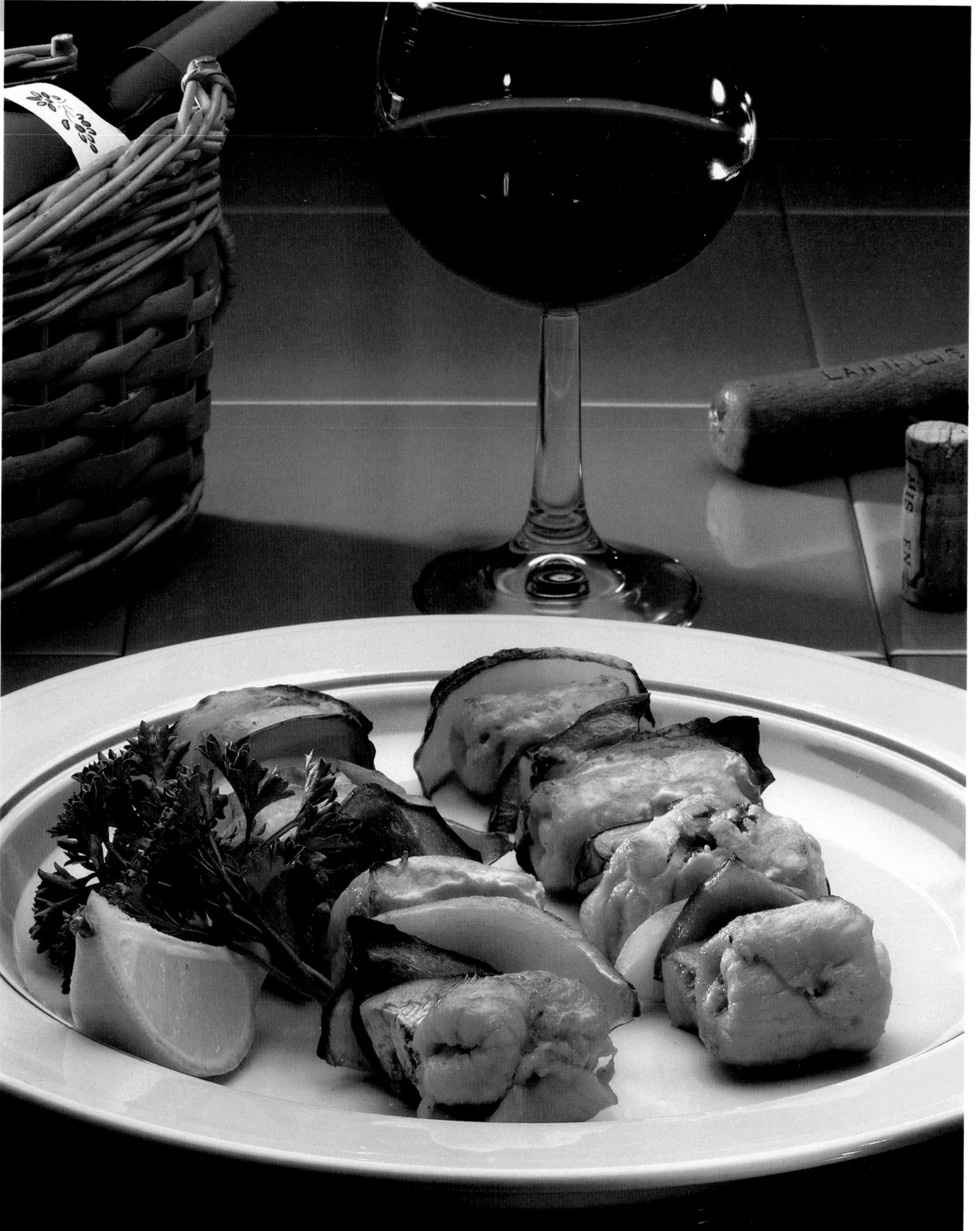

Stuffed Turkey on Skewers

(serves 4)

1 SERVING	321 CALORIES	4g CARBOHYDRATE
29g PROTEIN	21g FAT	0.7g FIBER

3 tbsp	(45 ml) butter
2	shallots, finely chopped
¼ tsp	(1 ml) tarragon
¼ lb	(125 g) mushrooms, finely chopped
1 tbsp	(15 ml) chopped parsley
3 tbsp	(45 ml) heavy cream
16	thin slices raw turkey breast, flattened
¼	red onion, in pieces
1	green pepper, in bite-size pieces
1 tbsp	(15 ml) lemon juice
	salt and pepper

Preheat oven to 400°F (200°C).

Heat 2 tbsp (30 ml) butter in frying pan. Cook shallots and tarragon 2 minutes.

Add mushrooms and parsley; continue cooking 4 minutes over medium-high heat. Season generously.

Pour in cream, mix and cook 2 to 3 minutes over high heat. Remove from heat and cool slightly.

1 The easiest way to flatten the turkey slices is with a mallet on waxed paper.

2 After shallots and tarragon have cooked for 2 minutes, add mushrooms and parsley; continue cooking 4 minutes over medium-high heat.

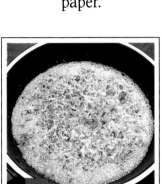

3 Pour in cream; mix and cook 2 to 3 minutes over high heat. Remove and cool slightly.

4 Spread about 1 tbsp (15 ml) of mushroom mixture over meat. Fold sides and roll.

Lay turkey slices flat on counter; spread about 1 tbsp (15 ml) of mushroom mixture over meat. Fold one side over and then the other side so that they overlap slightly. Start at one end and roll.

Alternate turkey rolls with onion and green pepper on skewers. Set aside in ovenproof platter.

Mix remaining butter with lemon juice; brush this over kebabs and season well.

Change oven setting to Grill (Broil) and cook 12 minutes 6 in (15 cm) from top element. Turn skewers over once and baste occasionally.

Strips of Beef and Vegetables

(serves 4)

1 SERVING	389 CALORIES	12g CARBOHYDRATE
47g PROTEIN	17g FAT	3.7g FIBER

2 tbsp	(30 ml) olive oil
1½ lb	(750 g) sirloin tip
3	garlic cloves, smashed and chopped
1	head broccoli (in flowerets), blanched 4 minutes
16	large cherry tomatoes
½	red onion, cut in 2 and sectioned
	juice 1 lemon
	salt and pepper

Heat 1 tsp (5 ml) oil in frying pan. When very hot, add whole piece of meat and sear on all sides. Season well.

Slice beef into ½ in (1.25 cm) strips. Place in bowl along with remaining oil, garlic and lemon juice. Marinate 15 minutes.

Drain beef and reserve marinade. Fold pieces in half and alternate on skewers along with vegetables.

Place on ovenproof platter and broil 6 minutes 6 in (15 cm) from top element. Turn skewers over once and baste several times with marinade.

Place remaining oil, garlic and lemon juice in bowl.
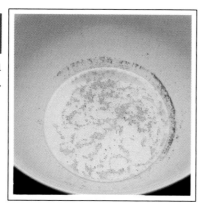

Drain beef and reserve marinade.

Add strips of beef and marinate 15 minutes.

Fold pieces of meat in half and alternate on skewers along with vegetables.

Meat and Potato Kebabs

(serves 4)

1 SERVING	441 CALORIES	27g CARBOHYDRATE
45g PROTEIN	17g FAT	4.8g FIBER

1 ½ lb	(750 g) sirloin steak, in 1 in (2.5 cm) long strips about ¾ in (2 cm) thick
3 tbsp	(45 ml) soya sauce
2	garlic cloves, smashed and chopped
2 tbsp	(30 ml) vegetable oil
16	small new round potatoes, peeled and cooked
2 tbsp	(30 ml) catsup
1 tbsp	(15 ml) honey
	salt and pepper

Preheat oven to 400°F (200°C).

Place beef, soya sauce, garlic and oil in bowl; marinate 15 minutes.

Alternate beef and potatoes on skewers; place on ovenproof platter.

Mix catsup with honey and brush over skewers; season generously. Broil 7 minutes in oven 6 in (15 cm) from top element. Turn skewers over once.

Serve with salad.

Beef Marinated in Bourbon

(serves 4)

1 SERVING 53g PROTEIN	435 CALORIES 19g FAT	13g CARBOHYDRATE 1.5g FIBER

2 lb	(900 g) sirloin tip, in 1 ¼ in (3 cm) cubes
¼ cup	(50 ml) bourbon
2 tbsp	(30 ml) soya sauce
1 tsp	(5 ml) Dijon mustard
¼ tsp	(1 ml) Worcestershire sauce
12	blanched mushroom caps
12	bite-size pieces bok choy (stem only)
2	white onions, cut in 4, blanched and sectioned
2	large carrots, cut in ½ in (1.2 cm) lengths and blanched
2 tbsp	(30 ml) vegetable oil
	salt and pepper

Marinate sirloin in mixture of bourbon, soya sauce, mustard and Worcestershire sauce for 1 hour.

Drain beef and reserve marinade. Alternate beef and vegetables on skewers and place on ovenproof platter; brush with oil.

Season skewers generously and broil 4 minutes in oven 4 in (10 cm) from top element. Turn skewers over once.

Move skewers 6 in (15 cm) from top element; finish broiling another 4 minutes turning skewers once. Baste with a bit of marinade.

Veal in Beer Marinade

(serves 4)

1 SERVING 13g PROTEIN	186 CALORIES 10g FAT	11g CARBOHYDRATE 1.4g FIBER

½ lb	(250 g) veal tenderloin, sliced in ¼ in (0.65 cm) thick rounds
1 cup	(250 ml) beer
1 tbsp	(15 ml) chopped fresh ginger
¼ tsp	(1 ml) Tabasco sauce
¼ tsp	(1 ml) Trinidad-style hot sauce
12	green onions, in 1 ¼ in (3 cm) long sticks
1	small zucchini, sliced ½ in (1.2 cm) thick
1	red pepper, in bite-size pieces
1 tbsp	(15 ml) vegetable oil
1 tbsp	(15 ml) honey
	salt and pepper

Marinate veal in mixture of beer, ginger, Tabasco, hot sauce and salt and pepper. Refrigerate 1 hour.

Drain veal and reserve marinade.

Alternate veal (fold each piece in two) along with onion sticks, zucchini and red pepper on skewers. Place in ovenproof dish and baste with marinade; sprinkle with oil and honey.

Broil 16 minutes in oven 6 in (15 cm) from top element. Turn skewers over twice.

Serve on rice.

1 Marinate veal in mixture of beer, ginger, Tabasco, hot sauce and salt and pepper. Refrigerate 1 hour.

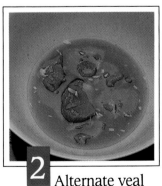

2 Alternate veal pieces folded in two along with vegetables on skewers.

Veal Scallopini on Skewers

(serves 4)

1 SERVING	216 CALORIES	6g CARBOHYDRATE
12g PROTEIN	16g FAT	0g FIBER

4	veal scallopini from leg
3 tbsp	(45 ml) olive oil
2 tbsp	(30 ml) maple syrup
¼ tsp	(1 ml) tarragon
1 tbsp	(15 ml) wine vinegar
	few drops Trinidad-style hot sauce
	salt and pepper
	lemon juice to taste
	paprika to taste

If butcher has not already pounded veal, place pieces between two sheets of waxed paper. Flatten with mallet until very thin. Trim away fat and season generously.

Roll scallopini lengthwise keeping meat fairly taut. Secure each roll on very long skewer. Refer to Photo 2 for visual help.

Place skewers on ovenproof platter and set aside.

Mix oil, maple syrup, tarragon, vinegar, hot sauce, salt, pepper and lemon juice together.

Brush mixture over skewers and broil 7 minutes in oven 6 in (15 cm) from top element.

Turn skewers over and season with paprika; baste with maple syrup mixture. Continue broiling 7 minutes.

Remove veal from skewers.

Serve with green vegetables and garnish with broiled tomatoes.

If butcher has not already pounded veal, place pieces between two sheets of waxed paper. Flatten with mallet until very thin.

Depending on the length of your veal rolls the skewer need only be inserted twice in order to keep meat in place.

Veal and Mushroom Caps

(serves 4)

1 SERVING	285 CALORIES	4g CARBOHYDRATE
20g PROTEIN	21g FAT	0.6g FIBER

½ lb	(250 g) veal tenderloin, in bite-size pieces
12	mushroom caps, cleaned
12	bite-size chunks of celery
8	slices red onion
¼ cup	(50 ml) wine vinegar
2	garlic cloves, smashed and chopped
3 tbsp	(45 ml) olive oil
¼ tsp	(1 ml) fresh ground pepper
1 tsp	(5 ml) chopped parsley
9	bay leaves
3	½ in (1.2 cm) thick slices cooked back bacon, cubed and sautéed in butter

Place veal, mushrooms, celery and onion in bowl; set aside.

Place vinegar, garlic, oil, pepper, parsley and 1 bay leaf in small saucepan; bring to boil and cook 5 minutes over medium heat.

Pour hot liquid over veal and vegetables in bowl; marinate 1 hour on countertop. Drain and reserve marinade.

Alternate bacon, veal, mushrooms, celery, remaining bay leaves and onion on skewers. Place in ovenproof platter and broil 12 minutes 6 in (15 cm) from top element. Turn skewers over once and baste occasionally with marinade.

Place veal, mushrooms, celery and onion in bowl; set aside.

Pour hot marinade into bowl and leave on countertop for 1 hour.

Lemon Veal Kebabs

(serves 4)

1 SERVING	265 CALORIES	11g CARBOHYDRATE
17g PROTEIN	17g FAT	2.0g FIBER

½ lb	(250 g) veal tenderloin, sliced in ¼ in (0.65 cm) thick rounds
16	mushroom caps, cleaned
1	yellow pepper, in large pieces
¼ cup	(50 ml) olive oil
¼ cup	(50 ml) wine vinegar
1 tbsp	(15 ml) chopped fresh tarragon
2	broccoli stalks, cubed and cooked
½	red onion, in large pieces
	juice 1 lemon

Place veal, mushrooms and pepper in bowl. Sprinkle in oil, vinegar, tarragon and lemon juice. Refrigerate 35 minutes.

Drain and reserve marinade. Alternate veal (fold each piece in 2), mushrooms, yellow pepper, broccoli and onion on skewers.

Place in ovenproof dish and pour marinade over skewers. Broil 12 minutes in oven 6 in (15 cm) from top element. Turn skewers over once.

Serve with baked potatoes or other vegetables.

Marinate veal, mushrooms and pepper in a mixture of oil, vinegar, tarragon and lemon juice. Refrigerate for 35 minutes.

Alternate veal and vegetables on skewers. It is important to fold each piece of veal in two as you add them to the skewers.

Spicy Meatballs

Veal and Prune Kebabs

(serves 4)

1 SERVING	480 CALORIES	44g CARBOHYDRATE
40g PROTEIN	16g FAT	8.8g FIBER

1½ lb	(750 g) veal sirloin, cut in strips
½ cup	(125 ml) rice wine
2 tbsp	(30 ml) oil
1 tsp	(5 ml) lemon juice
24	pitted prunes
1½	green peppers, diced large
24	¾ in (2 cm) celery pieces, blanched
12	fresh mint leaves
	pinch thyme
	salt and freshly ground pepper

Place meat in wine, oil, lemon juice and thyme; marinate 15 minutes on countertop.

Drain meat and reserve marinade. Alternate veal, prunes, green peppers, celery and mint leaves on skewers; place on ovenproof platter.

Generously brush with marinade and broil 10 minutes 6 in (15 cm) from top element. Turn skewers over once and season during cooking.

(serves 4)

1 SERVING	490 CALORIES	21g CARBOHYDRATE
52g PROTEIN	22g FAT	0.5g FIBER

¾ lb	(375 g) lean ground pork
¾ lb	(375 g) lean ground veal
2 tbsp	(30 ml) chili sauce
3 tbsp	(45 ml) breadcrumbs
¼ tsp	(1 ml) chili powder
1	egg
1 tsp	(5 ml) Worcestershire sauce
¼ tsp	(1 ml) paprika
½ cup	(125 ml) chili sauce
½ cup	(125 ml) catsup
2 tbsp	(30 ml) oil
2 tbsp	(30 ml) sherry
	salt and pepper

Preheat oven to 400°F (200°C).

Place pork, veal, 2 tbsp (30 ml) chili sauce, breadcrumbs, chili powder, egg, Worcestershire sauce and paprika in mixer; process until meat forms a ball and sticks to sides of bowl.

Cover with waxed paper and chill 1 hour.

Dust hands with flour and shape mixture into small meatballs; thread on skewers. Place on ovenproof platter.

Mix remaining ingredients together. Cook skewers 8 minutes 6 in (15 cm) from top element; turn over once and baste often with sauce.

Dinner Party Skewers

(serves 4)

1 SERVING	215 CALORIES	21g CARBOHYDRATE
17g PROTEIN	7g FAT	1.1g FIBER

¼ cup	(50 ml) molasses
¼ cup	(50 ml) vinegar
1 tbsp	(15 ml) tomato paste
3	anchovy filets, chopped and mashed
1	large pork tenderloin, sliced thick
2	large celery stalks, in 1 in (2.5 cm) lengths
1	large green pepper, in bite-size pieces
1	seedless orange
	juice ½ lemon
	juice 1 orange

Preheat oven to 500°F (260°C).

Mix molasses, vinegar and tomato paste together in large bowl. Add lemon and orange juices, anchovies and mix very well.

Place pork, celery and green pepper in marinade; set aside 1 hour on countertop.

Slice other orange in two; cut each half into ¼ in (0.65 cm) thick slices. Do not peel.

Alternate double slices of orange along with ingredients in bowl on skewers; place on ovenproof platter.

Cook 14 minutes, turning skewers over once.

1 Mix molasses, vinegar and tomato paste together in large bowl. Add anchovies, lemon and orange juices; mix very well.

2 Place pork, celery and green pepper in marinade; set aside 1 hour on countertop.

Ribs and Tomatoes

(serves 4)

1 SERVING	383 CALORIES	16g CARBOHYDRATE
19g PROTEIN	27g FAT	0.9g FIBER

2½ lb	(1.2 kg) pork back ribs
3 tbsp	(45 ml) maple syrup
¼ cup	(50 ml) catsup
2	garlic cloves, smashed and chopped
1	large yellow pepper, in large pieces
6	slices precooked bacon, cut in half and rolled
1	tomato, in thin wedges
	juice ½ lemon
	few drops Tabasco sauce
	salt and pepper

Place ribs in large saucepan and cover with water; bring to boil. Skim and continue cooking 1 hour over medium heat.

Remove ribs from water and cool; cut into 1 in (2.5 cm) pieces.

Mix maple syrup, catsup, garlic, lemon juice, Tabasco, salt and pepper together in bowl. Stir in ribs and let stand 15 minutes on countertop.

Alternate rib pieces, yellow pepper, rolled bacon and tomato on skewers. Place in ovenproof platter and broil 8 minutes 6 in (15 cm) from top element. Turn skewers once and baste with leftover catsup mixture.

After ribs have been cooked in hot water, remove and cool. Then cut into 1 in (2.5 cm) pieces.

Alternate rib pieces, yellow pepper, rolled bacon and tomato on skewers.

Pork and Vegetable Kebabs

(serves 4)

1 SERVING	224 CALORIES	12g CARBOHYDRATE
17g PROTEIN	12g FAT	1.6g FIBER

5 oz	(142 g) piece Polish sausage
1	pork tenderloin, fat trimmed
1	small zucchini, in ½ in (1.2 cm) thick slices
1	yellow pepper, in bite-size pieces
8	green onions, in 1½ in (4 cm) long sticks
¼ tsp	(1 ml) Worcestershire sauce
½ cup	(125 ml) catsup
1 tsp	(5 ml) horseradish
	few drops Tabasco sauce
	salt and pepper

Preheat oven to 500°F (260°C).

Remove skin from sausage and slice in 1½ in (4 cm) rings. Cube pork tenderloin and place in bowl along with sausage, zucchini, yellow pepper and onion sticks.

Add Worcestershire sauce, catsup, horseradish, Tabasco sauce, salt and pepper to bowl; mix until everything is evenly coated. Marinate 15 minutes on countertop.

Alternate ingredients on skewers and place on ovenproof platter. Cook 15 minutes 6 in (15 cm) from top element turning skewers over twice.

Serve with potatoes if desired.

Prepare ingredients as directed in recipe then place them in a bowl.

Add Worcestershire sauce, catsup, horseradish, Tabasco sauce, salt and pepper to bowl; mix until everything is evenly coated. Marinate 15 minutes on countertop.

Pork Kebabs with Sweet-Sour Sauce

(serves 4)

1 SERVING 34g PROTEIN	388 CALORIES 16g FAT	27g CARBOHYDRATE 2.8g FIBER

1 tbsp	(15 ml) vegetable oil
1	garlic clove, smashed and chopped
1	small onion, thinly sliced
1	small carrot, thinly sliced
2	pineapple rings, cubed
2 tbsp	(30 ml) soya sauce
2 tbsp	(30 ml) wine vinegar
1 tbsp	(15 ml) sugar
3 tbsp	(45 ml) catsup
1 cup	(250 ml) hot chicken stock
1 tbsp	(15 ml) cornstarch
3 tbsp	(45 ml) cold water
1 lb	(500 g) pork tenderloin, in strips
16	baby carrots, blanched
1 ½	yellow peppers, diced large
	salt and pepper

To prepare sauce, heat oil in frying pan. When hot, cook garlic, onion and carrot 3 minutes over medium heat.

Stir in pineapple, soya sauce and vinegar; cook 2 minutes.

Add sugar and catsup; mix well. Pour in chicken stock, season and bring to boil.

Mix cornstarch with water; stir into sauce and cook 2 minutes. Remove from heat.

Fold pork strips in half and alternate along with baby carrots and pepper pieces on skewers. Season well and place on ovenproof platter.

Generously brush sweet-sour sauce over skewers; broil 4 to 5 minutes each side 6 in (15 cm) from top element. Baste frequently.

Ham and Apple on Skewers

(serves 4)

1 SERVING 36g PROTEIN	355 CALORIES 7g FAT	37g CARBOHYDRATE 2.5g FIBER

2	slices Virginia ham, ¾ in (2 cm) thick and in ¾ in (2 cm) cubes
3	apples, in wedges with skin
3 tbsp	(45 ml) maple syrup
2 tsp	(10 ml) soya sauce
½ cup	(125 ml) catsup
¼ cup	(50 ml) apple juice
	pinch cinnamon
	pinch ground clove

Place all ingredients in bowl, mix and marinate 15 minutes.

Drain and reserve marinade. Alternate ham and apples on skewers; place on ovenproof platter.

Broil 8 to 10 minutes 6 in (15 cm) from top element. Turn skewers over once and baste with marinade.

These kebabs are very tasty for brunch.

Cabbage Rolls on Skewers

(serves 4)

1 SERVING	334 CALORIES	5g CARBOHYDRATE
38g PROTEIN	18g FAT	0.6g FIBER

1 tbsp	(15 ml) butter
½ lb	(250 g) ground pork
½ lb	(250 g) ground veal
¼ tsp	(1 ml) paprika
¼ tsp	(1 ml) ground clove
½ cup	(125 ml) grated cheddar cheese
½ cup	(125 ml) cooked chopped onion
1 tbsp	(15 ml) chopped parsley
1 tbsp	(15 ml) sour cream
1	egg, lightly beaten
8	large cabbage leaves, blanched
	salt and pepper

Heat butter in frying pan. When hot, brown pork and veal 4 to 5 minutes over medium heat; season with paprika and clove.

Transfer meat to bowl and add remaining ingredients except cabbage leaves. Mix until well combined, cover and chill 1 hour.

Lay cabbage leaves flat and spread about 3 tbsp (45 ml) of meat mixture over each leaf. Roll fairly tight and tuck in ends. Place tube-like rolls on plate and weight down with another plate; chill 15 minutes.

Cut each cabbage roll into 3 pieces and carefully thread on skewers. Broil 6 to 8 minutes in oven 6 in (15 cm) from top element; turn skewers over once.

This unusual kebab dish also serves well topped with a hint of tomato sauce.

Italian Sausage and Beef Kebabs

(serves 4)

1 SERVING	611 CALORIES	17g CARBOHYDRATE
39g PROTEIN	43g FAT	1.3g FIBER

1 lb	(500 g) sirloin tip, in bite-size pieces
1 lb	(500 g) Italian sausage, in ¾ in (2 cm) pieces
2	onions, cut in 4 and sectioned
1½	red peppers, in bite-size pieces
8	garlic cloves, peeled
½ cup	(125 ml) olive oil
¼ cup	(50 ml) chili sauce
	juice 1 lemon
	freshly ground pepper
	dash paprika

Alternate beef, sausage, onion, pepper and garlic on skewers. Place on ovenproof platter.

Mix oil, chili sauce, lemon juice, pepper and paprika together; brush over skewers.

Broil about 6 minutes on each side (depending on size) 6 in (15 cm) from top element. Baste once or twice.

Accompany with a spicy rice.

Polish Sausages and Bacon

(serves 4)

1 SERVING	169 CALORIES	10g CARBOHYDRATE
12g PROTEIN	9g FAT	0.8g FIBER

2	¾ in (2 cm) thick slices back bacon, diced large
½	red onion, cut in 3
4 oz	(115 g) Polish sausage, peeled and diced large
½	cucumber, peeled, seeded and cut in ¾ in (2 cm) thick slices
½ cup	(125 ml) catsup
1 tbsp	(15 ml) horseradish
	juice 1 lime
	few drops Tabasco sauce
	pepper

Preheat oven to 500°F (260°C).

Alternate bacon, onion, sausage and cucumber on skewers; place on ovenproof platter.

Mix remaining ingredients together and brush over skewers.

Cook 14 minutes 8 in (20 cm) from top element. Turn skewers over once and baste with leftover catsup mixture if desired.

Cocktail Sausages on Skewers

(serves 4)

1 SERVING	320 CALORIES	7g CARBOHYDRATE
10g PROTEIN	28g FAT	0.5g FIBER

8	slices bacon, precooked 2 minutes
8 oz	(230 g) can cocktail sausages
10 oz	(284 ml) can mandarin sections, drained
	barbecue sauce for basting

Cut bacon slices in two and roll; alternate along with sausages and mandarins on thin wooden skewers.

Place in ovenproof dish and baste with barbecue sauce. Broil 5 minutes in oven 6 in (15 cm) from top element.

Serve as an appetizer or snack.

Tasty Lamb Kebabs

(serves 4)

1 SERVING	266 CALORIES	10g CARBOHYDRATE
16g PROTEIN	18g FAT	0.4g FIBER

½ cup	(125 ml) mint sauce
1 tbsp	(15 ml) olive oil
2	garlic cloves, smashed and chopped
8	small lamb chops, ½ in (1.2 cm) thick, boned and fat removed
2	small onions, cut in 4 and sectioned
10	bay leaves
1½	celery stalks, cut in 1 in (2.5 cm) lengths and blanched
	salt and pepper
	juice ¼ lemon

Preheat oven to 400°F (200°C).

Place mint sauce, oil, garlic, pepper and lemon juice in bowl. Add lamb and mix thoroughly; marinate 15 minutes on countertop.

Alternate lamb, onion sections, bay leaves and celery pieces on skewers; season generously. Place on ovenproof platter.

Change oven setting to broil. Cook skewers 3 minutes each side 6 in (15 cm) from top element. Leave door ajar and baste with leftover mint marinade.

Serve with hot mustard if desired.

38

Hearty Lamb Kebabs

(serves 4)

1 SERVING	733 CALORIES	20g CARBOHYDRATE
44g PROTEIN	53g FAT	2.9g FIBER

2 lb	(900 g) boneless leg of lamb, in ¾ in (2 cm) pieces
2	onions, finely chopped
1 tbsp	(15 ml) crushed rosemary
½ cup	(125 ml) olive oil
2	bay leaves
1	large Spanish onion, cut in 8 and sectioned
1 tbsp	(15 ml) olive oil
2	garlic cloves, smashed and chopped
3	tomatoes, peeled and chopped
4	slices Italian bread, toasted
¼ cup	(50 ml) grated Parmesan cheese
	salt and pepper

Place lamb, chopped onions, rosemary, ¼ cup (125 ml) oil and bay leaves in bowl; mix and marinate 1 hour on countertop.

Alternate pieces of lamb and Spanish onion on skewers; place on ovenproof platter and set aside.

Heat remaining measure of oil in frying pan. Cook garlic and tomatoes 7 to 9 minutes over medium heat; season well. Reduce heat and simmer.

Place skewers in oven and broil 5 to 6 minutes 6 in (15 cm) from top element.

Spread tomato mixture over toasted bread slices and top with cheese; place in ovenproof dish.

Turn skewers over; broil another 5 to 6 minutes. Place bread beside skewers and broil, but for only 3 to 4 minutes.

To serve place one skewer on each slice of bread.

Salmon and Cucumber Kebabs

(serves 4)

1 SERVING	171 CALORIES	1g CARBOHYDRATE
26g PROTEIN	7g FAT	0.6g FIBER

2 tbsp	(30 ml) grated lemon rind
½ cup	(125 ml) dry white wine
1 tsp	(5 ml) tarragon
3	salmon steaks
½	English cucumber, peeled and diced large
8	fresh mint leaves
	juice 1 lemon
	salt and pepper

Mix lemon rind, wine, tarragon and lemon juice together in large bowl.

Remove middle bone from salmon steaks, leave on skin and cut in 2. Cut each half into 3 pieces. Add to bowl along with cucumber; marinate 15 minutes.

Drain and reserve marinade.

Alternate salmon, cucumber and mint leaves on skewers; place on ovenproof platter and season.

Broil 4 minutes 6 in (15 cm) from top element; baste once with marinade.

Turn skewers over and broil about 3 minutes, depending on size. Baste once more.

Perch Kebabs

(serves 4)

1 SERVING	392 CALORIES	8g CARBOHYDRATE
45g PROTEIN	20g FAT	1.1g FIBER

2	garlic cloves, smashed and chopped
1 tbsp	(15 ml) oyster sauce
2 lb	(900 g) perch filets, cut in half then in 1 in (2.5 cm) pieces
8	cherry tomatoes
4	small onions, blanched and cut in 4
3 tbsp	(45 ml) olive oil
2 tbsp	(30 ml) sherry
	juice 1 lemon
	salt and pepper

Preheat oven to 400°F (200°C).

Mix garlic, oyster sauce and lemon juice in bowl. Add fish and marinate 15 minutes.

Roll fish pieces and alternate along with tomatoes and onions on skewers. Place on ovenproof platter.

Mix oil and sherry together; brush over skewers. Season to taste.

Change oven setting to broil. Cook skewers 3 minutes each side 6 in (15 cm) from top element.

1 Mix garlic, oyster sauce and lemon in bowl.

2 Add fish and marinate 15 minutes.

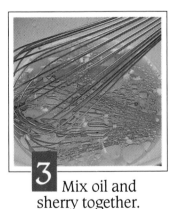

3 Mix oil and sherry together.

4 Brush sherry mixture over skewers before broiling.

Sturgeon, Brussels Sprouts and Carrots

(serves 4)

1 SERVING	254 CALORIES	18g CARBOHYDRATE
23g PROTEIN	10g FAT	4.8g FIBER

2	sturgeon steaks, $\frac{3}{4}$ in (2 cm) thick and in $\frac{3}{4}$ in (2 cm) cubes
24	cooked Brussels sprouts
24	cooked baby carrots
½ cup	(125 ml) sake
2 tbsp	(30 ml) oil
1	garlic clove, smashed and chopped
8	oyster mushrooms
	salt and pepper

Place fish, sprouts, carrots, sake, oil, garlic, salt and pepper in bowl; marinate 15 minutes.

Drain and reserve marinade. Alternate fish and vegetables on skewers. Note: It is best to fold mushrooms in half.

Place skewers on ovenproof platter and broil 8 to 10 minutes 6 in (15 cm) from top element. Turn skewers over once and baste with marinade.

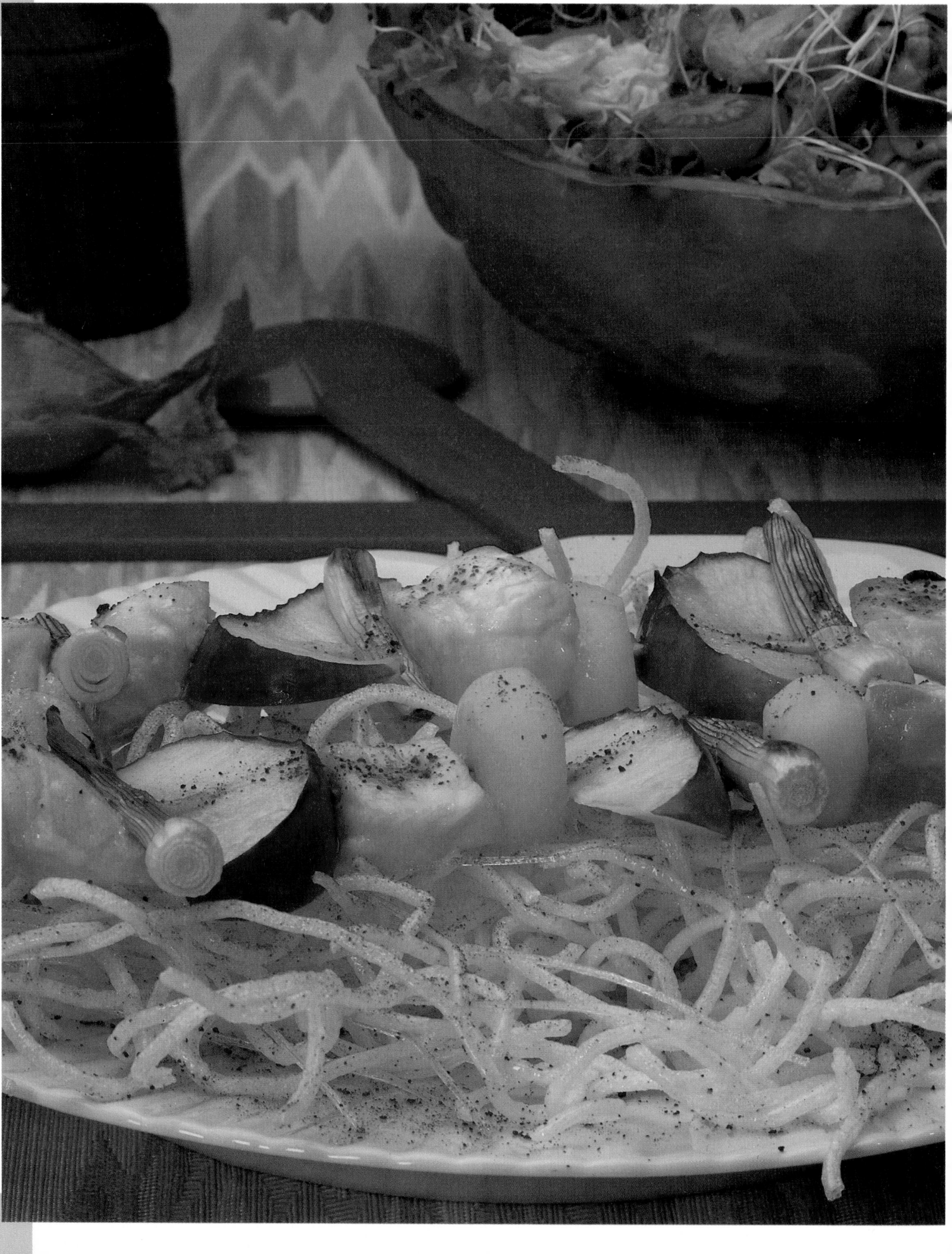

Clam Kebabs

Fish Lover's Kebabs

(serves 4)

1 SERVING	385 CALORIES	10g CARBOHYDRATE
48g PROTEIN	17g FAT	1.0g FIBER

2 lb	(900 g) halibut steaks, ¾ in (2 cm) thick and in 1 in (2.5 cm) pieces
1	onion, finely chopped
4 tbsp	(60 ml) oil
2 tbsp	(30 ml) lime juice
¼ tsp	(1 ml) Tabasco sauce
¼ cup	(50 ml) dry white wine
6	green onions, in 1 in (2.5 cm) sticks
7 oz	(199 ml) can water chestnuts, drained
12	lime slices
12	apple wedges with skin

Marinate halibut 15 minutes in chopped onion, oil, lime juice, Tabasco sauce and wine.

Drain and reserve marinade.

Alternate fish, green onions, water chestnuts, lime slices and apple wedges on skewers. Place on ovenproof platter.

Broil 8 to 10 minutes in oven 6 in (15 cm) from top element. Turn skewers over once and baste occasionally with marinade.

(serves 4)

1 SERVING	406 CALORIES	33g CARBOHYDRATE
28g PROTEIN	18g FAT	0.2g FIBER

24	large clams, scrubbed
1 tsp	(5 ml) lemon juice
1 tbsp	(15 ml) teriyaki sauce
1 cup	(250 ml) seasoned flour
2	beaten eggs
1 ½ cups	(375 ml) crushed Corn Flakes
	melted garlic butter
	pepper

Preheat oven to 450°F (240°C).

Spread clams in one layer in large roasting pan. Place in oven for 4 to 5 minutes or until shells open.

Shuck and discard shells. Place clams in bowl with lemon juice and teriyaki sauce; mix well and season with pepper.

Dredge clams in flour, dip in eggs and coat with corn flakes. Put on skewers with skewer going through each clam twice. Set all on ovenproof platter.

Change oven setting to broil. Baste skewers with garlic butter, leave oven door ajar, and broil 6 minutes 6 in (15 cm) from top element. Turn skewers over once and baste again if necessary.

Oyster Kebabs

(serves 4)

1 SERVING	681 CALORIES	50g CARBOHYDRATE
55g PROTEIN	29g FAT	0g FIBER

36	large shucked oysters
8	slices cooked bacon, cut in half
1 cup	(250 ml) flour
¼ tsp	(1 ml) paprika
1 tsp	(5 ml) chopped parsley
4 tbsp	(60 ml) butter, melted
¼ tsp	(1 ml) teriyaki sauce
	salt
	juice 1 lemon

Preheat oven to 400°F (200°C).

Alternate oysters and rolled pieces of bacon on skewers.

Mix flour with paprika and parsley. Roll skewers in this and place in ovenproof platter.

Mix butter, teriyaki sauce, salt and lemon juice together; pour over skewers. Change oven setting to broil and cook skewers 3 minutes each side 6 in (15 cm) from top element.

Serve with garlic bread.

Brandy Jumbo Shrimp

(serves 4)

1 SERVING	164 CALORIES	6g CARBOHYDRATE
17g PROTEIN	8g FAT	0.8g FIBER

20	raw jumbo shrimp, shelled and deveined
2	garlic cloves, smashed and chopped
½ cup	(125 ml) brandy
2 tbsp	(30 ml) olive oil
4	stems bok choy, in ¾ in (2 cm) pieces
	juice 1 lemon
	salt and pepper

Place all ingredients in bowl and marinate 30 minutes on countertop.

Alternate shrimp and bok choy on skewers. Place on ovenproof platter.

Broil 12 to 14 minutes in oven 6 in (15 cm) from top element. Turn skewers over once and season during cooking. Baste with marinade if desired.

Serve with tartare sauce.

Breaded Mussels on Skewers

(serves 4)

1 SERVING	610 CALORIES	60g CARBOHYDRATE
43g PROTEIN	22g FAT	0.2g FIBER

6½ lb	(3 kg) mussels, scrubbed and bearded
½ cup	(125 ml) dry white wine
4 tbsp	(60 ml) butter
1 tbsp	(15 ml) lemon juice
1 cup	(250 ml) seasoned flour
2	beaten eggs
2 cups	(500 ml) breadcrumbs
	few drops Tabasco sauce
	few drops lemon juice
	salt and pepper

Place mussels, wine, 2 tbsp (30 ml) butter, lemon juice and pepper in saucepan. Cover and bring to boil; continue cooking over medium heat until shells open.

Drain liquid into small bowl. Shuck mussels and pour any juices from shells into the small bowl. Set aside.

Dredge mussels in flour. Dip several at a time in eggs then coat with breadcrumbs.

Thread on wooden skewers and place on ovenproof platter. Broil 4 minutes very close to top element; turn skewers once.

Meanwhile, prepare sauce by transferring reserved mussel liquid in bowl to saucepan. Reduce by ⅔ over medium-high heat.

Stir in remaining butter, Tabasco sauce and few drops lemon juice; cook 1 minute.

Serve with kebabs.

Chinese Shrimp Kebabs

(serves 4)

1 SERVING	237 CALORIES	21g CARBOHYDRATE
27g PROTEIN	5g FAT	0g FIBER

16	chunks fresh pineapple
2 lb	(900 g) raw shrimp, shelled and deveined
24	fresh snow peas, blanched
½ cup	(125 ml) rice wine
2 tbsp	(30 ml) sesame sauce
1 tbsp	(15 ml) oil
1 tsp	(5 ml) lime juice
	salt and pepper

Preheat oven to 400°F (200°C).

Place pineapple, shrimp, pea pods, wine and sesame sauce in bowl; marinate 15 minutes.

Alternate ingredients on skewers and place on ovenproof platter. Mix oil with lime juice; set aside.

Cook skewers 6 to 8 minutes in oven 6 in (15 cm) from top element. Baste occasionally with oil mixture and turn skewers over once. Season to taste.

Serve with steamed rice and chopsticks.

Escargot Appetizer

(serves 4)

1 SERVING	462 CALORIES	20g CARBOHYDRATE
19g PROTEIN	34g FAT	0.2g FIBER

24	canned snails, drained
8	slices bacon, precooked and in 2 in (5 cm) pieces
16	cooked pearl onions
½ cup	(125 ml) melted garlic butter
1 ½ cups	(375 ml) seasoned breadcrumbs

Alternate snails, rolled pieces of bacon and pearl onions on short skewers. Place on ovenproof platter and baste generously with garlic butter.

Roll skewers in breadcrumbs until well coated. Broil 4 to 6 minutes in oven 4 in (10 cm) from top element. Turn skewers over once.

Serve with extra garlic butter and lemon wedges.

Scallop Kebabs with Fried Parsley

(serves 4)

1 SERVING	434 CALORIES	10g CARBOHYDRATE
31g PROTEIN	30g FAT	0.8g FIBER

½ cup	(125 ml) olive oil
3 tbsp	(45 ml) wine vinegar
½ tsp	(2 ml) crushed rosemary
2 tbsp	(30 ml) lemon juice
1 ½ lb	(750 g) large scallops
12	bay leaves
1	large lemon, sliced (remove seeds)
1	bunch fresh parsley
	freshly ground pepper

Reserve 3 tbsp (45 ml) oil. Place remaining oil in bowl along with vinegar, rosemary, lemon juice, scallops and pepper. Toss and marinate 1 hour on countertop.

Drain scallops and set marinade aside.

Alternate scallops, bay leaves and lemon slices on skewers; place on ovenproof platter.

Broil 3 minutes each side in oven 6 in (15 cm) from top element. Baste occasionally with marinade.

Before kebabs are done, heat reserved oil in frying pan. When hot, sauté parsley (as is, in bunch) about 2 minutes.

Serve as an unusual garnish with kebabs.

Stuffed Mushroom Caps

(serves 4)

1 SERVING	552 CALORIES	43g CARBOHYDRATE
32g PROTEIN	28g FAT	1.3g FIBER

1 lb	(500 g) ricotta cheese
¼ lb	(125 g) grated mozzarella cheese
1 tbsp	(15 ml) chopped parsley
¼ tsp	(1 ml) basil
32	blanched mushroom caps
2	beaten eggs
2 cups	(500 ml) seasoned breadcrumbs
	dash paprika
	salt and pepper
	Tabasco sauce to taste

Mix both cheeses, parsley, basil, paprika, salt, pepper and Tabasco together. Stuff mushroom caps.

Press two mushroom caps together (to keep stuffing in place) and thread 4 sets on each skewer.

Roll skewers in beaten eggs, then in breadcrumbs. Place on ovenproof platter and broil 6 minutes in oven 6 in (15 cm) from top element. Turn skewers over once.

Serve as an appetizer or with a main dish.

Mushroom Garnish

(serves 4)

1 SERVING	208 CALORIES	10g CARBOHYDRATE
24g PROTEIN	8g FAT	1.0g FIBER

1 tbsp	(15 ml) butter
1	onion, finely chopped
½ lb	(250 g) lean ground beef
1 tbsp	(15 ml) chopped parsley
¼ cup	(50 ml) grated Gruyère cheese
16	large mushrooms caps, blanched 3 minutes
3 tbsp	(45 ml) seasoned breadcrumbs
	salt and pepper

Heat butter in frying pan. Sauté onion 2 to 3 minutes over medium-low heat.

Add beef and parsley; season to taste. Continue cooking 3 to 4 minutes.

Mix in cheese and cook 1 minute. Remove from heat and stuff mushroom caps.

Thread mushroom caps on skewers with stuffing side up. Place on ovenproof platter and sprinkle breadcrumbs over stuffing.

Broil 3 to 4 minutes in oven 6 in (15 cm) from top element. Do not turn skewers over!

Serve as a vegetable garnish.

Assorted Pepper Kebabs

(serves 4)

1 SERVING	155 CALORIES	12g CARBOHYDRATE
2g PROTEIN	11g FAT	2.1g FIBER

4 tbsp	(60 ml) olive oil
¼ tsp	(1 ml) Tabasco sauce
½ tsp	(2 ml) lemon juice
2	garlic cloves, smashed and finely chopped
2	green peppers, seeded and halved
2	yellow peppers, seeded and halved
2	red peppers, seeded and halved
	freshly ground pepper

Preheat oven to 450°F (240°C).

Mix oil, Tabasco, lemon juice, garlic and pepper together. Place peppers in ovenproof dish and pour in mixture. Cook 10 minutes in middle of oven.

Remove and let cool slightly.

Cut pepper halves into 3 and alternate colours on skewers; brush with oil mixture. Broil 6 minutes 6 in (15 cm) from top element; turn over once.

Serve.

Eggplant and Bacon Skewers

(serves 4)

1 SERVING	88 CALORIES	9g CARBOHYDRATE
4g PROTEIN	4g FAT	0.8g FIBER

2	eggplant slices, ¾ in (2 cm) thick
1	back bacon slice, ¾ in (2 cm) thick
8	pieces of red onion
8	cherry tomatoes
¼ tsp	(1 ml) Worcestershire sauce
1 tbsp	(15 ml) oil
3 tbsp	(45 ml) plum sauce
	salt and pepper

Cut eggplant and bacon into ½ in (1.2 cm) cubes. Alternate along with onion and tomatoes on thin wooden skewers.

Place in ovenproof dish and season generously. Sprinkle on Worcestershire sauce, oil and plum sauce.

Broil 10 minutes in oven 6 in (15 cm) from top element. Turn skewers over once.

Cut eggplant and bacon into ½ in (1.2 cm) cubes.

Alternate along with onion and tomatoes on thin wooden skewers. Place in ovenproof dish and season generously. Sprinkle in Worcestershire sauce, oil and plum sauce.

New Potatoes

(serves 4)

1 SERVING	548 CALORIES	34g CARBOHYDRATE
22g PROTEIN	36g FAT	7.1g FIBER

24	new round potatoes, cooked in jackets
24	slices bacon, medium cooked
1 cup	(250 ml) finely grated cheddar cheese
	dash paprika
	freshly ground pepper

Wrap potatoes with bacon slices and place on skewers. Set on ovenproof platter.

Broil 3 minutes in oven 6 in (15 cm) from top element. Turn skewers over; sprinkle with cheese, paprika and pepper. Finish broiling another 3 minutes.

Serve with meat or fish.

Mixed Vegetable Kebabs

(serves 4)

1 SERVING	74 CALORIES	12g CARBOHYDRATE
2g PROTEIN	2g FAT	2.1g FIBER

2	red peppers, in bite-size pieces
1	zucchini, cut in two and sliced thick
1	red onion, in large pieces
2 tbsp	(30 ml) soya sauce
1 tsp	(5 ml) Worcestershire sauce
1 tsp	(5 ml) oil
2	garlic cloves, smashed and chopped
½ tsp	(2 ml) tarragon
½ cup	(125 ml) barbecue sauce

Preheat oven to 450°F (240°C).

Place vegetables in bowl. Add soya sauce, Worcestershire sauce, oil, garlic and tarragon. Marinate 30 minutes at room temperature.

Drain vegetables and reserve marinade.

Alternate vegetables on skewers and place on ovenproof platter; baste with barbecue sauce.

Cook 8 minutes in oven 4 in (10 cm) from top element. Baste several times with marinade and turn skewers twice.

Serve with barbecue sauce for dipping.

1 Place red peppers, zucchini and onion in bowl.

2 Add soya sauce, Worcestershire sauce, oil, garlic and tarragon; marinate 30 minutes at room temperature.

Tomato Fruit Kebabs

(serves 4)

1 SERVING	140 CALORIES	34g CARBOHYDRATE
1g PROTEIN	0g FAT	2.7g FIBER

2	small bananas, sliced thick
¼	pineapple, in large chunks
1	apple, peeled and sliced in wedges
1	large tomato, cored and sliced in wedges
1 tbsp	(15 ml) brown sugar
1 tsp	(5 ml) cinnamon
2 tbsp	(30 ml) maple syrup

Place fruit, tomato, brown sugar, cinnamon and maple syrup in bowl; toss gently. Set aside 15 minutes on countertop.

Alternate pineapple, tomato, banana and apple on thin wooden skewers; repeat until ingredients are used.

Place on ovenproof platter and pour juices from bowl over kebabs. Broil 6 minutes in oven 6 in (15 cm) from top element. Turn skewers over once.

Serve as an interesting dessert or with a meat dish.

Pineapple Chunks and Water Chestnuts

(serves 4)

1 SERVING	143 CALORIES	15g CARBOHYDRATE
5g PROTEIN	7g FAT	0.4g FIBER

16	chunks fresh pineapple
8	slices bacon, medium cooked and cut in half
12	canned water chestnuts
2 tbsp	(30 ml) maple syrup
1 tsp	(5 ml) lemon juice

Wrap pineapple chunks with bacon. Alternate with water chestnuts on skewers and place on ovenproof platter.

Mix maple syrup with lemon juice; brush over skewers. Broil 3 minutes each side in oven 6 in (15 cm) from top element.

Serve as an appetizer or as a snack.

Apricot Dessert

(serves 4)

1 SERVING	259 CALORIES	47g CARBOHYDRATE
2g PROTEIN	7g FAT	2.9g FIBER

24	apricots, pitted
½ cup	(125 ml) Tia Maria
2 tbsp	(30 ml) butter
2 tbsp	(30 ml) sugar
	juice 1 orange
	juice ½ lemon
	whipped cream for topping

Marinate apricots in Tia Maria for 30 minutes.

Drain and reserve liquid; thread apricots on skewers.

Heat butter in frying pan. Stir in sugar and cook until golden brown; stir constantly!

Pour in reserved marinade and flambé. Add orange and lemon juices; cook 2 minutes.

Pour sauce into fairly deep baking dish and place skewers on top. Broil 6 minutes in oven.

Top with whipped cream if desired.

Double Orange Skewer Dessert

(serves 4)

1 SERVING	400 CALORIES	70g CARBOHYDRATE
3g PROTEIN	12g FAT	2.4g FIBER

2	mandarins, peeled and sectioned
1	seedless orange, peeled and sectioned
½	orange honeydew melon, cut in bite-size pieces
2 tbsp	(30 ml) granulated sugar
2 tbsp	(30 ml) orange liqueur
2 oz	(60 g) unsweetened chocolate
¼ cup	(50 ml) heavy cream
1 cup	(250 ml) icing sugar
	few drops vanilla

Place fruit in bowl with granulated sugar and liqueur. Toss and let stand while you make the sauce.

Place chocolate, cream, icing sugar and vanilla in double boiler. Cook until mixture is completely melted; stir constantly.

Alternate fruit on wooden skewers and place on individual dessert plates. Drizzle chocolate sauce over kebabs and serve.

Passion Fruit Kebabs

(serves 4)

1 SERVING	141 CALORIES	29g CARBOHYDRATE
4g PROTEIN	1g FAT	0g FIBER

4	passion fruit*, cut in half
2 tbsp	(30 ml) orange liqueur
2	egg whites
2 tbsp	(30 ml) sugar

Carefully thread fruit halves on short skewers. Sprinkle liqueur over each and place on ovenproof platter.

Beat egg whites until fairly stiff. Slowly incorporate sugar and continue beating 1½ minutes.

Spoon a large dollop of egg whites on each fruit half. Broil 2 minutes in oven 6 in (15 cm) from top element.

Serve immediately. Diners should eat passion fruit with a spoon.

* Choose your passion fruit carefully. Look for dark purple skin with a lumpy texture that is fairly firm.

Strawberry and Kiwi Kebabs

(serves 4)

1 SERVING	104 CALORIES	23g CARBOHYDRATE
3g PROTEIN	0g FAT	1.2g FIBER

24	ripe strawberries, hulled
4	ripe kiwis, peeled and cut in 4
3 tbsp	(45 ml) sugar
¼ cup	(50 ml) Lamb's Caribbean Cream
1 tbsp	(15 ml) grated lemon rind
2	egg whites

Preheat oven to 400°F (200°C).

Place strawberries and kiwis in bowl; add 1 tbsp (15 ml) sugar, Caribbean Cream and lemon rind. Toss and marinate 1 hour.

Alternate fruit on wooden skewers and place on ovenproof platter.

Beat egg whites until fairly stiff. Slowly incorporate remaining sugar and continue beating 1½ minutes.

Carefully arrange dollops of egg whites on top portion of skewers. Change oven setting to broil and brown 2 to 3 minutes 6 in (15 cm) from top element.

Serve immediately.

Skewer Sundae

(serves 4)

1 SERVING	429 CALORIES	54g CARBOHYDRATE
6g PROTEIN	21g FAT	1.6g FIBER

1	banana, sliced
12	strawberries, cut in half
12	chunks fresh pineapple
8	scoops French vanilla ice cream
2 tbsp	(30 ml) butter
2 tbsp	(30 ml) sugar
½ cup	(125 ml) orange juice
	grated rind ½ lemon
	grated rind ½ orange

Alternate fruit on short wooden skewers. Divide ice cream scoops between four sundae dishes and set skewers on top; refrigerate.

Heat butter in frying pan. Stir in sugar and cook until golden brown; mix constantly!

Add orange juice and rinds; continue cooking to reduce by half.

Cool slightly then pour over kebabs and serve.

Plums with Jubilee Sauce

(serves 4)

1 SERVING	175 CALORIES	36g CARBOHYDRATE
1g PROTEIN	3g FAT	2.9g FIBER

8	ripe plums, pitted and cut in half
¼ cup	(50 ml) kirsch
1 tbsp	(15 ml) butter
2 tbsp	(30 ml) sugar
¾ cup	(175 ml) cherry juice
½ cup	(125 ml) canned cherries
1 tsp	(5 ml) cornstarch
2 tbsp	(30 ml) cold water
	juice 1 orange

Marinate plums in half of kirsch for 10 minutes. Drain and reserve marinade; thread plum halves on short wooden skewers.

Heat butter with sugar in frying pan. Stir constantly and cook 1 minute.

Add cherry juice, cherries and orange juice; mix well. Add remaining kirsch and marinade; bring to boil.

Set skewers in sauce and cook 2 to 3 minutes over medium heat. Transfer skewers to dessert dishes and continue cooking sauce 2 to 3 minutes.

Mix cornstarch with water; stir into sauce and cook 1 minute.

Pour over kebabs and serve.

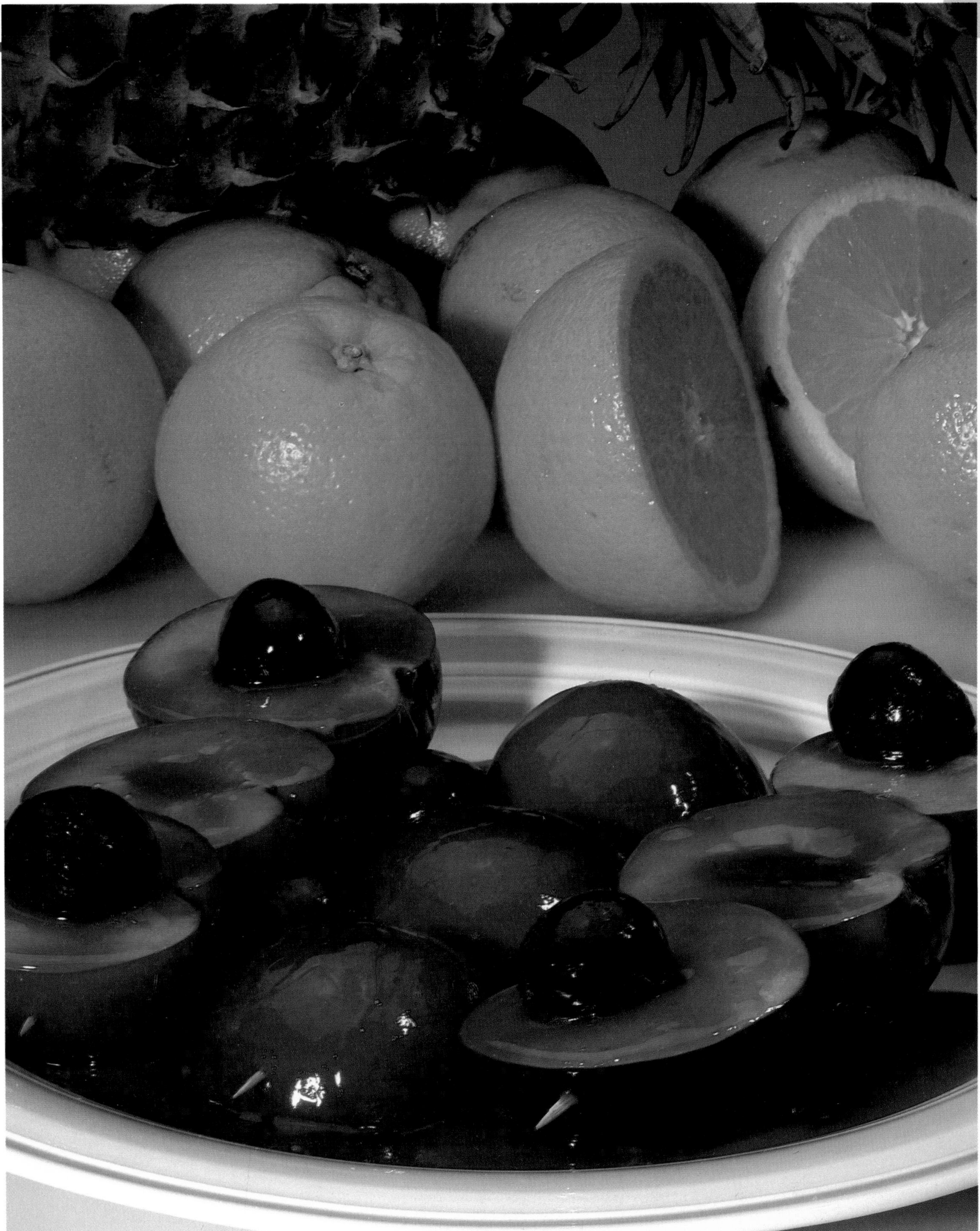

Onion Mustard Sauce

1 SERVING	17 CALORIES	2g CARBOHYDRATE
0g PROTEIN	1g FAT	0.1g FIBER

1 tbsp	(15 ml) olive oil
1	onion, chopped
¼ cup	(50 ml) wine vinegar
2 tbsp	(30 ml) capers
1 tsp	(5 ml) chopped parsley
¼ tsp	(1 ml) freshly ground pepper
1 cup	(250 ml) dry red wine
1½ cups	(375 ml) brown sauce, heated
2 tbsp	(30 ml) Dijon mustard

Heat oil in deep frying pan. When hot, add onion and cook 3 minutes over medium heat.

Stir in vinegar, capers, parsley and pepper; cook 3 minutes.

Pour in wine and cook 6 to 7 minutes over high heat.

Mix in brown sauce, correct seasoning and simmer 6 to 7 minutes over low heat.

Remove pan from stove, stir in mustard and serve sauce with beef or veal.

After onion has cooked 3 minutes, stir in vinegar, capers, parsley and pepper; continue cooking 3 minutes.

Mix in brown sauce, correct seasoning and simmer 6 to 7 minutes over low heat.

Pour in wine and cook 6 to 7 minutes over high heat.

Remove pan from stove and stir in mustard before serving.

Parsley Sauce

1 SERVING	13 CALORIES	1g CARBOHYDRATE
0g PROTEIN	1g FAT	0g FIBER

1 tbsp	(15 ml) butter
2 tbsp	(30 ml) chopped parsley
1 tsp	(5 ml) oregano
1 tbsp	(15 ml) tarragon
2	shallots, chopped
2 tbsp	(30 ml) wine vinegar
½ cup	(125 ml) dry white wine
1 ½ cups	(375 ml) hot chicken stock
1 tbsp	(15 ml) cornstarch
3 tbsp	(45 ml) cold water
	salt and pepper

Heat butter in deep frying pan. Cook parsley, oregano, tarragon and shallots 2 minutes over medium heat; season well.

Pour in vinegar and cook 1 minute over high heat.

Add wine; cook 3 to 4 minutes over high heat.

Pour in chicken stock, bring to boil and continue cooking 3 to 4 minutes. Correct seasoning.

Mix cornstarch with water; stir into sauce and cook 2 to 3 minutes.

Serve this sauce with chicken or veal.

Cook parsley, oregano, tarragon and shallots 2 minutes in hot butter over medium heat; season well.

Pour in chicken stock, bring to boil and continue cooking 3 to 4 minutes. Correct seasoning.

Pour in vinegar, cook 1 minute, then add wine. Cook another 3 to 4 minutes over high heat.

Stir diluted cornstarch into sauce and cook 2 to 3 minutes to thicken.

Curry Sauce

1 SERVING	48 CALORIES	3g CARBOHYDRATE
0g PROTEIN	4g FAT	0.1g FIBER

2 tbsp	(30 ml) butter
2	large onions, finely chopped
3 tbsp	(45 ml) curry powder
2 cups	(500 ml) hot chicken stock
1½ tbsp	(25 ml) cornstarch
3 tbsp	(45 ml) cold water
¼ cup	(50 ml) heavy cream
	dash paprika
	salt and pepper

Heat butter in deep frying pan. When hot, add onions and season with paprika; cook 4 to 5 minutes over medium heat.

Mix in curry powder and cook 3 to 4 minutes over very low heat.

Pour in stock and season well; mix and cook 4 to 5 minutes over medium heat.

Mix cornstarch with water; stir into sauce along with cream. Cook 4 to 5 minutes over low heat.

Serve with a variety of kebabs.

Cook onions seasoned with paprika 4 to 5 minutes over medium heat.

Mix in curry powder and cook 3 to 4 minutes over very low heat.

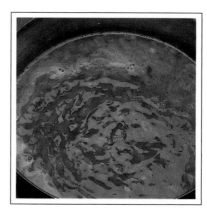

Pour in stock and season well; mix and cook 4 to 5 minutes over medium heat.

Stir diluted cornstarch and cream into sauce; cook 4 to 5 minutes over low heat.

Bourguignonne Sauce

1 SERVING	43 CALORIES	3g CARBOHYDRATE
1g PROTEIN	3g FAT	0.2g FIBER

1 tbsp	(15 ml) vegetable oil
2	shallots, chopped
2	garlic cloves, smashed and chopped
1 tbsp	(15 ml) chopped parsley
1 tbsp	(15 ml) tarragon
1 cup	(250 ml) dry red wine
1	bay leaf
1½ cups	(375 ml) brown sauce, heated
1 cup	(250 ml) diced mushrooms, sautéed
	salt and pepper

Heat oil in deep frying pan. When hot, add shallots, garlic, parsley and tarragon; cook 2 minutes over medium heat.

Add wine, bay leaf and season with pepper; cook 6 to 7 minutes over high heat.

Mix in brown sauce; cook 4 to 5 minutes over medium heat.

Add mushrooms, correct seasoning and cook 2 to 3 minutes.

Serve with beef kebabs. Remember to discard bay leaf before serving.

Cook shallots, garlic, parsley and tarragon in hot oil 2 minutes over medium heat.

Mix in brown sauce; cook 4 to 5 minutes over medium heat.

Pour in wine, bay leaf and season with pepper; cook 6 to 7 minutes over high heat.

Add mushrooms, correct seasoning and cook 2 to 3 minutes.

Orange Honey Sauce

1 SERVING	70 CALORIES	13g CARBOHYDRATE
0g PROTEIN	2g FAT	0.2g FIBER

1	onion, finely chopped
1 tbsp	(15 ml) oil
1 cup	(250 ml) orange juice
4 tbsp	(60 ml) honey
1 tbsp	(15 ml) finely chopped fresh ginger
2 tbsp	(30 ml) wine vinegar
	few drops Tabasco sauce

Mix all ingredients together in small saucepan. Bring to boil and continue cooking 2 minutes.

Cool slightly and baste over chicken or pork before broiling.

Peppercorn Sauce

1 SERVING	82 CALORIES	5g CARBOHYDRATE
2g PROTEIN	6g FAT	0.1g FIBER

1 tbsp	(15 ml) butter
1	onion, finely chopped
1 tbsp	(15 ml) chopped parsley
3 tbsp	(45 ml) green peppercorns
½ cup	(125 ml) dry white wine
1 ½ cups	(375 ml) hot white sauce
1 tsp	(5 ml) cumin
	salt and pepper
	dash paprika

Heat butter in saucepan. When hot, add onion and parsley; cook 2 minutes.

Stir in peppercorns and wine; cook 5 minutes over high heat.

Mix in white sauce, cumin and remaining spices; cook 6 to 7 minutes over low heat.

Correct seasoning and serve with almost any kebab.

Tartare Sauce

1 SERVING	99 CALORIES	0g CARBOHYDRATE
0g PROTEIN	11g FAT	0.2g FIBER

1 cup	(250 ml) mayonnaise
3	pickles, finely chopped
24	stuffed green olives, finely chopped
1 tsp	(5 ml) chopped fresh parsley
1 tbsp	(15 ml) capers
¼ tsp	(1 ml) paprika
1 tsp	(5 ml) lemon juice
	salt and pepper

Mix all ingredients together in bowl until well combined. Correct seasoning and chill until serving time.

Stroganoff Sauce

1 SERVING	43 CALORIES	3g CARBOHYDRATE
1g PROTEIN	3g FAT	0.2g FIBER

1 tbsp	(15 ml) olive oil
1	medium onion, finely chopped
¼ lb	(125 g) mushrooms, finely chopped
1 tsp	(5 ml) chopped parsley
½ cup	(125 ml) dry red wine
1 ½ cups	(375 ml) brown sauce, heated
¼ cup	(50 ml) heavy cream
	salt and pepper

Heat oil in deep frying pan. Cook onion 3 minutes over medium heat.

Mix in mushrooms and parsley; cook 2 to 3 minutes.

Pour in wine; cook 4 to 5 minutes over high heat.

Mix in brown sauce, correct seasoning and cook 6 to 7 minutes over medium-low heat.

Stir in cream and finish cooking 2 minutes.

Serve sauce with either beef or chicken.

After onion has cooked 3 minutes, mix in mushrooms and parsley; cook 2 to 3 minutes.

Pour in wine; cook 4 to 5 minutes over high heat.

Mix in brown sauce, correct seasoning and cook 6 to 7 minutes over medium-low heat.

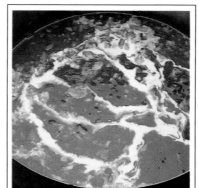

Stir in cream and finish cooking 2 minutes.

Paprika Sauce

1 SERVING	74 CALORIES	4g CARBOHYDRATE
1g PROTEIN	6g FAT	0.2g FIBER

Spicy Kebab Sauce

1 SERVING	61 CALORIES	12g CARBOHYDRATE
1g PROTEIN	1g FAT	0.3g FIBER

2 tbsp	(30 ml) horseradish
1 ½ cups	(375 ml) catsup
½ cup	(125 ml) chili sauce
1 tsp	(5 ml) Worcestershire sauce
	few drops Tabasco sauce
	few drops lime juice
	dash salt

Mix all ingredients together in bowl until well combined. Spread over kebabs and broil as directed in recipe.

1 cup	(250 ml) chopped onions
2 tbsp	(30 ml) butter
2 tbsp	(30 ml) paprika
½ cup	(125 ml) dry white wine
1 ½ cups	(375 ml) hot white sauce
	few drops Tabasco sauce
	dash salt
	few drops lemon juice

Place onions in small saucepan and pour in water to cover. Bring to boil and continue cooking 2 minutes; drain and set aside.

Heat butter in saucepan. Cook drained onion and paprika 5 to 6 minutes over low heat.

Pour in wine; cook 5 minutes over high heat to reduce liquid by ⅔.

Mix in white sauce and remaining ingredients; cook 6 to 7 minutes over low heat.

Serve sauce with a variety of kebabs.

PASTA

How To Cook Perfect Pasta

We have allowed ¼ lb (125 g) or less of dry pasta per serving, depending on the recipe.

Allow 16 cups (4 l) of water per 1 lb (500 g) of pasta as the water must be able to circulate easily.

To help keep pasta from sticking, add about 1 tbsp (15 ml) of oil or vinegar to the water before adding pasta.

To draw out the pasta's flavor you can add about 1 tsp (5 ml) of salt.

Be sure to bring the water to a full boil before adding pasta and when you do so, stir the noodles well.

During cooking keep the water boiling and stir several times or as often as needed to prevent the pasta from sticking.

One way to check if the pasta is cooked is by biting into a strand or piece and deciding by your preference. The package directions will give you a guideline for cooking times.

When pasta is 'al dente', stop the cooking process by draining pasta into a colander or large sieve and rinsing with cold water. Shake off excess water and set aside until ready to use. If you need to heat pasta quickly simply rinse with hot water.

For your convenience we have given these measurements in cups, which are equivalent to ¼ lb (125 g) of the pasta listed. All measurements are for dry pasta.

Rotini	1 cup	250 ml
Conch Shells (medium)	1⅓ cups	325 ml
Penne	1¾ cups	425 ml
Fusilli	1¾ cups	425 ml
Macaroni	1 cup	250 ml
Broad Egg Noodles	2¼ cups	550 ml

Last Minute White Spaghetti

(serves 4)

1 SERVING	579 CALORIES	94g CARBOHYDRATE
17g PROTEIN	15g FAT	0.3g FIBER

1 tbsp	(15 ml) white vinegar
1 tsp	(5 ml) salt
1 lb	(500 g) spaghetti
3 tbsp	(45 ml) butter
¼ cup	(50 ml) grated Parmesan cheese
¼ cup	(50 ml) grated mozzarella cheese
¼ cup	(50 ml) grated Gruyère cheese
¼ tsp	(1 ml) celery seed
	white pepper
	dash paprika

Bring 16 cups (4 L) water, vinegar and salt to full boil in large saucepan. Add pasta and stir; cook at full boil uncovered, stirring occasionally. Using package directions as a guideline, test pasta several times by biting into strand. When 'al dente', drain into colander reserving ¼ cup (50 ml) of cooking liquid. Rinse pasta with cold water and set aside.

Melt butter in same saucepan. Mix in cheeses and reserved cooking liquid; blend together well.

Add pasta and seasonings; mix well but gently and cook about 2 minutes over medium heat. Stir constantly!

Sprinkle with more paprika and serve immediately.

Four Cheese Sauce and Noodles

(serves 4)

1 SERVING	882 CALORIES	111g CARBOHYDRATE
33g PROTEIN	34g FAT	0.5g FIBER

4 tbsp	(60 ml) butter
4½ tbsp	(65 ml) flour
4 cups	(1 L) hot milk
½ tsp	(2 ml) nutmeg
¼ tsp	(1 ml) ground clove
¼ cup	(50 ml) grated Fontina cheese
¼ cup	(50 ml) crumbled Gorgonzola cheese
¼ cup	(50 ml) diced mozzarella cheese
¼ cup	(50 ml) grated Parmesan cheese
1 lb	(500 g) broad egg noodles, cooked
	salt and pepper

Heat butter in saucepan. Mix in flour and cook 2 to 3 minutes over low heat.

Add half of milk, whisk well and pour in remaining milk. Add seasonings and cook sauce 8 to 10 minutes over low heat.

Stir in cheeses and cook 4 to 5 minutes over low heat. Stir as required.

Serve with noodles.

Basic Tomato Sauce

1 SERVING	154 CALORIES	21g CARBOHYDRATE
4g PROTEIN	6g FAT	2.2g FIBER

2 tbsp	(30 ml) vegetable oil
1 tbsp	(15 ml) melted butter
2	onions, finely chopped
2	garlic cloves, smashed and chopped
12	large tomatoes, peeled and chopped
3	parsley sprigs
1 tsp	(5 ml) oregano
½ tsp	(2 ml) thyme
1	bay leaf
¼ tsp	(1 ml) crushed chillies
5½ oz	(156 ml) can tomato paste
	salt and pepper
	pinch sugar

Heat oil and butter in skillet. Add onions and garlic; mix well, cover and cook 4 to 5 minutes over low heat.

Stir in tomatoes, seasonings, parsley and sugar; continue cooking covered 15 minutes over low heat. Stir occasionally.

Remove cover and stir in tomato paste. Finish cooking 10 to 15 minutes over low heat uncovered.

Force sauce through sieve. This recipe will yield about 4 cups (1 L).

Meat Sauce for Spaghetti

(serves 6 to 8)

1 SERVING	265 CALORIES	15g CARBOHYDRATE
22g PROTEIN	13g FAT	1.7g FIBER

2 tbsp	(30 ml) olive oil
1	onion, chopped
1	carrot, diced small
1	celery stalk, diced small
3	garlic cloves, smashed and chopped
½ lb	(250 g) lean ground pork
½ lb	(250 g) ground beef
¼ lb	(125 g) sausage meat
¼ tsp	(1 ml) crushed chillies
½ tsp	(2 ml) thyme
½ tsp	(2 ml) oregano
¼ tsp	(1 ml) chili powder
¼ tsp	(1 ml) sugar
1	bay leaf
1 cup	(250 ml) dry white wine Chardonnay
2	28 oz (796 ml) cans tomatoes, drained and chopped
5 ½ oz	(156 ml) can tomato paste
	salt and pepper

Heat oil in deep skillet. Add onion, carrot, celery and garlic; cover and cook 3 minutes over medium heat.

Add pork, beef and sausage meat; mix well and continue cooking 4 minutes. Do not cover.

Add seasonings, sugar and wine; cook 3 minutes over high heat.

Stir in tomatoes, tomato paste and correct seasoning; bring to boil. Cook sauce, partially covered, about 1 hour over low heat; stir occasionally.

Serve this sauce with spaghetti or use it in a variety of pasta dishes as it is versatile.

Cook vegetables and garlic 3 minutes over medium heat. Cover pan.

Add seasonings, sugar and wine; cook 3 minutes over high heat.

Add pork, beef and sausage meat; mix well and continue cooking 4 minutes uncovered.

Stir in tomatoes, tomato paste and correct seasoning; bring to boil. Cook sauce, partially covered, about 1 hour over low heat.

White Sauce

1 SERVING	60 CALORIES	4g CARBOHYDRATE
2g PROTEIN	4g FAT	0g FIBER

4 tbsp	(60 ml) butter
5 tbsp	(75 ml) flour
5 cups	(1.2 L) hot milk
1	onion, studded with 1 clove
¼ tsp	(1 ml) nutmeg
	salt and white pepper

Heat butter in large saucepan. When melted, add flour and mix well. Cook 2 minutes over low heat stirring constantly.

Whisk in half of milk. Incorporate remaining milk and season. Drop in onion, stir in nutmeg and bring to boil.

Cook sauce 8 to 10 minutes over low heat, stirring occasionally. Use this sauce in a variety of pasta recipes.

Spicy Tomato Sauce

1 SERVING	182 CALORIES	15g CARBOHYDRATE
8g PROTEIN	10g FAT	1.5g FIBER

1 tbsp	(15 ml) olive oil
4	slices bacon, diced
1	large onion, finely chopped
2	garlic cloves, smashed and chopped
6	large tomatoes, peeled, seeded and chopped
1	fresh jalapeno pepper, finely chopped
1 tbsp	(15 ml) basil
1 tsp	(5 ml) chili powder
¼ tsp	(1 ml) sugar
¼ cup	(50 ml) grated Parmesan cheese
	salt and pepper

Heat oil in skillet. Cook bacon until crisp then remove, leaving fat in pan. Set bacon aside.

Add onion and garlic to pan; cook 3 to 4 minutes over low heat.

Stir in tomatoes, jalapeno pepper, seasonings and sugar. Cover and cook 20 minutes over low heat; stir occasionally.

Remove cover and continue cooking 15 minutes.

Mix in cheese and bacon. This recipe will yield about 2 cups (500 ml).

Perogies in Sauce

(serves 4)

1 SERVING	465 CALORIES	48g CARBOHYDRATE
21g PROTEIN	21g FAT	2.9g FIBER

2 tbsp	(30 ml) olive oil
1	onion, chopped
½	medium eggplant, cubed
1	zucchini, sliced
½ tsp	(2 ml) oregano
1 lb	(500 g) package perogies, cooked
2 tbsp	(30 ml) butter
28 oz	(796 ml) can tomatoes, drained and chopped
1	garlic clove, smashed and chopped
1 cup	(250 ml) chicken stock, heated
4 tbsp	(60 ml) tomato paste
3 tbsp	(45 ml) ricotta cheese
	salt and pepper

Heat oil in skillet and cook onion 2 minutes over medium heat.

Add eggplant, zucchini, oregano, salt and pepper. Cover and cook 10 to 12 minutes over medium heat stirring occasionally.

Meanwhile brown cooked perogies in 2 tbsp (30 ml) butter. When lightly browned on both sides remove from pan and set aside.

Add tomatoes and garlic to eggplant in skillet; mix very well and pour in chicken stock. Correct seasoning and stir in tomato paste; bring to boil and continue cooking uncovered 8 to 10 minutes.

Mix in cheese and perogies; simmer 2 to 3 minutes or until heated.

After onions have **1** cooked 3 minutes, mix in curry and continue cooking another 3 minutes. Do not cover.

Add mushrooms **2** and cook another 3 to 4 minutes.

3 Pour in chicken stock and season; bring to boil and cook 15 to 18 minutes over medium heat.

4 After sauce has thickened, add grapes, banana and water chestnuts and cook 1 minute.

Tortellini with Curry Sauce

(serves 4)

1 SERVING	325 CALORIES	43g CARBOHYDRATE
9g PROTEIN	13g FAT	2.6g FIBER

2 tbsp	(30 ml) oil
2	onions, chopped
2 tbsp	(30 ml) curry powder
½ lb	(250 g) mushrooms, sliced
3 cups	(750 ml) chicken stock, heated
2 tbsp	(30 ml) cornstarch
3 tbsp	(45 ml) cold water
1 cup	(250 ml) seedless green grapes
1	banana, sliced thick
10 oz	(284 ml) can water chestnuts, drained and sliced
½ lb	(250 g) cheese tortellini, cooked
	salt and pepper

Heat oil in skillet. Add onions and cook 3 minutes over medium heat covered.

Mix in curry; continue cooking 3 minutes uncovered.

Add mushrooms and cook another 3 to 4 minutes. Pour in chicken stock and season; bring to boil and cook 15 to 18 minutes over medium heat.

Mix cornstarch with water; stir into sauce and cook 1 minute.

Stir grapes, banana and water chestnuts into mixture; cook 1 minute.

Add tortellini and simmer 3 to 4 minutes.

Yellow Peppers Stuffed with Spaghetti

(serves 4)

1 SERVING	417 CALORIES	70g CARBOHYDRATE
14g PROTEIN	9g FAT	3.6g FIBER

2½ cups	(375 ml) spaghetti, broken into 1 in (2.5 cm) lengths
4	large yellow peppers, blanched 4 minutes
1 tbsp	(15 ml) butter
½ lb	(250 g) mushrooms, diced
2 tbsp	(30 ml) chopped pimento
1¼ cups	(300 ml) tomato sauce, heated
½ cup	(125 ml) ricotta cheese
	salt and pepper

Cook spaghetti al dente. Drain well and set aside.

Using small knife cut tops off peppers and remove white fibers and seeds; set aside on ovenproof platter.

Heat butter in saucepan. Cook mushrooms 3 minutes over medium heat; season well.

Add pimento and spaghetti; mix well and cook 2 minutes.

Stir in tomato sauce and cheese; correct seasoning. Pour into peppers and broil 4 to 5 minutes in oven.

Tortellini in Sauce

(serves 4)

1 SERVING	320 CALORIES	24g CARBOHYDRATE
11g PROTEIN	20g FAT	0.9g FIBER

3 tbsp	(45 ml) butter
1	onion, chopped
1 tbsp	(15 ml) chopped parsley
1	garlic clove, smashed and chopped
¼ lb	(125 g) mushrooms, diced
1 cup	(250 ml) dry red wine
2 cups	(500 ml) beef stock, heated
2 tbsp	(30 ml) cornstarch
3 tbsp	(45 ml) cold water
½ lb	(250 g) tortellini, cooked
¼ cup	(50 ml) crumbled cooked bacon
½ cup	(125 ml) grated Parmesan cheese
	salt and pepper

Heat butter in skillet. Add onion, parsley and garlic; cook 3 minutes over low heat.

Mix in mushrooms and season; cook 3 to 4 minutes over medium heat.

Pour in wine and cook 4 minutes over high heat. Add beef stock and cook 3 to 4 minutes over medium heat; correct seasoning.

Mix cornstarch with water; stir into sauce and cook 2 minutes.

Add tortellini, simmer 3 to 4 minutes then serve with bacon and cheese.

Fettuccine and Mussels

(serves 4)

1 SERVING	828 CALORIES	113g CARBOHYDRATE
58g PROTEIN	16g FAT	0.7g FIBER

8½ lb	(4 kg) fresh mussels, scrubbed and bearded
3	shallots, finely chopped
1 tbsp	(15 ml) chopped parsley
2 tbsp	(30 ml) butter
1 cup	(250 ml) dry white wine
2 cups	(500 ml) tomato sauce, heated
1 lb	(500 g) fettuccine, cooked
½ cup	(125 ml) grated Parmesan cheese
	salt and pepper

Place mussels in large pan with shallots, parsley, butter and wine. Cover and bring to boil; cook about 4 to 5 minutes or until shells open.

Remove shells, pouring liquid back into pan. Discard shells and set mussels aside.

Strain cooking liquid through cheesecloth into saucepan. Bring to boil and continue cooking 2 to 3 minutes.

Mix in tomato sauce, season and cook 4 to 5 minutes over medium heat.

Stir mussels and fettuccine into sauce. Cook 3 to 4 minutes over low heat or until heated through.

Serve with cheese.

Fettuccine with Peas

(serves 4)

1 SERVING	737 CALORIES	103g CARBOHYDRATE
25g PROTEIN	25g FAT	1.0g FIBER

3 tbsp	(45 ml) butter
2 tbsp	(30 ml) grated onion
3 tbsp	(45 ml) flour
2¼ cups	(550 ml) hot milk
¼ tsp	(1 ml) nutmeg
¼ tsp	(1 ml) white pepper
1 lb	(500 g) white fettuccine, cooked
1 cup	(250 ml) snow peas*, blanched
4	slices crisp bacon, finely chopped
½ cup	(125 ml) grated Parmesan cheese
	salt
	few drops Tabasco sauce

Heat butter with onion in saucepan. Mix in flour and cook 2 minutes over low heat, stirring only once.

Pour in half of milk, whisk well and add remaining milk along with seasonings; cook sauce 10 minutes over low heat. Stir at least 2 to 3 times.

Add pasta and peas to sauce; stir and cook 2 to 3 minutes more.

Correct seasoning and garnish portions with bacon and cheese.

* Snow peas are available fresh in the pod. Be careful not to accidently choose the green garden peas which are also sold fresh. After shelling the peas you can save the pods for another recipe such as a stir-fry.

Stuffed Cold Tomatoes

(serves 4)

1 SERVING	216 CALORIES	23g CARBOHYDRATE
4g PROTEIN	12g FAT	3.4g FIBER

8	large tomatoes
3	mint leaves, chopped
2 tbsp	(30 ml) olive oil
1 tsp	(5 ml) wine vinegar
1½ cups	(375 ml) cooked ready-cut macaroni
3 tbsp	(45 ml) mustard vinaigrette or substitute
1 tbsp	(15 ml) chopped parsley
1	green pepper, finely chopped
2 tbsp	(30 ml) pickled sweet pimento
	salt and pepper

Using sharp knife and spoon, hollow tomatoes. Discard insides and set shells aside.

Mix chopped mint, oil and vinegar together. Season well and sprinkle in tomatoes; let stand 15 minutes.

Mix macaroni with remaining ingredients; let stand 15 minutes.

Fill tomatoes with macaroni mixture, chill 15 minutes, and serve.

Meaty Macaroni and Cheese

(serves 4)

1 SERVING	826 CALORIES	88g CARBOHYDRATE
60g PROTEIN	26g FAT	2.0g FIBER

2 tbsp	(30 ml) olive oil
1	onion, finely chopped
1	garlic clove, smashed and chopped
½ tsp	(2 ml) oregano
1 tbsp	(15 ml) chopped parsley
½ lb	(250 g) ground beef
½ lb	(250 g) lean ground pork
1½	28 oz (796 ml) cans tomatoes, drained and chopped
¾ lb	(375 g) macaroni, cooked
¾ lb	(375 g) ricotta cheese
	salt and pepper

Heat oil in skillet. Add onion and cook 3 minutes over low heat.

Stir in garlic, seasonings and meats; cook 5 to 6 minutes over medium heat stirring often.

Mix in tomatoes and correct seasoning. Continue cooking 10 to 12 minutes over low heat.

Add macaroni and cheese; cook 4 to 5 minutes over low heat and serve.

Seafood Macaroni

(serves 4)

1 SERVING	795 CALORIES	112g CARBOHYDRATE
53g PROTEIN	15g FAT	5.1g FIBER

5	large tomatoes, cut in 2 and seeded
1 tbsp	(15 ml) olive oil
1	large onion, finely chopped
½ tsp	(2 ml) basil
½ tsp	(2 ml) tarragon
½ tsp	(2 ml) chopped parsley
1 lb	(500 g) small cooked shrimp
1 lb	(500 g) macaroni, cooked
1 cup	(250 ml) ricotta cheese
	pinch sugar
	salt and pepper

Purée tomatoes in blender for 3 minutes.

Heat oil in large frying pan. Cook onion 3 minutes over low heat.

Add basil, tarragon, parsley, sugar and tomatoes; season well. Cook 25 to 30 minutes over low heat.

Stir in shrimp, macaroni and cheese; cook 3 minutes or until heated through.

Serve.

Garnished Penne

(serves 4)

1 SERVING	623 CALORIES	90g CARBOHYDRATE
23g PROTEIN	19g FAT	0.5g FIBER

2 tbsp	(30 ml) butter
¼ cup	(50 ml) Monterey Jack or cheddar, crumbled or grated
½ cup	(125 ml) grated Parmesan cheese
1 lb	(500 g) penne, cooked and still hot
12	thin slices salami, in julienne
	salt and pepper
	chopped parsley

Heat butter in large saucepan over medium-low heat. Stir in cheeses and cook 2 minutes over low heat. Mix to avoid sticking.

Add hot penne and season generously. Mix well and continue cooking 2 to 3 minutes over low heat.

Stir in salami, garnish with chopped parsley and serve.

Penne Vegetable Salad

(serves 4)

1 SERVING	591 CALORIES	95g CARBOHYDRATE
31g PROTEIN	43g FAT	1.7g FIBER

1 lb	(500 g) penne, cooked
1	yellow pepper, in julienne
½	zucchini, in julienne and blanched
4	slices cooked ham, in julienne
1	large tomato, cored and in wedges
½ cup	(125 ml) pitted black olives
1 tbsp	(15 ml) chopped parsley
½ tsp	(2 ml) chopped fresh oregano
3	mint leaves, chopped
1	egg yolk
2 tbsp	(30 ml) catsup
3 tbsp	(45 ml) wine vinegar
½ cup	(125 ml) olive oil
½ cup	(125 ml) grated Parmesan cheese
1 tbsp	(15 ml) chopped jalapeno peppers
	salt and pepper

In large serving bowl, toss together penne, yellow pepper, zucchini, ham, tomato, olives, parsley, oregano and mint.

In another bowl mix egg yolk with catsup. Incorporate vinegar then slowly add oil while mixing constantly.

Add remaining ingredients and poor over salad. Toss and serve.

Linguine with Artichoke Hearts

(serves 4)

1 SERVING	707 CALORIES	195g CARBOHYDRATE
20g PROTEIN	23g FAT	1.3g FIBER

5 tbsp	(75 ml) butter
4½ tbsp	(65 ml) flour
2 cups	(500 ml) hot chicken stock
8	artichoke hearts, quartered
1	garlic clove, smashed and chopped
½ cup	(125 ml) stuffed green olives, halved
1 tbsp	(15 ml) chopped parsley
¼ cup	(50 ml) dry white wine Chardonnay
1 lb	(500 g) linguine, cooked
½ cup	(125 ml) grated Parmesan cheese
	salt and pepper
	dash paprika

Heat 4 tbsp (60 ml) butter in saucepan. Mix in flour and cook 2 minutes over low heat while stirring.

Pour in chicken stock, mix very well and season generously. Cook 8 to 10 minutes over low heat.

Meanwhile, heat remaining butter in frying pan. Cook artichoke hearts, garlic, olives and parsley 2 to 3 minutes over medium heat. Season well.

Incorporate white wine and continue cooking mixture 2 to 3 minutes.

Add artichoke mixture to sauce and mix well. Pour over pasta and sprinkle with cheese and paprika before serving.

Meaty Lasagne

(serves 6)

1 SERVING	785 CALORIES	85g CARBOHYDRATE
64g PROTEIN	21g FAT	2.4g FIBER

1½ cups	(375 ml) cottage cheese
¼ tsp	(1 ml) allspice
½ tsp	(2 ml) oregano
1 tbsp	(15 ml) chopped lemon rind
½ cup	(125 ml) grated Parmesan cheese
2 tbsp	(30 ml) vegetable oil
2	onions, chopped
1	celery stalk, chopped
2	garlic cloves, smashed and chopped
1 lb	(500 g) ground beef
½ lb	(250 g) ground veal
1 lb	(500 g) mushrooms, chopped
1 lb	(500 g) lasagne, cooked
1¼ cups	(300 ml) grated mozzarella cheese
4 cups	(1 L) hot tomato sauce
	salt and pepper

Preheat oven to 375°F (190°C). Grease lasagne dish.

Mix cottage cheese, allspice, oregano, lemon rind and Parmesan cheese together in bowl; set aside.

Heat oil in large skillet; cook onions, celery and garlic 3 to 4 minutes over medium heat.

Add meats, mix well and brown 5 to 6 minutes; season well. Mix in mushrooms and finish cooking 3 to 4 minutes over high heat. Correct seasoning and remove from stove.

Dividing ingredients equally build lasagne with layers of pasta, meat, cottage cheese, mozzarella and tomato sauce. End with a layer of pasta then cover with sauce and remaining mozzarella.

Bake 50 minutes in oven.

Lasagne Rolls

(serves 4)

1 SERVING	949 CALORIES	57g CARBOHYDRATE
70g PROTEIN	49g FAT	0.9g FIBER

2 tbsp	(30 ml) vegetable oil
1	small onion, finely chopped
¼ tsp	(1 ml) thyme
1 tsp	(5 ml) oregano
1 tbsp	(15 ml) chopped parsley
¼ tsp	(1 ml) ground clove
1 lb	(500 g) ground veal
3	slices ham, finely chopped
¼ cup	(50 ml) hot chicken stock
1 cup	(250 ml) cooked spinach, chopped
3 oz	(90 g) diced mozzarella cheese
1	beaten egg
8	strips lasagne, cooked
4 cups	(1 L) hot white sauce
1 cup	(250 ml) grated Gruyère cheese
	salt and pepper
	paprika to taste

Preheat oven to 375°F (190°C).

Heat oil in large frying pan. Add onion, thyme, oregano, parsley and clove; cover and cook 3 minutes.

Stir in veal and ham; season and cook 3 minutes uncovered.

Add chicken stock and spinach; cook 3 to 4 minutes. Stir in mozzarella and cook 2 to 3 minutes while mixing. Remove pan from heat and cool.

Add egg to bind stuffing. Lay lasagne strips flat and sprinkle with paprika. Spread stuffing over full length of strips and roll.

Place rolls in baking dish and cover with white sauce; top with cheese. Bake 20 minutes in oven. Serve with a vegetable garnish or salad.

Lay lasagne strips flat and sprinkle with paprika for extra taste.

Spread stuffing over full length of each strip then roll.

Place rolls in baking dish and cover with white sauce.

Top with cheese and bake 20 minutes in oven.

Vegetable Lasagne

(serves 6)

1 SERVING	666 CALORIES	81g CARBOHYDRATE
27g PROTEIN	26g FAT	4.7g FIBER

½ cup	(125 ml) grated Parmesan cheese
½ cup	(125 ml) grated Gruyère cheese
½ cup	(125 ml) grated Romano cheese
3 tbsp	(45 ml) butter
1	red onion, finely diced
1	celery stalk, finely diced
1	small zucchini, diced
½	small cauliflower, diced
1	yellow pepper, diced
1	small eggplant, finely diced
1 tbsp	(15 ml) chopped parsley
1 tbsp	(15 ml) grated lemon rind
½ tsp	(2 ml) nutmeg and ground clove
2	garlic cloves, smashed and chopped
¼ cup	(50 ml) chicken stock, heated
1 lb	(500 g) lasagne, cooked
6	tomatoes, thinly sliced
3 cups	(750 ml) thin white sauce, heated
½ cup	(125 ml) tomato sauce, heated
	salt and pepper
	sliced mozzarella for topping
	paprika to taste

Preheat oven to 375°F (190°C). Grease lasagne dish.

Mix grated cheeses together; set aside.

Heat butter in large skillet; cook onion and celery 4 minutes over low heat.

Add remaining vegetables (except tomatoes), parsley, lemon rind, seasonings, garlic and chicken stock. Mix well, cover and cook 10 to 12 minutes over low heat.

Dividing ingredients equally, build lasagne with layers of pasta, vegetables, tomatoes, grated cheeses and white sauce. End with a layer of pasta then cover with tomato sauce and mozzarella cheese; sprinkle with paprika.

Place lasagne dish on cookie sheet and bake about 50 minutes.

Cook vegetables  (except tomatoes), seasonings, garlic and chicken stock in large skillet for 10 to 12 minutes. Be sure to cover pan and keep heat low.

 After the layers of lasagne, vegetables, tomatoes and grated cheeses, top with white sauce.

When building  the lasagne try to spread layers evenly.

 End with a layer of pasta then cover with tomato sauce and mozzarella cheese; sprinkle with paprika.

Fusilli, Broccoli and Cheese

(serves 4)

1 SERVING	892 CALORIES	101g CARBOHYDRATE
32g PROTEIN	40g FAT	1.1g FIBER

2	small heads broccoli, in flowerets
1½ cups	(375 ml) cold light cream
½ lb	(250 g) Gorgonzola cheese, crumbled
1 tbsp	(15 ml) butter
1 tbsp	(15 ml) chopped parsley
1 lb	(500 g) fusilli, cooked
	few drops lemon juice
	salt and pepper

Cook broccoli in boiling salted water for 3 to 4 minutes. Drain and set aside. Sprinkle with lemon juice.

Pour cream into saucepan and bring to boiling point. Add cheese and butter; mix very well and season.

Cook 4 to 5 minutes over low heat to melt cheese. Stir occasionally.

Stir in broccoli, parsley and lemon juice; simmer 1 to 2 minutes then serve with pasta.

Fusilli and Chicken Livers

(serves 4)

1 SERVING	648 CALORIES	87g CARBOHYDRATE
39g PROTEIN	16g FAT	1.8g FIBER

1 tbsp	(15 ml) oil
1 lb	(500 g) chicken livers, cut in 2
2 tbsp	(30 ml) butter
1	onion, finely chopped
½ lb	(250 g) mushrooms, diced
1	red pepper, diced
½ cup	(125 ml) dry red wine
1 cup	(250 ml) tomato sauce, heated
1 cup	(250 ml) beef stock, heated
¼ tsp	(1 ml) thyme
½ tsp	(2 ml) basil
1 tsp	(5 ml) cornstarch
2 tbsp	(30 ml) cold water
¾ lb	(375 g) fusilli, cooked and still hot
	salt and pepper

Heat oil in frying pan and cook livers 3 minutes each side; season well. Remove and set aside.

Add butter, onion and mushrooms to pan; cook 3 minutes over medium heat. Add red pepper and cook 2 minutes; season well.

Pour in wine and cook 3 minutes over high heat. Mix in tomato sauce, beef stock and seasonings; cook 2 minutes.

Mix cornstarch with water; stir into sauce and cook 1 minute. Add livers, simmer 5 minutes then pour over hot fusilli.

Eggplant and Conch Shells

(serves 4)

1 SERVING	567 CALORIES	92g CARBOHYDRATE
16g PROTEIN	15g FAT	2.8g FIBER

2	medium eggplants
3 tbsp	(45 ml) olive oil
1	garlic clove, smashed and chopped
1 tbsp	(15 ml) chopped parsley
1 tsp	(5 ml) marjoram
2 cups	(500 ml) spicy tomato sauce, heated
¾ lb	(375 g) medium conch shells, cooked
½ cup	(125 ml) marinated pitted black olives, sliced
	salt and pepper

Preheat oven to 375°F (190°C).

Cut eggplants in half lengthwise. Score flesh and brush with 2 tbsp (30 ml) oil. Bake 50 minutes in oven.

When cooked, remove and chop flesh.

Heat remaining oil in skillet and cook garlic 1 minute. Add eggplant and seasonings; mix and cook 3 to 4 minutes over high heat.

Pour in tomato sauce, mix well and simmer 5 minutes over low heat.

Stir in conch shells and olives; simmer 2 to 3 minutes over low heat.

Rotini
with Mushrooms

(serves 4)

1 SERVING	623 CALORIES	77g CARBOHYDRATE
18g PROTEIN	27g FAT	0.8g FIBER

2 tbsp	(30 ml) olive oil
2 cups	(500 ml) quartered mushrooms
2 tbsp	(30 ml) capers
1 tsp	(5 ml) chopped fresh parsley
½ tsp	(2 ml) oregano
½ cup	(125 ml) dry red wine Valpolicella
1½ cups	(375 ml) hot light cream
2 tbsp	(30 ml) tomato paste
2	green onions, chopped
¾ lb	(375 g) rotini, cooked
¼ cup	(375 g) grated Parmesan cheese
	salt and pepper

Heat oil in saucepan. Add mushrooms, capers, parsley, oregano, salt and pepper; cook 3 to 4 minutes over medium heat.

Pour in red wine and cook 3 to 4 minutes over high heat.

Add cream and mix well. Stir in tomato paste and onions; cook 3 to 4 minutes over low heat.

Correct seasoning and serve sauce with pasta. Sprinkle with cheese before serving.

Egg Noodles and Anchovies

(serves 4)

1 SERVING	677 CALORIES	80g CARBOHYDRATE
24g PROTEIN	29g FAT	2.3g FIBER

5	large tomatoes, peeled
2 tbsp	(30 ml) olive oil
1	garlic clove, smashed and chopped
3	fresh basil leaves, chopped
1	small jalapeno pepper, in 2 pieces
4	anchovy filets, chopped
1 cup	(250 ml) marinated black olives, pitted
3 tbsp	(45 ml) capers
1 cup	(250 ml) grated Emmentaler cheese
¾ lb	(375 g) extra-broad egg noodles, cooked
	salt and pepper

Purée tomatoes in blender; set aside.

Heat oil in skillet and cook garlic and basil 1 minute over medium heat.

Add tomatoes and pieces of jalapeno; mix well and stir in anchovies. Bring to boil and cook 18 to 20 minutes over low heat. During cooking, taste sauce occasionally; remove jalapeno pieces when they have imparted enough flavour.

Add remaining ingredients and mix well. Cook 3 to 4 minutes before serving.

Purée tomatoes in blender.
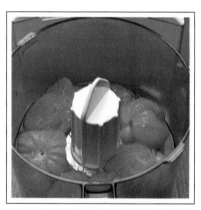

Add tomatoes and pieces of jalapeno to cooking garlic and basil leaves.

Mix well and stir in anchovies. Bring sauce to boil and cook 18 to 20 minutes over low heat.

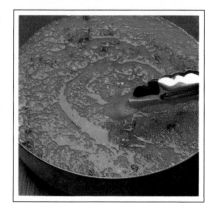
During cooking, taste sauce occasionally and when pleased with taste remove jalapeno pieces.

Spinach Egg Noodles Stroganoff

(serves 4)

1 SERVING	781 CALORIES	80g CARBOHYDRATE
59g PROTEIN	25g FAT	1.3g FIBER

1 tbsp	(15 ml) vegetable oil
1½ lb	(750 g) sirloin steak, cut in 1 in (2.5 cm) strips
2 tbsp	(30 ml) melted butter
2	shallots, chopped
1	onion, thinly sliced
½ lb	(250 g) mushrooms, diced
1 tbsp	(15 ml) chopped parsley
¼ tsp	(1 ml) thyme
1 cup	(250 ml) dry red wine Valpolicella
2 cups	(500 ml) beef stock, heated
1½ tbsp	(25 ml) cornstarch
3 tbsp	(45 ml) cold water
¾ lb	(375 g) broad spinach egg noodles, cooked
½ cup	(125 ml) ricotta cheese
	salt and pepper

Heat oil in frying pan. Add meat and cook 2 minutes over medium-high heat. Turn over, season and cook 1 more minute. Remove meat from pan.

Add butter, shallots and onion; cook 3 minutes over low heat.

Add mushrooms, parsley and thyme; cook 3 minutes over medium heat.

Correct seasoning and add wine; cook 3 minutes over high heat. Stir in beef stock; cook 3 minutes over low heat.

Mix cornstarch with water; stir into sauce and cook about 2 minutes.

Replace meat in sauce, fold in noodles and simmer 2 minutes. Stir in cheese and serve.

Continental Egg Noodles

(serves 4)

1 SERVING	765 CALORIES	128g CARBOHYDRATE
16g PROTEIN	21g FAT	1.7g FIBER

3 tbsp	(45 ml) butter
2	onions, finely chopped
2	green onions, finely chopped
3 tbsp	(45 ml) curry powder
1 tsp	(5 ml) cumin
3 cups	(750 ml) chicken stock, heated
2 tbsp	(30 ml) cornstarch
3 tbsp	(45 ml) cold water
½ cup	(125 ml) golden raisins
½ cup	(125 ml) grated coconut
1 lb	(500 g) broad egg noodles, cooked
½ cup	(125 ml) plain yogurt
	salt and pepper
	sesame seeds

Heat butter in large skillet. Add both onions and cook 3 to 4 minutes over low heat. Stir in curry and cumin; continue cooking 3 to 4 minutes.

Add chicken stock, season and bring to boil. Cook 15 minutes over low heat.

Mix cornstarch with water; stir into sauce and cook 1 minute.

Add raisins, coconut and noodles; simmer 2 to 3 minutes.

Stir in yogurt and top with sesame seeds.

Vermicelli and Spinach

(serves 4)

1 SERVING	701 CALORIES	110g CARBOHYDRATE
27g PROTEIN	17g FAT	1.9g FIBER

1 lb	(500 g) spinach leaves
2 tbsp	(30 ml) olive oil
2	garlic cloves, smashed and chopped
3 cups	(750 ml) tomato sauce, heated
1 lb	(500 g) vermicelli, cooked
1 cup	(250 ml) grated Parmesan cheese
	salt and pepper

Wash spinach very well. Cool about 3 to 4 minutes in salted boiling water; cover pan.

Drain spinach, shape into balls and squeeze out all excess water. Chop and set aside.

Heat oil in skillet. When hot, add garlic and spinach; cook 3 minutes over high heat.

Add tomato sauce, vermicelli, salt and pepper; simmer 2 to 3 minutes over medium-low heat.

Serve with cheese.

Vermicelli, Bacon and Peas

(serves 4)

1 SERVING	489 CALORIES	83g CARBOHYDRATE
19g PROTEIN	9g FAT	5.8g FIBER

2 tbsp	(30 ml) butter
1	Spanish onion, chopped
½ tsp	(2 ml) oregano
½ tsp	(2 ml) paprika
4	slices back bacon, in strips
¼ cup	(50 ml) dry red wine
1½ cups	(375 ml) beef stock, heated
1½ tbsp	(25 ml) cornstarch
3 tbsp	(45 ml) cold water
1½ cups	(375 ml) frozen green peas, cooked
¾ lb	(375 g) vermicelli, cooked
¼ cup	(125 ml) grated Parmesan cheese
	salt and pepper

Heat butter in skillet; cook onion and seasonings 8 to 10 minutes over low heat.

Add bacon and cook 3 to 4 minutes. Stir in wine and cook 3 minutes over high heat.

Mix in beef stock and cook 5 to 6 minutes over medium heat. Mix cornstarch with water; stir into sauce and cook 1 minute.

Add peas and vermicelli; mix well and simmer 3 minutes. Stir in cheese and serve.

Cook onion and seasonings 8 to 10 minutes over low heat.

Add bacon and cook 3 to 4 minutes. Pour in wine, stir and cook 3 minutes over high heat.

Stir diluted cornstarch into sauce and cook 1 minute to thicken.

Add peas and vermicelli; mix well and simmer 3 minutes. Stir in cheese before serving.

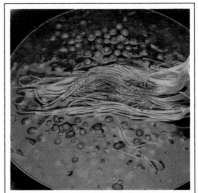

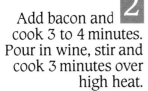

Layered Gnocchi *(serves 4)*

1 SERVING	488 CALORIES	42g CARBOHYDRATE
26g PROTEIN	24g FAT	0.3g FIBER

½ cup	(125 ml) ricotta cheese
2	eggs
1 cup	(250 ml) grated Parmesan cheese
1½ cups	(375 ml) sifted flour
1 cup	(250 ml) grated Gruyère cheese
1½ cups	(375 ml) thin white sauce, heated
1 cup	(250 ml) tomato sauce, heated
1 tbsp	(15 ml) chopped parsley
	salt and pepper
	paprika

Preheat oven to 375°F (190°C).

Place ricotta, eggs, Parmesan, salt and pepper in blender; mix 1 minute.

Add flour and mix 1 minute; transfer dough to bowl, cover and refrigerate 1 hour.

Bring plenty of salted water to boiling point. Drop in small pieces of dough and cook 8 minutes. Keep water at boiling point and when cooked, remove with slotted spoon and drain on paper towels. Depending on the size of pan you may have to cook gnocchi in two batches.

Place half of gnocchi in lightly greased baking dish. Add half of Gruyère, half of white sauce and paprika.

Pour in half of tomato sauce and finish with remaining gnocchi, cheese, parsley and sauces.

Bake 30 to 35 minutes in oven.

After dough has been chilled, drop small pieces into hot water and cook 8 minutes. Do not crowd.

Place half of gnocchi in lightly greased baking dish. Add half of Gruyère, half of white sauce and paprika.

Pour in half of tomato sauce.

Finish with remaining gnocchi, cheese, parsley and sauces.

Potato Gnocchi

(serves 4)

1 SERVING	400 CALORIES	42g CARBOHYDRATE
13g PROTEIN	20g FAT	1.0g FIBER

1 cup	(250 ml) flour
2 cups	(500 ml) cooked riced potatoes
4 tbsp	(60 ml) butter
½ cup	(125 ml) grated mozzarella cheese
1½ cups	(375 ml) tomato sauce, heated
½ cup	(125 ml) ricotta cheese
	salt and white pepper
	pinch nutmeg

Place flour in bowl and form well in center. Add potatoes, nutmeg and 3 tbsp (45 ml) butter; pinch dough to incorporate.

Season and remove dough from bowl. Place on counter and knead with the heel of your hand until smooth.

Shape dough into ball and cut into 4 quarters. Roll each quarter into a cylindrical shape with a diameter of about 1 in (2.5 cm). Slice into ½ in (1.2 cm) pieces.

Cook in salted simmering water for about 5 minutes. Monitor heat to keep water simmering without breaking into a boil.

When cooked, gnocchi should rise to the surface. Remove with slotted spoon and set aside to drain on paper towel.

Preheat oven to 375°F (190°C).

With remaining butter grease large baking dish.

Season mozzarella with salt and pepper. Mix ricotta cheese with tomato sauce over low heat for 1 minute.

Layer gnocchi, mozzarella and sauce in baking dish. Bake 12 minutes.

Change oven setting to broil and continue cooking 4 minutes. Serve.

BUDGET COOKING

Economical cooking should not imply that you're getting the bottom of the barrel nor should it be an indication of a meal with little taste, variety or nutrition. But rather, inexpensive eating should simply mean that you're getting your money's worth and making the most of what you buy. As you are probably well aware, there are many ways of literally saving cash such as using coupons, taking advantage of in-store sales or just generally 'shopping around'. But the best rule of thumb I can offer you is to never settle for poor quality and pay for it! Treat food shopping as you would any other — if the goods are damaged or not up to par, the price should be adjusted accordingly. If on Tuesday the red peppers are a sorry lot then substitute them for another vegetable that is fresh and worth your money — in other words be ready to compromise! Aside from being flexible, be prepared to spend a little extra time in the kitchen as some foods like inexpensive cuts of meat may need marinating or longer cooking times to bring out the best flavor and tenderness. And lastly, think of your freezer as you would your best friend. Let's get started...

Corned Beef and Cabbage

(serves 4)

1 SERVING	1777 CALORIES	54g CARBOHYDRATE
73g PROTEIN	141g FAT	6.3g FIBER

4 lb	(1.8 kg) corned beef brisket
3	cloves
1	bay leaf
3	parsley sprigs
½ tsp	(2 ml) thyme
1	large cabbage, cut in 4
8	carrots, pared
4	large potatoes, peeled and cut in half
2	leeks, cut in 4 lengthwise to within 1 in (2.5 cm) of base, washed
	salt and pepper

Place brisket in large saucepan and pour in enough cold water to cover beef by 3 in (7.5 cm). Bring to boil, then skim.

Add cloves, bay leaf, parsley and thyme; partially cover and cook 3 hours over low heat. Skim if necessary.

Meanwhile, blanch cabbage and carrots in salted boiling water about 10 minutes. Drain well.

Add blanched vegetables, potatoes and leeks to beef. Continue cooking 1 hour partially covered.

To serve, remove beef and vegetables from liquid and arrange on serving platter. Moisten beef with a little bit of cooking liquid, slice and serve.

Boiled Beef

(serves 4)

1 SERVING	486 CALORIES	7g CARBOHYDRATE
56g PROTEIN	26g FAT	1.5g FIBER

4 lb	(1.8 kg) cross-rib roast, tied
2	celery stalks, cut in ½
2	leeks, cut in 4 lengthwise to within 1 in (2.5 cm) of base, washed
1	Spanish onion, cut in 4
2	garlic cloves, peeled and whole
4	cloves
½ tsp	(2 ml) allspice
4	parsley sprigs
2	bay leaves
	salt and pepper

Place all ingredients in large saucepan and pour in enough cold water to cover; bring to boil.

Skim then continue cooking 4 hours over low heat; partially cover. Serve with horseradish sauce.

Horseradish Sauce

1 SERVING	51 CALORIES	5g CARBOHYDRATE
1g PROTEIN	3g FAT	0.5g FIBER

4 tbsp	(60 ml) horseradish
2 tbsp	(30 ml) sour cream
1 tbsp	(15 ml) breadcrumbs
⅓ cup	(75 ml) whipped heavy cream
	few drops Tabasco sauce
	fresh ground pepper

Mix horseradish, sour cream and breadcrumbs together.

Add remaining ingredients and season generously. Serve with boiled beef.

Pot Roast

(serves 4)

1 SERVING	488 CALORIES	21g CARBOHYDRATE
56g PROTEIN	20g FAT	3.0g FIBER

2 tbsp	(30 ml) vegetable oil
3 lb	(1.4 kg) sirloin tip roast
5	onions, peeled, cut in 4
2 cups	(500 ml) dry red wine
2 cups	(500 ml) tomato sauce, heated
1	garlic clove, smashed and chopped
½ tsp	(2 ml) thyme
½ tsp	(2 ml) basil
½ tsp	(2 ml) allspice
	salt and pepper

Preheat oven to 350°F (180°C).

Heat oil in large ovenproof casserole. Sear beef 6 to 8 minutes over medium-high heat on all sides; season well.

Add onions and continue cooking 6 to 8 minutes over medium heat.

Pour in wine and tomato sauce. Add garlic, seasonings and bring to boil.

Cover and cook 2½ hours in oven.

Serve with additional vegetables if desired.

Sear beef 6 to 8 minutes over medium-high heat on all sides; season well.

Add onions and continue cooking 6 to 8 minutes over medium heat.

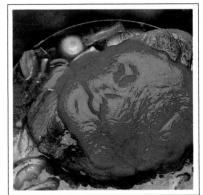

Pour in wine.

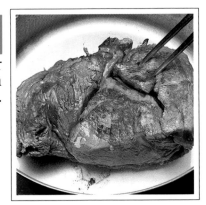

Pour in tomato sauce. Add garlic, seasonings and bring to boil. Finish cooking 2½ hours in oven.

Beef Stew

(serves 4)

1 SERVING	513 CALORIES	36g CARBOHYDRATE
36g PROTEIN	25g FAT	3.0g FIBER

2 tbsp	(30 ml) vegetable oil
2 lb	(900 g) stewing beef, cubed
½ tsp	(2 ml) chili powder
4 tbsp	(60 ml) flour
1 tbsp	(15 ml) butter
1	garlic clove, smashed and chopped
1	onion, coarsely chopped
1	celery stalk, diced
¼ tsp	(1 ml) thyme
1	clove
½ tsp	(2 ml) tarragon
½ tsp	(2 ml) basil
28 oz	(796 ml) can tomatoes
2½ cups	(625 ml) beef stock, heated
2 tbsp	(30 ml) tomato paste
2	large potatoes, peeled and cubed
2	large carrots, pared and cubed
	salt and pepper

Preheat oven to 350°F (180°C).

Heat oil in ovenproof casserole. Sear meat (in two batches) 3 minutes over medium-high heat. Turn pieces over and add chili powder, salt and pepper; finish searing 3 minutes.

With all meat in casserole sprinkle in flour. Mix well and cook 2 to 3 minutes over medium heat.

Remove meat and set aside.

Add butter to casserole. Cook garlic, onion, celery and seasonings 3 to 4 minutes over medium heat.

Pour in tomatoes with juice and correct seasoning. Replace meat and mix well.

Add beef stock, mix and stir in tomato paste; cover and bring to boil. Finish cooking 2 hours in oven.

1 hour before beef is cooked, add vegetables to casserole, forty minutes later, remove cover.

Serve stew with garlic bread.

Sear meat (in two batches) 3 minutes over medium-high heat. Turn pieces over and add chili powder, salt and pepper; finish searing 3 minutes.

Cook garlic, onion, celery and seasonings 3 to 4 minutes over medium heat.

With all meat in casserole sprinkle in flour. Mix well and cook 2 to 3 minutes over medium heat.

Pour in tomatoes with juice and correct seasoning.

Stir-fry meat and garlic for 2 minutes then pour in soya sauce. Mix well to coat meat strips then remove.

Add yellow pepper and pea pods; continue cooking 2 to 3 minutes over high heat stirring frequently.

Add onions and cucumbers to pan; cook 2 minutes over high heat. Season with pepper.

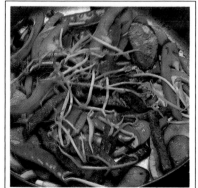

Replace meat in pan along with sprouts; simmer 2 to 3 minutes over medium-low heat before serving.

Beef Stir-Fry

(serves 4)

1 SERVING	410 CALORIES	11g CARBOHYDRATE
51g PROTEIN	18g FAT	2.2g FIBER

2 tbsp	(30 ml) vegetable oil
2 lb	(900 g) strip loin steak, cut in strips
1	garlic clove, smashed and chopped
2 tbsp	(30 ml) soya sauce
4	green onions, in 2.5 cm lengths
1	red onion, cut in half and sliced
2	dill cucumbers, sliced
1	yellow pepper, sliced
7 oz	(200 g) snow peas, ends trimmed
1 cup	(250 ml) bean sprouts
	salt and pepper

Heat oil in large frying pan. When hot, add meat and garlic; stir-fry 2 minutes.

Season and pour in soya sauce; mix well and remove meat from pan.

Add onions and cucumbers to pan; cook 2 minutes over high heat. Season with pepper.

Add yellow pepper and snow peas; continue cooking 2 to 3 minutes over high heat stirring frequently.

Replace meat in pan along with sprouts; simmer 2 to 3 minutes over medium-low heat before serving.

Chuck Roast with Vegetables

(serves 4)

1 SERVING	749 CALORIES	24g CARBOHYDRATE
71g PROTEIN	41g FAT	3.7g FIBER

2 tbsp	(30 ml) vegetable oil
4-5 lb	(1.8-2.3 kg) chuck short rib roast, tied
3	onions, peeled, cut in 4
1	bay leaf
¼ tsp	(1 ml) thyme
¼ tsp	(1 ml) basil
1½ cups	(375 ml) beer
1½ cups	(375 ml) brown sauce
4	carrots, pared
4	leeks, cut in 4 lengthwise to within 1 in (2.5 cm) of base, washed
1 tbsp	(15 ml) cornstarch
3 tbsp	(45 ml) cold water
	salt and pepper

Preheat oven to 350°F (180°C).

Heat oil in ovenproof casserole. Sear meat 8 to 10 minutes on all sides.

Add onions, bay leaf and seasonings; continue cooking 4 to 5 minutes.

Pour in beer and bring to boil. Add brown sauce and bring to boil again.

Cover and cook 2½ hours in oven.

About 1 hour before roast is cooked, add carrots to casserole. And 20 minutes later, add leeks.

Arrange beef and vegetables on serving platter.

Place casserole over medium-high heat and bring liquid to boil. Mix cornstarch with water; stir into sauce and cook 3 to 4 minutes over medium heat to thicken.

Correct seasoning and serve sauce with beef and vegetables.

Mock Pepper Steak

(serves 4)

1 SERVING	387 CALORIES	12g CARBOHYDRATE
51g PROTEIN	15g FAT	1.5g FIBER

1½ lb	(750 g) ground beef
1	egg
2 tbsp	(30 ml) breadcrumbs
1 tbsp	(15 ml) chopped parsley
½ tsp	(2 ml) Worcestershire sauce
2 tbsp	(30 ml) vegetable oil
1	onion, chopped
1 lb	(500 g) mushrooms, sliced
2 tbsp	(30 ml) green peppercorns
1½ cups	(375 ml) beef stock, heated
1 tbsp	(15 ml) cornstarch
3 tbsp	(45 ml) cold water
	salt

Mix meat, egg, breadcrumbs, parsley and Worcestershire sauce in mixer for 2 minutes at high speed; season to taste. Shape into steaks.

Heat oil in large frying pan. Cook steaks 8 to 10 minutes over medium heat turning over 4 times. When cooked, remove and keep hot in oven.

Add onion to frying pan and cook 2 minutes. Add mushrooms and peppercorns, season and continue cooking 3 to 4 minutes over medium heat.

Pour in beef stock, mix and bring to boil. Mix cornstarch with water and stir into sauce. Cook 2 minutes more to thicken.

Remove steaks from oven and serve with sauce.

Salisbury Steak

(serves 4)

1 SERVING	436 CALORIES	16g CARBOHYDRATE
57g PROTEIN	16g FAT	2.1g FIBER

2 lb	(900 g) ground beef
2 tbsp	(30 ml) breadcrumbs
1	egg
1 tbsp	(15 ml) chopped parsley
½ tsp	(2 ml) chili powder
2 tbsp	(30 ml) vegetable oil
4	onions, thinly sliced
2 tbsp	(30 ml) tomato paste
½ tsp	(2 ml) basil
2 cups	(500 ml) beef stock, heated
1½ tbsp	(25 ml) cornstarch
3 tbsp	(45 ml) cold water
	salt and pepper

Preheat oven to 150°F (70°C).

Mix meat, breadcrumbs, egg, parsley, chili powder, salt and pepper together until well incorporated. Shape into steaks.

Heat oil in large frying pan. Cook 8 to 10 minutes over medium heat. Turn over 4 times and season twice. When cooked, remove from pan and keep hot in oven.

Add onions to pan; cook 4 minutes over medium heat.

Add tomato paste and mix well. Stir in basil and beef stock; bring to boil. Correct seasoning.

Mix cornstarch with water; stir into sauce and cook 3 to 4 minutes.

Pour onion sauce over steaks and serve.

Braised Beef Brisket

(serves 4)

1 SERVING	558 CALORIES	5g CARBOHYDRATE
22g PROTEIN	50g FAT	0.5g FIBER

2 tbsp	(30 ml) vegetable oil
4 lb	(1.8 kg) beef brisket, tied
2	large onions, thinly sliced
1	clove
2 tbsp	(30 ml) paprika
¼ tsp	(1 ml) thyme
1 tsp	(5 ml) chopped parsley
1 cup	(250 ml) beer
2 cups	(500 ml) light beef stock, heated
2 tbsp	(30 ml) cornstarch
4 tbsp	(60 ml) cold water
¼ cup	(50 ml) sour cream
	salt and pepper

Preheat oven to 350°F (180°C).

Heat oil in ovenproof casserole. Sear beef 8 minutes on all sides over medium heat. Remove and season well.

Add onions to casserole and cook 4 minutes.

Stir in seasonings and parsley; cook 2 minutes.

Pour in beer, bring to boil and cook 3 minutes over medium heat. Replace meat in casserole and add beef stock; correct seasoning and bring to boil again.

Cover casserole and finish cooking 2-2½ hours in oven. Meat should be very tender when served.

When done, remove meat from casserole and set aside.

Place casserole over medium heat and bring liquid to boil. Mix cornstarch with water; stir into sauce and continue cooking 3 minutes.

Remove from heat, stir in sour cream and serve sauce with meat.

Italian Sausages and Vegetables

(serves 4)

1 SERVING	276 CALORIES	31g CARBOHYDRATE
11g PROTEIN	12g FAT	3.6g FIBER

2	carrots, pared and sliced on the bias 1 in (2.5 cm) thick
24	fresh pearl onions
1	small zucchini, sliced on the bias 1 in (2.5 cm) thick
2 tbsp	(30 ml) vegetable oil
2	apples, peeled, cored and in wedges
4	Italian sausages, sliced on the bias 1 in (2.5 cm) thick
2	garlic cloves, smashed and chopped
1½ cups	(375 ml) chicken stock, heated
1 tbsp	(15 ml) tomato paste
1 tbsp	(15 ml) cornstarch
3 tbsp	(45 ml) cold water
	salt and pepper

Place carrots in saucepan, cover with water and boil 6 minutes uncovered.

Add onions and zucchini; season and cook 3 minutes. Drain vegetables and let cool slightly.

Heat oil in large frying pan. Cook vegetables, apples, sausages and garlic 4 to 5 minutes over high heat; season well.

Pour in chicken stock and bring to boil.

Stir in tomato paste and cook 1 minute over medium-low heat. Mix cornstarch with water; stir into sauce and finish cooking 1 minute.

Serve with rice.

Creamy Chicken Stew

(serves 4)

1 SERVING	333 CALORIES	29g CARBOHYDRATE
25g PROTEIN	13g FAT	2.7g FIBER

3½ lb	(1.6 kg) chicken, cut in 10 pieces and skinned
1	small onion, coarsely chopped
1	celery stalk, diced
1	bay leaf
1	parsley sprig
¼ tsp	(1 ml) celery salt
½ tsp	(2 ml) basil
3 tbsp	(45 ml) butter
4 tbsp	(60 ml) flour
2	large cooked carrots, diced large
1	large cooked potato, diced large
1	cooked parsnip, diced large
	salt and pepper
	paprika

Season chicken pieces with salt, pepper and paprika. Place leg and thigh pieces in large skillet and cover with cold water.

Add onion, celery, bay leaf, parsley and seasonings. Cover and bring to boil. Continue cooking 16 minutes over medium heat.

Add remaining chicken pieces and continue cooking 20 minutes covered.

Transfer chicken pieces to bowl and strain cooking liquid through fine sieve into second bowl.

Heat butter in skillet. Mix in flour and cook 2 to 3 minutes over low heat, stirring occasionally.

Pour in half of strained cooking liquid and whisk well. Incorporate remaining and season. Cook sauce 3 to 4 minutes over medium heat.

Place cooked vegetables in sauce and cook 3 to 4 minutes over medium-low heat.

Add chicken and finish cooking 8 to 10 minutes over low heat. Do not cover.

Cut chicken in **1** 10 pieces and skin. Season with salt, pepper and paprika.

3 Cover with cold water. Add onion, celery, bay leaf, parsley and seasonings. Cover pan and bring to boil.

Place leg and **2** thigh pieces in large skillet.

4 After all chicken has been cooked and removed, add vegetables to sauce.

Roast Chicken

(serves 4)

1 SERVING	321 CALORIES	12g CARBOHYDRATE
30g PROTEIN	17g FAT	1.9g FIBER

4-5 lb	(1.8 - 2.3 kg) chicken, cleaned
1	large carrot
2	celery stalks
1	onion, cut in half
2-3	parsley sprigs
1	bay leaf
3 tbsp	(45 ml) melted butter
1	onion, diced
½ tsp	(2 ml) tarragon
1½ cups	(375 ml) hot chicken stock
1½ tbsp	(25 ml) cornstarch
3 tbsp	(45 ml) cold water
	salt and pepper

Preheat oven to 425°F (220°C).

Stuff cleaned chicken with carrot, celery, halved onion, parsley and bay leaf. Force inside and dribble in 1 tsp (5 ml) melted butter.

Secure legs with string and baste with remaining butter. Place in roasting pan, season generously and sear about 15 minutes in oven.

Reduce heat to 350°F (180°C) and finish cooking chicken 25 to 30 minutes per 1 lb (500 g).

When cooked, remove chicken and set aside.

Place roasting pan over high heat; add diced onion and tarragon and cook 4 minutes.

Pour in chicken stock and bring to boil. Season and continue cooking 3 to 4 minutes.

Mix cornstarch with water; stir into sauce and cook 1 to 2 minutes or until thickened.

Serve onion gravy with chicken.

Stuff cleaned chicken with vegetables, parsley and bay leaf. Force inside and dribble in 1 tsp (5 ml) melted butter.

Secure chicken by drawing a string threaded on a trussing needle through the legs twice. Knot string between legs.

Place in roasting pan, season generously and baste with remaining butter. Sear about 15 minutes in oven.

After chicken is cooked, prepare gravy by using juices that have collected in roasting pan.

Pineapple Chicken

(serves 4)

1 SERVING	252 CALORIES	14g CARBOHYDRATE
22g PROTEIN	12g FAT	0.5g FIBER

2 tbsp	(30 ml) vegetable oil
2	chicken breasts, skinned, halved and cubed
1 tbsp	(15 ml) chopped ginger
3 tbsp	(45 ml) pine nuts
14 oz	(398 ml) can pineapple chunks
3 tbsp	(45 ml) wine vinegar
1½ cups	(375 ml) chicken stock, heated
1 tsp	(5 ml) soya sauce
1 tbsp	(15 ml) cornstarch
3 tbsp	(45 ml) cold water
	salt and pepper

Heat oil in large frying pan. Add chicken, ginger and pine nuts; season and cook 4 to 5 minutes. Stir once.

Drain pineapple and reserve ½ cup (125 ml) of juice. Add pineapple chunks to pan and continue cooking 3 to 4 minutes over low heat.

Remove chicken pieces and set aside.

Add vinegar to sauce and boil 1 minute. Stir in pineapple juice, chicken stock and soya sauce; season well and bring to boil. Cook 3 minutes.

Mix cornstarch with water; stir into sauce and bring to boil. Cook 1 more minute.

Replace chicken in pan, correct seasoning and simmer over low heat until heated through.

Chicken Livers Marsala

(serves 4)

1 SERVING	397 CALORIES	21g CARBOHYDRATE
40g PROTEIN	17g FAT	0.8g FIBER

1½ lb	(750 g) chicken livers, cleaned, fat trimmed and halved
½ cup	(125 ml) seasoned flour
2 tbsp	(30 ml) vegetable oil
1 tbsp	(15 ml) butter
1	small onion, finely chopped
½ lb	(250 g) mushrooms, sliced
1 tbsp	(15 ml) chopped parsley
½ cup	(125 ml) Marsala wine
1 cup	(250 ml) chicken stock, heated
1 tsp	(5 ml) cornstarch
2 tbsp	(30 ml) cold water
	salt and pepper

Dredge livers in flour. Heat oil and butter in large frying pan. Cook livers 4 minutes over high heat, stirring once.

Add onion, mushrooms and parsley; season and continue cooking 4 to 5 minutes over medium heat.

Pour in wine and chicken stock; mix and cook 4 minutes over low heat.

Mix cornstarch with water; stir into sauce and bring to boil. Simmer 2 minutes over low heat and serve with noodles.

Pork Tenderloin Sauté

(serves 4)

1 SERVING	357 CALORIES	12g CARBOHYDRATE
30g PROTEIN	21g FAT	1.5g FIBER

2	pork tenderloins
2 tbsp	(30 ml) soya sauce
¼ cup	(50 ml) dry sherry
3 tbsp	(45 ml) vegetable oil
1	leek, (white part only) thinly sliced
½ lb	(250 g) mushrooms, sliced
3	green onions, in sticks
1	green pepper, thinly sliced
½ cup	(125 ml) frozen peas, cooked
2 cups	(500 ml) chicken stock, heated
2 tbsp	(30 ml) cornstarch
4 tbsp	(60 ml) cold water
	salt and pepper

Trim meat of fat and slice on the bias ¾ in (2 cm) thick. Place in bowl with soya sauce and sherry; marinate 30 minutes.

Remove meat from bowl; reserve marinade.

Heat 1½ tbsp (25 ml) oil in frying pan. Cook half of meat for 3 to 4 minutes over medium heat; turn pieces over once and season well.

Remove cooked meat, set aside and repeat for remaining meat but avoid adding any more oil.

When all meat is cooked and removed, add rest of oil to pan. Cook vegetables 3 to 4 minutes over high heat; season well.

Pour in chicken stock and reserved marinade; bring to boil.

Mix cornstarch with water; stir into sauce and cook 1 to 2 minutes over medium heat.

Replace meat in sauce, simmer 3 to 4 minutes and serve.

1 For convenience gather all the ingredients needed before you start the recipe.

2 Place all meat, parsley and seasonings in large bowl. Add onion and garlic; mix well.

The Best Meatloaf

(serves 6 to 8)

1 SERVING	317 CALORIES	14g CARBOHYDRATE
36g PROTEIN	13g FAT	0.3g FIBER

1 lb	(500 g) ground beef
½ lb	(250 g) ground pork
½ lb	(250 g) ground veal
1 tbsp	(15 ml) chopped parsley
¼ tsp	(1 ml) thyme
¼ tsp	(1 ml) chili powder
¼ tsp	(1 ml) basil
1	onion, chopped and cooked
2	garlic cloves, smashed and chopped
1½ cups	(375 ml) breadcrumbs
2	eggs
1 cup	(250 ml) light cream
	salt and pepper
	several bay leaves

Preheat oven to 350°F (180°C).

Set aside 10 × 4 in (25 × 10 cm) mold.

Place all meat, parsley and seasonings in large bowl. Add onion and garlic; mix well.

Add breadcrumbs and eggs; mix, then stir in cream.

To double-check seasoning, cook a tiny patty of mixture in hot oil. Taste and adjust remaining mixture if necessary.

Press mixture into loaf pan, place bay leaves on top and set in roasting pan with hot water. Cook 1½ hours in oven.

Serve plain or with mushroom sauce.

Mushroom Sauce for Meatloaf

1 SERVING	30 CALORIES	2g CARBOHYDRATE
1g PROTEIN	2g FAT	0.2g FIBER

2 tbsp	(30 ml) vegetable oil
½ lb	(250 g) mushrooms, sliced
2 tbsp	(30 ml) chopped onion
1 cup	(250 ml) peeled diced eggplant
2 cups	(500 ml) beef stock, heated
1 tbsp	(15 ml) chopped chives
2 tbsp	(30 ml) cornstarch
4 tbsp	(60 ml) cold water
	salt and pepper

Heat oil in frying pan. Add mushrooms, onion and eggplant; cover and cook 10 minutes over low heat. Season well.

Add beef stock, chives and season well; bring to boil.

Mix cornstarch with water; stir into sauce and cook 4 to 5 minutes over low heat.

Pour sauce over meatloaf or serve with burgers.

3 Add breadcrumbs and eggs, mix then stir in cream.

4 Press mixture into loaf pan, place bay leaves on top and set in roasting pan with hot water.

Meatballs and Garlic Spinach

(serves 4)

1 SERVING	446 CALORIES	14g CARBOHYDRATE
57g PROTEIN	18g FAT	1.9g FIBER

1½ lb	(750 g) lean ground pork
1	onion, chopped and cooked
¼ tsp	(1 ml) chili powder
1 tsp	(5 ml) Worcestershire sauce
1	egg
2 tbsp	(30 ml) vegetable oil
1½ cups	(375 ml) chicken stock, heated
1 tbsp	(15 ml) soya sauce
1 tbsp	(15 ml) cornstarch
3 tbsp	(45 ml) cold water
2	garlic cloves, smashed and chopped
2 lb	(900 g) spinach, cooked and chopped
	salt and pepper

In mixer blend together pork, onion, chili powder, Worcestershire sauce, egg, salt and pepper. When mixture is smooth, shape into small meatballs.

Heat half of oil in large frying pan. Add meatballs and cook 3 to 4 minutes on all sides; season generously.

Using small spoon remove most of fat from pan and discard. Add chicken stock and soya sauce to meatballs. Cover and cook 6 minutes over low heat.

Mix cornstarch with water; stir into meatball mixture and continue cooking 3 minutes.

Meanwhile, heat remaining oil in second frying pan. When hot, cook garlic and spinach 3 minutes over medium heat; season well.

Serve spinach with meatballs.

Pork Shoulder Roast with Cider

(serves 4)

1 SERVING	1107 CALORIES	32g CARBOHYDRATE
112g PROTEIN	59g FAT	2.2g FIBER

2 tbsp	(30 ml) vegetable oil
5 lb	(2.3 kg) pork shoulder, fat trimmed and tied
2	onions, thinly sliced
2	apples, peeled, cored and in wedges
2 cups	(500 ml) apple cider
1 cup	(250 ml) chicken stock, heated
¼ tsp	(1 ml) thyme
½ tsp	(2 ml) basil
½ cup	(125 ml) sultana raisins
1 tbsp	(15 ml) cornstarch
2 tbsp	(30 ml) cold water
	salt and pepper

Preheat oven to 300°F (150°C).

Heat oil in ovenproof casserole. Sear meat 8 minutes on all sides over medium heat. Remove and season well; set aside.

Add onions and apple to casserole; cook 5 to 6 minutes.

Add cider and bring to boil; cook 2 minutes.

Add chicken stock, mix well and replace meat in sauce. Add seasonings and bring to boil with cover.

Finish cooking meat 2 to 2½ hours in oven with cover.

When done, transfer meat to serving platter. Place casserole over medium heat; bring liquid to boil and skim.

Stir in raisins. Mix cornstarch with water; stir into sauce and cook 1 minute. Correct seasoning.

Serve sauce with pork.

Rice Hash Pancakes

(serves 4)

1 SERVING	396 CALORIES	28g CARBOHYDRATE
17g PROTEIN	24g FAT	1.0g FIBER

3 tbsp	(45 ml) oil
1	onion, finely chopped
¾ cup	(175 ml) ground beef
1 tbsp	(15 ml) chopped parsley
¼ tsp	(1 ml) ground clove
2 tbsp	(30 ml) flour
1½ cups	(375 ml) leftover cooked rice
½ cup	(125 ml) grated Gruyère cheese
1	egg
2 tbsp	(30 ml) butter
2 cups	(500 ml) spicy tomato sauce, heated
	salt and pepper
	Parmesan cheese to taste

Heat oil in frying pan. Cook onion 3 minutes over low heat.

Add beef, season. Add parsley and clove; mix and cook 3 to 4 minutes over medium heat.

Mix in flour and rice. Add Gruyère cheese and mix again; cook 3 minutes.

Cool, then add egg. Transfer to mixer; blend 2 minutes.

Dust hands with flour and shape mixture into pancakes. Cook 4 minutes each side in hot butter.

Serve with tomato sauce and Parmesan cheese.

Tomato Rice

(serves 4)

1 SERVING	209 CALORIES	35g CARBOHYDRATE
6g PROTEIN	5g FAT	1.5g FIBER

1 tbsp	(15 ml) olive oil
1	onion, chopped
1	garlic clove, smashed and chopped
1 tbsp	(15 ml) chopped parsley
1½ cups	(375 ml) canned tomatoes, drained and chopped
1 cup	(250 ml) long grain rice, rinsed
1 tbsp	(15 ml) tomato paste
1¼ cups	(300 ml) tomato juice
½ cup	(125 ml) grated Parmesan cheese
	salt and pepper

Preheat oven to 350°F (180°C).

Heat oil in ovenproof casserole. Cook onion, garlic and parsley 2 minutes over medium heat.

Stir in tomatoes and cook 3 minutes over high heat; season.

Mix in rice, tomato paste and juice; bring to boil.

Cover and cook 18 minutes in oven.

About 5 minutes before rice is cooked, stir in cheese with fork.

Vegetable Baked Rice

(serves 4)

1 SERVING	242 CALORIES	33g CARBOHYDRATE
5g PROTEIN	10g FAT	3.7g FIBER

1 tbsp	(15 ml) olive oil
3	green onions, finely chopped
1 cup	(250 ml) long grain rice, rinsed
¼ tsp	(1 ml) thyme
1	bay leaf
1½ cups	(375 ml) chicken stock, heated
2 tbsp	(30 ml) butter
¼	celery stalk, diced
½ cup	(125 ml) cooked green peas
½ cup	(125 ml) cooked diced carrots
½ cup	(125 ml) diced zucchini
½ cup	(125 ml) diced mushrooms
	salt and pepper

Preheat oven to 350°F (180°C).

Heat oil in ovenproof casserole and cook onions 3 minutes over low heat.

Stir in rice; cook 2 minutes over medium heat. Season and mix in thyme and bay leaf.

Pour in chicken stock; cover and bring to boil. Finish cooking 18 minutes in oven.

Meanwhile, heat butter in frying pan. When hot, add all vegetables and cook about 3 to 4 minutes. Season generously. Add these vegetables to casserole about 5 minutes before rice is done.

Celeriac Pancakes

(serves 4)

1 SERVING	409 CALORIES	37g CARBOHYDRATE
18g PROTEIN	21g FAT	1.6g FIBER

1 lb	(500 g) celeriac, peeled and in lemony water
4	large potatoes, peeled and blanched 15 minutes
1½ cups	(375 ml) grated Gruyère cheese
2 tbsp	(30 ml) vegetable oil
	salt and pepper

Preheat oven to 425°F (220°C).

Dry celeriac and cut into very fine julienne; place in bowl. Cut potatoes in fine julienne and add to bowl along with cheese; season everything well and mix. Chill 1 hour.

Heat oil in large frying pan. When hot, place celeriac mixture in pan and press down with spatula. Cook 15 minutes over medium heat.

Wrap frying pan handle in foil and finish cooking pancake in oven for 15 minutes.

Slice as you would a pizza and serve.

Potato Pancakes

(serves 4)

1 SERVING	408 CALORIES	34g CARBOHYDRATE
5g PROTEIN	28g FAT	2.0g FIBER

8	potatoes, peeled and boiled
3 tbsp	(45 ml) butter
2	egg yolks
½ tsp	(2 ml) ginger
½ tsp	(2 ml) savory
1 tsp	(5 ml) sesame seeds
¼ cup	(50 ml) heavy cream
3 tbsp	(45 ml) peanut oil
	salt and white pepper

Mash potatoes through food mill. Add remaining ingredients (except oil) and mix until thoroughly blended. Set aside to cool.

Dust hands with flour and shape mixture into small pancakes. Heat oil in large frying pan and cook 3 minutes each side over medium-high heat.

Serve immediately.

Shepherd's Pie

(serves 4 to 6)

1 SERVING	587 CALORIES	44g CARBOHYDRATE
42g PROTEIN	27g FAT	3.9g FIBER

2 tbsp	(30 ml) oil
½	red onion, chopped
1 tbsp	(15 ml) chopped parsley
½ lb	(250 g) mushrooms, coarsely chopped
¼ tsp	(1 ml) ground clove
¼ tsp	(1 ml) allspice
1 lb	(500 g) ground beef
½ lb	(250 g) ground pork
½ tsp	(2 ml) basil
¼ tsp	(1 ml) thyme
12 oz	(341 ml) can whole kernel corn, drained
1½ cups	(375 ml) hot tomato sauce
½ cup	(125 ml) grated Romano cheese
3-3½ cups	(750-875 ml)) mashed potatoes
2 tbsp	(30 ml) melted butter
	salt and pepper
	dash paprika

Preheat oven to 375°F (190°C).

Heat oil in skillet and cook onion and parsley 2 minutes. Add mushrooms, clove and allspice; continue cooking 3 minutes over medium heat.

Stir in beef and pork, add basil and thyme; cook 5 to 6 minutes over medium-high heat.

Mix in corn, season and cook 3 to 4 minutes. Add tomato sauce, cheese and continue cooking 2 to 3 minutes over medium heat.

Spoon mixture into large baking dish and completely cover with mashed potatoes. Use a pastry bag for a fancy top as shown in the picture.

Sprinkle potatoes with paprika and moisten slightly with melted butter. Bake 45 minutes in oven.

Cook mushrooms, clove and allspice 3 minutes over medium heat.

Mix in corn, season and cook 3 to 4 minutes. Then add tomato sauce, cheese and continue cooking 2 to 3 minutes.

Add beef, pork, basil and thyme; cook 5 to 6 minutes over medium-high heat.

Spoon mixture into large baking dish and cover with mashed potatoes. If you desire a fancy top, use a pastry bag.

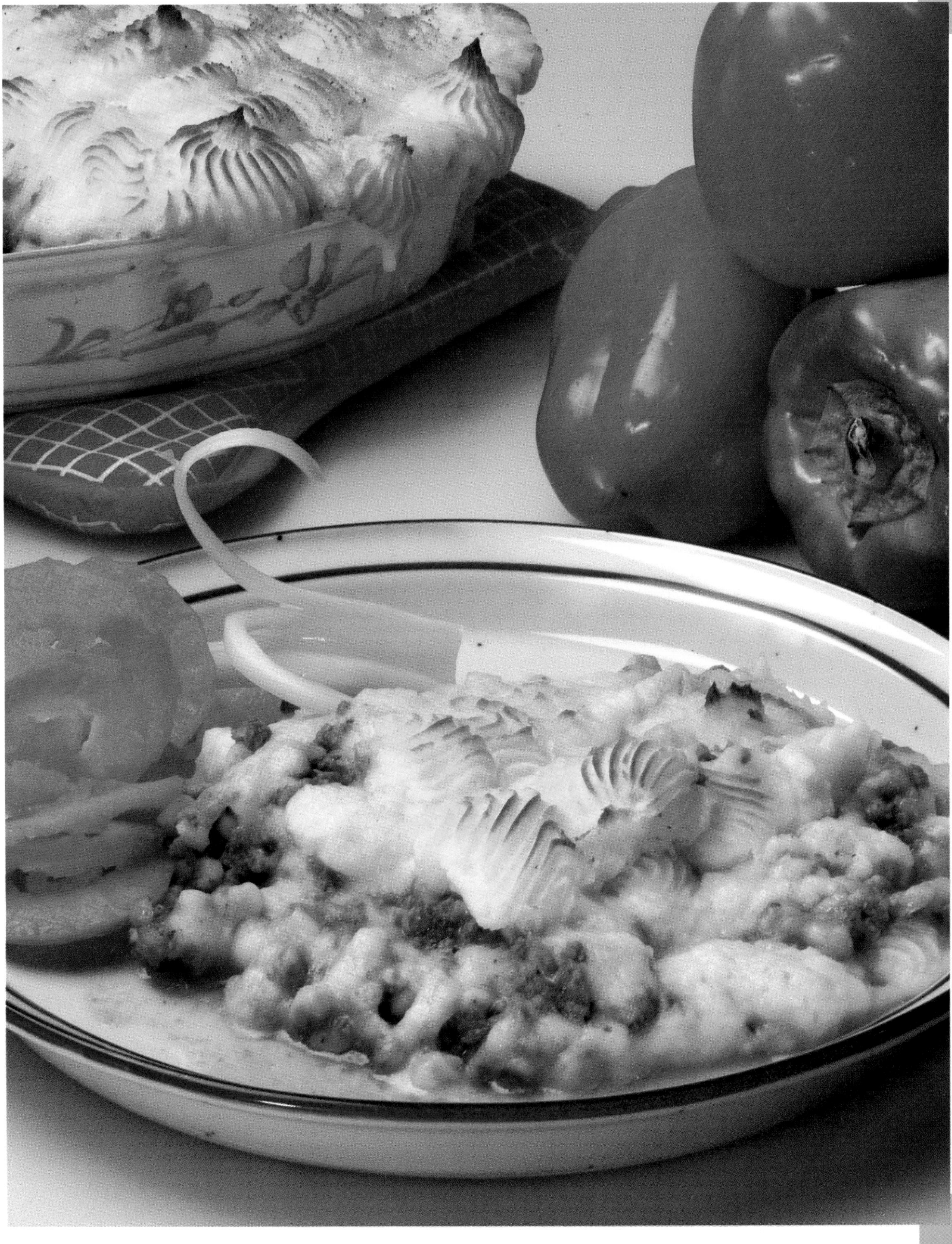

Pita Pizza

(serves 4)

1 SERVING	553 CALORIES	57g CARBOHYDRATE
25g PROTEIN	25g FAT	3.9g FIBER

4	small whole wheat pita bread
1 - 1½ cups	tomato sauce, heated
12	mushrooms, sliced
½	green pepper, in rings
½	red pepper, in rings
12	pitted black olives, sliced
2	raw sausages
1 cup	(250 ml) grated mozzarella cheese
1¼ cups	(300 ml) grated cheddar cheese
	chopped parsley to taste
	salt and pepper

Preheat oven to 425°F (220°C).

Place pita bread on cookie sheet and cover with tomato sauce. Add mushrooms, peppers and olives.

Remove sausage meat from casing and arrange on pizzas in tiny clumps. Top with a mixture of grated cheeses and season with parsley, salt and pepper.

Cook pizzas in the middle of the oven for 10 minutes.

Pita pizzas are a great way to use leftover vegetables — be creative with what's in your fridge.

Hot Potato Salad

(serves 4)

1 SERVING	180 CALORIES	27g CARBOHYDRATE
9g PROTEIN	4g FAT	1.4g FIBER

4	large potatoes, boiled with skin and still hot
4	slices bacon, diced
3	green onions, chopped
1	stalk celery heart, finely chopped
1	garlic clove, smashed and chopped
½ cup	(125 ml) red wine vinegar
¾ cup	(175 ml) chicken stock, heated
1 tbsp	(15 ml) chopped chives
	salt and pepper

Peel and cut potatoes in thick slices. Place in oven at 150°F (70°C) to keep hot.

Cook bacon in frying pan for 4 minutes or until crisp. Remove bacon leaving fat in pan and set aside.

Add onions, celery and garlic to pan; cook 3 minutes over medium heat.

Mix in vinegar; cook 1 minute over high heat. Add chicken stock and continue cooking 2 minutes.

Stir in chives and season generously. Pour over hot potatoes and let stand 10 minutes on counter.

Serve on lettuce leaves and sprinkle portions with reserved bacon.

Sole Croquettes

(serves 4)

1 SERVING	543 CALORIES	42g CARBOHYDRATE
33g PROTEIN	27g FAT	0.2g FIBER

4 tbsp	(60 ml) butter
3½ tbsp	(50 ml) flour
1 cup	(250 ml) hot milk
3	sole filets, cooked and chopped
1	small envelope unflavored gelatine, softened in water
1	egg yolk
¼ cup	(50 ml) heavy cream
1 tbsp	(15 ml) chopped parsley
3	egg whites
1 tbsp	(15 ml) oil
2 cups	(500 ml) breadcrumbs
	salt and pepper
	juice ¼ lemon

Heat butter in saucepan. Add flour and mix; cook 2 minutes over low heat.

Whisk in milk and season; continue cooking 5 minutes.

Remove saucepan from heat. Stir in fish and gelatine. Mix egg yolk with cream and incorporate.

Stir in parsley, lemon juice and correct seasoning. Spread mixture on large dinner plate, cover with plastic wrap and chill 2 minutes.

Beat egg whites with oil just until slightly foamy.

Shape croquette mixture into tubes; roll in breadcrumbs then dip in egg whites and finish by rolling in breadcrumbs again.

Deep-fry sole croquettes in hot oil until evenly browned.

Cheese Stuffed Tomatoes

(serves 4)

1 SERVING	180 CALORIES	18g CARBOHYDRATE
9g PROTEIN	8g FAT	3.2g FIBER

4	large tomatoes
1 tbsp	(15 ml) vegetable oil
1	small onion, finely chopped
1	garlic clove, smashed and chopped
½ tsp	(2 ml) oregano
15	mushrooms, sliced
1 tbsp	(15 ml) chopped parsley
½ cup	(125 ml) ricotta cheese
⅓ cup	(75 ml) breadcrumbs
	salt and pepper

Preheat oven to 375°F (190°C).

Core tomatoes, turn them upside-down and cut away a top. Scoop out most of flesh but leave a sturdy shell. Place shells in baking dish, season insides and moisten with a sprinkle of oil. Set tomato flesh aside.

Heat oil in frying pan and cook onion and garlic 3 to 4 minutes.

Add tomato flesh, oregano, mushrooms and parsley. Season well and cook 4 to 5 minutes over medium heat.

Mix in cheese and breadcrumbs; cook 2 to 3 minutes over medium heat.

Fill tomato shells with mixture and bake 30 to 35 minutes in oven.

Core tomatoes, **1** turn them upside-down and cut away a top. You can keep the tops for decoration at serving time.

3 After onion and garlic have cooked, add tomato flesh, oregano, mushrooms and parsley. Season well and cook 4 to 5 minutes over medium heat.

Scoop out most **2** of flesh but leave a sturdy shell. Season insides and set shells aside.

4 Mix in cheese and breadcrumbs; cook 2 to 3 minutes then fill tomato shells with mixture. Bake 30 to 35 minutes in oven.

Potato Salad with Lemon Dressing

(serves 4)

1 SERVING	291 CALORIES	18g CARBOHYDRATE
3g PROTEIN	23g FAT	1.4g FIBER

½ cup	(125 ml) mayonnaise
1 tbsp	(15 ml) chopped parsley
2 tbsp	(30 ml) grated lemon rind
4	boiled potatoes, peeled and diced large
2	celery stalks, diced
¼ cup	(50 ml) chopped red onion
	juice ½ lemon
	salt and pepper

Mix mayonnaise, parsley, lemon rind and juice together; season to taste.

Place potatoes, celery and onion in bowl; toss together.

Pour in lemon dressing, toss again and serve.

Beef Tongue Salad

(serves 4)

1 SERVING	232 CALORIES	10g CARBOHYDRATE
12g PROTEIN	16g FAT	

1	large cucumber, peeled, seeded and in julienne
1	apple, peeled, cored and in wedges
1 cup	(250 ml) cooked beets, in julienne
2 cups	(500 ml) cooked beef tongue, in julienne
3 tbsp	(45 ml) capers
¼ cup	(50 ml) mayonnaise
1 tbsp	(15 ml) strong mustard
1 tbsp	(15 ml) anchovy paste
	few drops lemon juice
	salt and pepper

Place cucumber in bowl, sprinkle with salt and marinate 30 minutes on counter.

Drain liquid and transfer cucumber to clean bowl. Add apple, beets, tongue and capers; mix.

Stir mayonnaise, mustard, anchovy paste, lemon juice and salt and pepper together. Pour over salad ingredients and mix until well coated.

Serve on lettuce leaves.

Delicious Turkey Salad

(serves 4)

1 SERVING	262 CALORIES	11g CARBOHYDRATE
23g PROTEIN	14g FAT	2.3g FIBER

2 cups	(500 ml) leftover cooked turkey, diced
2	carrots, pared and grated
½ cup	(125 ml) finely chopped onion
2	green onions, finely chopped
1	celery stalk, diced
1	cucumber, peeled, seeded and sliced
24	mushrooms, sliced
¼ cup	(50 ml) lime juice
2	mint leaves, chopped
3 oz	(90 g) cream cheese, soft
1 tbsp	(15 ml) oil
1 tsp	(5 ml) wine vinegar
	few drops Worcestershire sauce
	salt and pepper

Place all vegetables in large salad bowl.

In blender, mix together remaining ingredients until smooth. Pour dressing over salad, chill and serve.

Leftover Vegetable Soup

(serves 6 to 8)

1 SERVING	140 CALORIES	22g CARBOHYDRATE
4g PROTEIN	4g FAT	2.4g FIBER

2 tbsp	(30 ml) melted butter
2	onions, chopped
2	green onions, sliced
2	carrots, pared and sliced
2	potatoes, peeled and diced
1	small turnip, peeled and sliced
1	parsnip, pared and sliced
1	bay leaf
3	parsley sprigs
½ tsp	(2 ml) basil
¼ tsp	(1 ml) rosemary
½ tsp	(2 ml) chervil
¼ tsp	(1 ml) marjoram
¼	cabbage, in leaves
8 cups	(2 L) chicken stock, heated
1	yellow pepper, diced
1	red pepper, diced
1½ cups	(375 ml) large croutons
¼ cup	(50 ml) grated Gruyère cheese
	salt and pepper

Heat butter in very large saucepan. Add both onions and cook 3 minutes covered over medium heat.

Add carrots, potatoes, turnip and parsnip; mix well. Cover and continue cooking 5 minutes.

Add all seasonings including bay leaf and parsley; mix well and stir in cabbage. Pour in chicken stock and bring to boil uncovered over high heat.

Cook soup 35 minutes uncovered over medium-low heat.

About 5 minutes before soup is done, add peppers. Serve with croutons and garnish portions with grated cheese.

Scrambled Eggs with Vegetables

(serves 4)

1 SERVING	251 CALORIES	5g CARBOHYDRATE
15g PROTEIN	19g FAT	1.3g FIBER

2 tbsp	(30 ml) butter
12	cherry tomatoes
¼	cucumber, diced small
4	green onions, in 1 in (2.5 cm) sticks
8	beaten eggs, seasoned
6	slices salami, in strips
	salt and pepper

Heat butter in nonstick pan. When hot, add vegetables and cook 3 to 4 minutes over medium-high heat. Season well and stir once.

Reduce heat to medium and pour in eggs. Mix rapidly and continue cooking 1 to 2 minutes while stirring.

Add salami strips, mix and serve immediately. Accompany with bacon if desired.

Flat Spinach and Cheese Omelet

(serves 2)

1 SERVING	441 CALORIES	5g CARBOHYDRATE
31g PROTEIN	33g FAT	0.8g FIBER

2 tbsp	(30 ml) butter
1½ cups	(375 ml) cooked chopped spinach
6	eggs
½ cup	(125 ml) grated Gruyère cheese
	salt and pepper

Heat 1 tbsp (15 ml) butter in nonstick frying pan. When hot, add spinach and season well. Cook 3 minutes over high heat.

Break eggs into bowl and beat with fork; season well.

Remove spinach from pan and pour into eggs; mix well.

Heat remaining butter in nonstick pan. When hot, pour in egg mixture and cook 3 minutes over medium heat.

Sprinkle top with cheese; cover and cook 2 to 3 minutes over medium-low heat.

Slide omelet out of pan and serve.

Potato Omelet

(serves 2)

1 SERVING	441 CALORIES	18g CARBOHYDRATE
18g PROTEIN	33g FAT	1.1g FIBER

2 tbsp	(30 ml) butter
1 tsp	(5 ml) vegetable oil
2	potatoes, peeled and sliced
2 tbsp	(30 ml) chopped onion
1 tbsp	(15 ml) chopped fresh parsley
5	eggs
	pinch nutmeg
	salt and pepper

Heat 1 tbsp (15 ml) butter and oil in small frying pan.

When hot, add potatoes and season well. Cook 2 to 3 minutes on each side over medium heat. Stir once during cooking process.

Sprinkle nutmeg over potatoes and mix; cover and continue cooking 8 to 10 minutes.

Mix well; add onion and parsley. Cook, uncovered, 3 to 4 minutes. Meanwhile, break eggs into bowl and beat with fork; season well.

Heat remaining butter in nonstick frying pan or omelet pan.

When hot, pour in eggs and cook 1 minute over high heat.

Stir eggs rapidly and add potatoes. Roll omelet (see technique) and continue cooking 1 minute.

Serve with cooked broccoli and decorate with several cooked potatoes.

Stuffed Egg Halves with Mustard

(serves 4 to 6)

1 SERVING	241 CALORIES	0g CARBOHYDRATE
13g PROTEIN	21g FAT	0.2g FIBER

12	hard-boiled eggs, cut in half lengthwise
2 tbsp	(30 ml) Dijon mustard
4 tbsp	(60 ml) mayonnaise
	several drops Tabasco sauce
	lemon juice to taste
	salt and white pepper
	chopped fresh parsley
	several lettuce leaves, washed and dried

Force egg yolks through sieve using back of wooden spoon. Place in mixing bowl.

Add mustard, mayonnaise, Tabasco sauce, lemon juice, salt and pepper. Mix until well combined and correct seasoning.

Spoon mixture into pastry bag fitted with star nozzle. Stuff egg whites; sprinkle with some parsley.

Place stuffed eggs on lettuce leaves and serve.

If desired, refrigerate until serving time. Cover with plastic wrap.

Poached Eggs with Bacon

(serves 2)

1 SERVING	288 CALORIES	1g CARBOHYDRATE
17g PROTEIN	24g FAT	0g FIBER

6 cups	(1.5 L) water
1 tsp	(5 ml) white vinegar
4	eggs
6	slices bacon, cooked crisp
	salt
	buttered toast

Place water, vinegar and salt in large saucepan; bring to boil.

Reduce heat so that water simmers. Carefully slide eggs, one at a time, into water. Cook 3 minutes over medium heat.

Remove eggs with slotted spoon and drain.

Serve on buttered toast and with bacon. Decorate with tomato slices.

OUTDOOR COOKING

Tips for Barbecuing

Whether you are barbecuing with gas or over coals or an open fire, make a habit of preheating your barbecue.

After the barbecue has warmed up a bit, oil the grill; it will help prevent foods from sticking.

Keep an eye on foods being barbecued and turn as needed to avoid charring.

Because of the variety of barbecues available, treat our cooking times as guidelines and use your own judgement; taste when in doubt.

Remove fat from meats to prevent it from dropping on the coals and creating flames which will tend to increase charring.

If you are using charcoal be sure the coals have turned grey before adding any food.

If you do not use a marinade always oil meat before placing on the hot grill. This will not only give the meat taste but will also speed up and improve searing.

Barbecuing fish takes some patience because it tends to stick to the grill more than other foods. You can eliminate this by using a stainless-steel fish grill equipped with a long handle for easy turning.

Barbecued Steak Diane

(serves 2)

1 SERVING	445 CALORIES	1g CARBOHYDRATE
35g PROTEIN	26g FAT	trace FIBER

4 tbsp	(60 ml) melted butter
4 tbsp	(60 ml) cognac
4 tbsp	(60 ml) sherry
2 tbsp	(30 ml) chopped chives
2	strip loin steaks, 8-10 oz (250-300 g) each
	salt and pepper

Preheat barbecue at HIGH.

Place butter, cognac, sherry and chives in small saucepan; bring to boil.

Meanwhile, trim all excess fat from steaks.

Pour hot liquid over meat and let stand 15 minutes.

Place steaks on hot grill. Cook 8 to 10 minutes depending on taste. Season well and turn 3 to 4 times.

Fabulous Flank Steak

(serves 4)

1 SERVING	1064 CALORIES	11g CARBOHYDRATE
46g PROTEIN	94g FAT	trace FIBER

Marinade

1 ½ cups	(375 ml) vegetable oil
½ cup	(125 ml) soya sauce
¼ cup	(50 ml) Worcestershire sauce
½ cup	(125 ml) wine vinegar
½ cup	(125 ml) lemon juice
2 tbsp	(30 ml) dry mustard
1 tsp	(5 ml) salt
1 tbsp	(15 ml) pepper
1 tbsp	(15 ml) chopped parsley
2	garlic cloves, smashed and chopped

Recipe

2	large flank steaks, excess fat trimmed

Preheat barbecue at HIGH.

Mix marinade ingredients together, pour over meat and refrigerate 4 hours.

Drain meat and slice on an angle into large pieces. Set on hot grill and cook 3 to 4 minutes each side. Season and baste once with leftover marinade.

Serve with potatoes.

Strip Loin Steaks

(serves 4)

1 SERVING	314 CALORIES	13g CARBOHYDRATE
33g PROTEIN	14g FAT	trace FIBER

4	strip loin steaks, 8-10 oz (250-300 g) each
2 tbsp	(30 ml) butter
3	medium onions, chopped
1	garlic clove, smashed and chopped
1 tbsp	(15 ml) chopped parsley
¼ cup	(50 ml) raspberry wine vinegar
½ cup	(125 ml) taco sauce
	oil
	salt and pepper

Preheat barbecue at HIGH.

Brush steaks with oil and place on hot grill. Cook 8 to 10 minutes depending on taste. Turn 3 to 4 times and season after searing.

Meanwhile, heat butter in saucepan. Cook onions, garlic and parsley 3 to 4 minutes over low heat.

Add vinegar; cook 3 to 4 minutes over medium-high heat.

Season and stir in taco sauce; cook 2 to 3 minutes over low heat.

Serve with steaks.

When not using a marinade it is important to brush steaks with oil.

Cook onions, garlic and parsley in hot butter for 3 to 4 minutes over low heat.

Add vinegar and increase heat to medium-high. Cook 3 to 4 minutes to reduce liquid.

Season and stir in taco sauce; finish cooking 2 to 3 minutes over low heat.

Tangy T-Bone Steaks

(serves 4)

1 SERVING	319 CALORIES	18g CARBOHYDRATE
24g PROTEIN	17g FAT	trace FIBER

4	T-bone steaks, 1-1 ¼ in (2.5-3 cm) thick
½ cup	(125 ml) catsup
2 tbsp	(30 ml) melted butter
1 tbsp	(15 ml) Worcestershire sauce
½ tsp	(2 ml) chopped ginger
2 tbsp	(30 ml) wine vinegar
2 tbsp	(30 ml) honey
1 tbsp	(15 ml) lemon juice
1 tbsp	(15 ml) strong mustard
	salt and pepper
	oil

Preheat barbecue at HIGH.

Trim most of fat from steaks and slash remaining fat with knife to prevent curling. Moisten meat with a bit of oil then set aside.

Cook catsup, butter and Worcestershire sauce 2 to 3 minutes over low heat in saucepan.

Add ginger, vinegar and honey; continue cooking 2 to 3 minutes.

Remove from heat and stir in lemon juice and mustard.

Spread mixture over steaks and place on hot grill. Cook 12 to 14 minutes depending on taste. Turn 4 times, baste occasionally and season well.

Trim most of fat from steaks and slash remaining fat with knife to prevent curling. Moisten meat with a bit of oil.

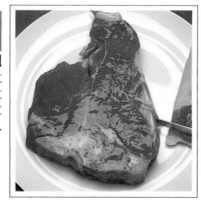

Cook catsup, butter and Worcestershire sauce 2 to 3 minutes over low heat.

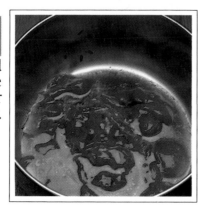

Add ginger, vinegar and honey; continue cooking 2 to 3 minutes. Remove from heat and stir in lemon juice and mustard.

Spread mixture over steaks before cooking.

Juicy Burgers

(serves 4)

1 SERVING	437 CALORIES	7g CARBOHYDRATE
70g PROTEIN	13g FAT	trace FIBER

2 lb	(900 g) lean ground beef
1	medium onion, chopped and cooked
½ tsp	(2 ml) chili powder
2 tbsp	(30 ml) tomato paste
3 tbsp	(45 ml) breadcrumbs
1	egg
	dash paprika
	salt and pepper
	oil for basting

Preheat barbecue at MEDIUM.

Place all ingredients, except oil, in mixer; blend until well incorporated and meat forms ball.

Shape into patties and brush with oil. Place on hot grill and season well. Cover and cook 8 to 10 minutes depending on taste. Turn patties 2 to 3 times and season once again.

Serve burgers with the usual condiments and a side order of onion rings.

Onion Rings

(serves 4)

1 SERVING	259 CALORIES	31g CARBOHYDRATE
8g PROTEIN	11g FAT	trace FIBER

2	medium onions, in rings
1½ cups	(375 ml) milk
2	beaten eggs
1½ cups	(375 ml) crushed soda crackers, well seasoned
	dash paprika

Place onion rings in milk and let stand about 15 minutes.

Drain onion rings, dip in beaten eggs and coat with crushed crackers; season with paprika.

Cook onion rings in hot oil for 3 minutes or until golden brown. Serve with burgers.

Rib-Eye Steaks

(serves 4)

1 SERVING	426 CALORIES	11g CARBOHYDRATE
40g PROTEIN	24g FAT	0.5g FIBER

Marinade

3	green onions, finely chopped
¼ cup	(50 ml) soya sauce
¼ cup	(50 ml) sesame oil
1 tbsp	(15 ml) sugar
2 tbsp	(30 ml) sesame seeds
	fresh ground pepper

Recipe

4	rib-eye steaks

Preheat barbecue at HIGH.

Mix marinade ingredients together and pour over steaks. Set aside in refrigerator for 1 hour.

Place steaks on hot grill and cook 5 to 6 minutes each side depending on taste. Baste occasionally and season with pepper.

Steaks with Vegetable Sauce

(serves 4)

1 SERVING	328 CALORIES	19g CARBOHYDRATE
34g PROTEIN	13g FAT	1.0g FIBER

2 tbsp	(30 ml) oil
3	fresh jalapeno peppers, very finely chopped
2	onions, chopped
1	yellow pepper, chopped
2	tomatoes, peeled and diced
1	zucchini, diced small
1 cup	(250 ml) diced pineapple
½ tsp	(2 ml) cumin
½ tsp	(2 ml) oregano
½ tsp	(2 ml) basil
3 tbsp	(45 ml) tomato paste
4	strip loin steaks, 8-10 oz (250-300 g) each
	salt and pepper

Preheat barbecue at HIGH.

Heat half of oil in saucepan. Cook jalapeno peppers, onions and yellow pepper 3 to 4 minutes over medium heat.

Mix in tomatoes and zucchini; cover and cook 5 to 6 minutes.

Mix in pineapple, season and add cumin, oregano and basil. Cover and cook 13 minutes over medium heat. About 3 minutes before end, stir in tomato paste.

While vegetables are cooking you might want to start steaks.

Brush meat with remaining oil and place on hot grill. Cook 8 to 10 minutes depending on taste. Turn 3 to 4 times and season well after searing.

Serve vegetable sauce with steaks.

1 Cook jalapeno peppers, onions and yellow pepper 3 to 4 minutes over medium heat.

3 Add pineapple and all seasonings. Cover and cook 13 minutes over medium heat.

2 Mix in tomatoes and zucchini; continue cooking 5 to 6 minutes with cover.

4 About 3 minutes before end of cooking time, stir in tomato paste.

New York Steaks

(serves 4)

1 SERVING	341 CALORIES	2g CARBOHYDRATE
41g PROTEIN	15g FAT	trace FIBER

2	garlic cloves, smashed and chopped
2	bay leaves, finely chopped
1 tsp	(5 ml) green peppercorns
½ cup	(125 ml) dry white wine
2 tbsp	(30 ml) wine vinegar
1 tbsp	(15 ml) oil
4	New York steaks, 8-10 oz (250-300 g) each
	salt and pepper

Preheat barbecue at HIGH.

Place all ingredients in deep plate; let stand 15 minutes.

Place steaks on hot grill and cook 8 to 10 minutes depending on taste. Turn at least three times, baste and season.

Marinated Pork Back Ribs

(serves 4)

1 SERVING	1014 CALORIES	15g CARBOHYDRATE
47g PROTEIN	84g FAT	trace FIBER

Marinade

¾ cup	(175 ml) pineapple juice
3 tbsp	(45 ml) soya sauce
2	garlic cloves, smashed and chopped
¼ cup	(50 ml) catsup
1 tbsp	(15 ml) honey

Recipe

3 lb	(1.4 kg) pork back ribs
	salt and pepper

Preheat barbecue at LOW.

Place pineapple juice, soya sauce and garlic in large bowl.

Mix well, add remaining marinade ingredients and season to taste. Add ribs and let stand 15 minutes.

Place ribs on hot grill. Partially cover and cook 40 to 45 minutes, turning frequently and basting as needed. Season well.

Veal Chops with Tomato Hollandaise

(serves 4)

1 SERVING	665 CALORIES	3.2g CARBOHYDRATE
52g PROTEIN	49g FAT	0.3g FIBER

3 tbsp	(45 ml) oil
1 tsp	(5 ml) Worcestershire sauce
1 tsp	(5 ml) curry powder
1 tsp	(5 ml) chili powder
4	large veal chops
1 tbsp	(15 ml) hot water
2 tbsp	(30 ml) horseradish
3	egg yolks
1 tbsp	(15 ml) tomato paste
½ tsp	(2 ml) cumin powder
½ cup	(125 ml) melted butter
	juice 1 lime
	salt and pepper

Preheat barbecue at HIGH.

Mix oil, Worcestershire sauce, curry, chili powder and lime juice together; brush over chops and season well.

Place chops on hot grill. Cook 5 to 6 minutes each side depending on thickness. Baste occasionally and season.

Meanwhile, mix water, horseradish, egg yolks, tomato paste and seasonings in blender for 30 seconds at high speed.

Reduce blender speed to low; very slowly incorporate butter. Keep mixing until butter is well blended. Season and serve with veal.

Juicy Veal Chops

(serves 4)

1 SERVING	576 CALORIES	18g CARBOHYDRATE
52g PROTEIN	30g FAT	0.6g FIBER

2 tbsp	(30 ml) butter
2	green onions, chopped
1	garlic clove, smashed and chopped
1	large tomato, peeled and diced
1½ cups	(375 ml) brown sauce, heated
2 tbsp	(30 ml) chili sauce
1 tbsp	(15 ml) teriyaki sauce
1 tsp	(5 ml) chopped ginger
4	large veal chops
	salt and pepper

Preheat barbecue at HIGH.

Heat butter in saucepan. Cook onions, garlic and tomato 3 to 4 minutes over high heat; season well.

Mix in brown sauce, chili sauce, teriyaki sauce and ginger; continue cooking 3 to 4 minutes over low heat.

Brush mixture over chops and set on hot grill. Cook 5 to 6 minutes on each side depending on thickness. Season well and baste several times.

If desired serve with baked potatoes.

Tomato Veal Chops

(serves 4)

1 SERVING	402 CALORIES	11g CARBOHYDRATE
50g PROTEIN	16g FAT	trace FIBER

4	loin veal chops, ¾ in (2 cm) thick
1 cup	(250 ml) tomato juice
2 tbsp	(30 ml) corn syrup
2 tbsp	(30 ml) vegetable oil
½ tsp	(2 ml) tarragon
½ tsp	(2 ml) chervil
1 tbsp	(15 ml) green peppercorns, mashed
1 tbsp	(15 ml) lime juice
	salt and pepper

Preheat barbecue at HIGH.

Trim excess fat from chops and place them in deep dish; set aside.

Mix tomato juice, corn syrup and oil together in bowl.

Add seasonings, peppercorns and lime juice; mix well and pour over veal. Marinate 30 minutes.

Place chops on hot grill. Partly cover and cook 15 minutes. Turn 4 times, baste often and season once or twice.

Trim excess fat from chops and place them in deep dish; set aside.

Mix tomato juice, corn syrup and oil together in bowl.

Add seasonings, peppercorns and lime juice; mix well.

Pour over veal and marinate 30 minutes.

Veal Scallopini

(serves 4)

1 SERVING	279 CALORIES	2g CARBOHYDRATE
33g PROTEIN	15g FAT	trace FIBER

Marinade

¼ cup	(50 ml) oil
1 tbsp	(15 ml) tarragon
1 tbsp	(15 ml) soya sauce
1	garlic clove, smashed and chopped
1 tbsp	(15 ml) lemon juice

Recipe

4	veal scallopini, ¼ in (0.65 cm) thick
	salt and pepper

Preheat barbecue at HIGH.

Mix marinade ingredients together in large bowl. Add veal and let stand 30 minutes.

Place veal on hot grill. Cook 8 minutes turning once and basting occasionally. Season generously.

Serve with grilled eggplant.

Stuffed Veal Scallopini

(serves 4)

1 SERVING	292 CALORIES	13g CARBOHYDRATE
34g PROTEIN	14g FAT	0.7g FIBER

1 tbsp	(15 ml) butter
1	onion, finely chopped
1 cup	(250 ml) finely diced eggplant
1 tbsp	(15 ml) chopped parsley
1 tbsp	(15 ml) tomato paste
4	large veal scallopini
8	vine leaves
2 tbsp	(30 ml) vegetable oil
1 tbsp	(15 ml) lemon juice
	salt and pepper

Preheat barbecue at MEDIUM.

Heat butter in small saucepan. Add onion, eggplant and parsley; cover and cook 7 to 8 minutes over low heat.

Mix in tomato paste and continue cooking 2 to 3 minutes.

Spread stuffing over scallopini, roll tightly and wrap in double vine leaves. Secure with toothpicks.

Place rolls on hot grill and baste with mixture of oil and lemon juice. Partially cover and cook 12 to 14 minutes, turning often.

Serve with hot barbecue sauce.

Stuffed Veal Loin

(serves 4)

1 SERVING	462 CALORIES	20g CARBOHYDRATE
55g PROTEIN	17g FAT	0.5g FIBER

2	¾ lb (375 g) veal loins
10 oz	(284 ml) can mandarin segments
2 tbsp	(30 ml) honey
2 tbsp	(30 ml) butter
1	onion, finely chopped
⅓ lb	(150 g) mushrooms, finely chopped
½ tsp	(2 ml) tarragon
2 tbsp	(30 ml) ricotta cheese
1 tbsp	(15 ml) breadcrumbs
	salt and pepper

Preheat barbecue at HIGH.

Trim excess fat from veal. Slice both loins open lengthwise so that they can be stuffed. See Technique for visual help.

Drain mandarins and pour juice into small saucepan. Set fruit aside. Add honey and cook 15 minutes on high to thicken. Remove from stove and let cool.

Heat butter in second saucepan. Cook onion 2 minutes over medium heat.

Add mushrooms and seasonings; cook 4 minutes over high heat. Remove from stove; stir in cheese and breadcrumbs.

Spread stuffing on both sides of meat. Add a row of mandarin segments (save some for decoration) and close; secure with kitchen string.

Brush loins with mandarin/honey mixture. Place on hot grill and partially cover. Cook 30 minutes turning often; baste occasionally with mandarin mixture.

Heat reserved mandarin segments with leftover basting mixture in small saucepan. Pour over loins before serving.

Trim excess fat from veal.

Spread cooked stuffing on both sides of meat and add a row of mandarin segments.

Slice loins open as shown so they can be stuffed.

Close and secure with kitchen string.

Curried Veal Scallopini

(serves 4)

1 SERVING	337 CALORIES	8g CARBOHYDRATE
34g PROTEIN	14g FAT	0.7g FIBER

1 cup	(250 ml) dry white wine
3 tbsp	(45 ml) olive oil
1 cup	(250 ml) tomato sauce
½ tsp	(2 ml) caraway seed
1 tbsp	(15 ml) curry powder
1	garlic clove, smashed and chopped
4	large veal scallopini
	salt and pepper

Preheat barbecue at HIGH.

Bring wine to boil in small saucepan; continue cooking 3 minutes over medium heat.

Mix in oil, tomato sauce, seasonings and garlic; simmer 3 to 4 minutes.

Brush mixture generously over veal. Roll tightly and secure with toothpicks; brush again with sauce.

Place veal rolls on hot grill. Cook 8 to 10 minutes, turning often and basting occasionally. Season to taste.

Garlic Veal Chops

(serves 4)

1 SERVING	370 CALORIES	1g CARBOHYDRATE
37g PROTEIN	23g FAT	trace FIBER

½ lb	(250 g) soft butter
2	garlic cloves, smashed and chopped
1 tbsp	(15 ml) finely chopped parsley
1 tbsp	(15 ml) smashed green peppercorns
¼ tsp	(1 ml) lemon juice
4	veal chops, ½ in (1.2 cm) thick
	salt and pepper

Preheat barbecue at HIGH.

Place butter, garlic, parsley, peppercorns, lemon juice and some salt in mixer or food processor; blend until well incorporated and smooth.

Melt ⅓ cup (75 ml) of butter mixture in small saucepan. Wrap remaining in foil and store in refrigerator for further uses.

Place chops on hot grill and generously brush with garlic butter. Partially cover and cook 8 minutes, turning 2 to 3 times. Baste often and season once.

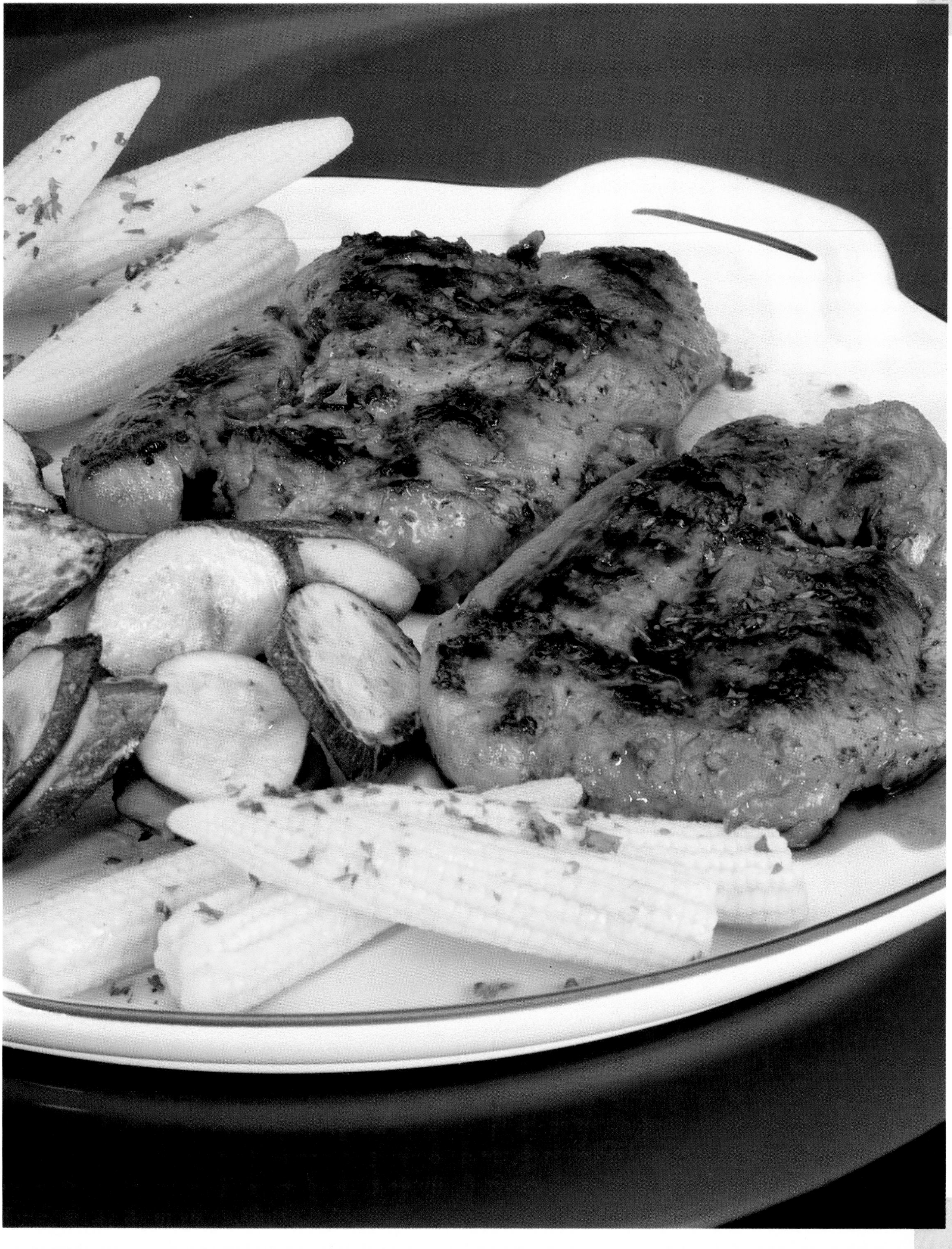

Veal Bites

(serves 4)

1 SERVING	556 CALORIES	1g CARBOHYDRATE
68g PROTEIN	29g FAT	--g FIBER

12	bite-size cubes Gruyère cheese
12	4 in (10 cm) squares veal scallopini, seasoned
3 tbsp	(45 ml) melted butter
	salt and pepper

Preheat barbecue at HIGH.

Wrap cheese cubes in scallopini squares; secure with toothpicks.

Baste with butter and place on hot grill. Cook 3 minutes each side depending on thickness. Season generously.

If desired serve with caper sauce or other dipping sauce.

Caper Sauce for Veal

1 SERVING	172 CALORIES	12g CARBOHYDRATE
4g PROTEIN	13g FAT	0.8g FIBER

1 tbsp	(15 ml) butter
2	shallots, chopped
3 tbsp	(45 ml) capers
2 tbsp	(30 ml) vinegar
1¼ cups	(300 ml) white sauce, heated
1 tbsp	(15 ml) tomato paste
	salt and pepper

Heat butter in saucepan over medium heat. Add shallots, capers and vinegar; cook 2 minutes over high heat.

Stir in white sauce and tomato paste; correct seasoning. Cook 5 to 6 minutes over low heat.

Serve with barbecued veal.

Best Veal Burgers

(serves 4)

1 SERVING	593 CALORIES	34g CARBOHYDRATE
51g PROTEIN	27g FAT	0.6g FIBER

¼ cup	(50 ml) melted butter
8	small medallions veal, about ¼ in (0.65 cm) thick
4	kaiser buns
4	slices fresh tomato
4	slices mozzarella cheese
	salt and pepper

Preheat barbecue at LOW.

Brush butter over veal medallions. Place on hot grill and cook 2 to 3 minutes each side; season very well.

Remove and transfer medallions to bottom parts of buns. Top with slices of tomato and cheese; close buns.

Squeeze buns slightly to help them hold; place on hot grill. Barbecue 2 minutes each side for added taste.

Serve with decorative fries.

Club Steak Bahamas

(serves 4)

1 SERVING	348 CALORIES	22g CARBOHYDRATE
36g PROTEIN	13g FAT	trace FIBER

1 cup	(250 ml) catsup
½ cup	(125 ml) wine vinegar
2	garlic cloves, smashed and chopped
1	onion, grated
4 tbsp	(60 ml) butter
1 tsp	(5 ml) Tabasco sauce
1 tbsp	(15 ml) dry mustard
4	club steaks, fat trimmed
	salt and pepper
	juice 3 limes

Preheat barbecue at HIGH.

Place catsup, vinegar, garlic and onion in saucepan; mix together.

Stir in butter, Tabasco, mustard, salt, pepper and lime juice. Bring to boil over medium-high heat. Continue cooking 4 to 5 minutes.

Remove saucepan from stove and spread mixture over steaks. Place meat on hot grill and cook 8 to 10 minutes depending on taste. Turn meat 3 to 4 times, season and baste occasionally.

Lamb Surprise

(serves 4)

1 SERVING	533 CALORIES	11g CARBOHYDRATE
58g PROTEIN	27g FAT	0.6g FIBER

12	pieces of lamb, 1½ in (4 cm) long and 1½ in (4 cm) thick
12	pieces of mozzarella, sized to fit over lamb
1 cup	(250 ml) hot barbecue sauce
¼ tsp	(1 ml) paprika
¼ tsp	(1 ml) sage
12	vine leaves
	salt and pepper

Preheat barbecue at HIGH.

Season lamb and place pieces of cheese on top. Brush with barbecue sauce and sprinkle with seasonings.

Wrap in vine leaves and secure with toothpicks. Place bundles on hot grill and cook 10 to 12 minutes. Turn several times and season vine leaves once.

Serve as appetizer.

Lamb Steaks with Sweet Marinade

(serves 4)

1 SERVING	318 CALORIES	11g CARBOHYDRATE
35g PROTEIN	14g FAT	trace FIBER

Marinade

2 tbsp	(30 ml) maple syrup
2 tbsp	(30 ml) wine vinegar
1 tsp	(5 ml) chopped parsley
¼ tsp	(1 ml) aniseed
¼ tsp	(1 ml) celery seed
¼ tsp	(1 ml) marjoram
2	garlic cloves, smashed and chopped
	juice 1 orange

Recipe

4	lamb steaks, (from leg), ½ in (1.2 cm) thick
2 tbsp	(30 ml) oil
	salt and pepper

Preheat barbecue at HIGH.

Mix marinade ingredients together; pour over lamb and marinate 2 hours in refrigerator.

Place lamb steaks on hot grill and brush with oil. Cook 10 to 12 minutes depending on taste. Turn 3 times, season well and baste occasionally with leftover marinade.

Serve with vegetables.

1 Your butcher will prepare the lamb steaks for you as it is necessary to use a saw to cut through the middle bone.

3 Add seasonings and garlic.

2 Prepare marinade by mixing maple syrup, vinegar, parsley and orange juice together.

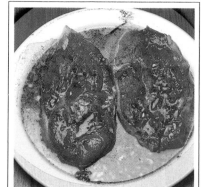

4 Pour over lamb and marinate 2 hours in refrigerator.

Lamb Roulade

(serves 4)

1 SERVING	287 CALORIES	5g CARBOHYDRATE
38g PROTEIN	12g FAT	1.0g FIBER

8	lamb cutlets (from leg)
1	onion, chopped and cooked
2 tbsp	(30 ml) green peppercorns
1 tbsp	(15 ml) coriander
	salt and pepper
	oil for basting

Preheat barbecue at MEDIUM.

Trim excess fat from cutlets. Place between waxed paper and flatten with mallet; season lightly.

Divide chopped onion, peppercorns and coriander between flattened cutlets. Roll and wrap in foil as shown in Technique; refrigerate 12 hours.

Unwrap lamb rolls and baste with oil. Place on hot grill and cook 14 to 16 minutes with cover. Turn at least 4 times.

Trim execss fat from cutlets.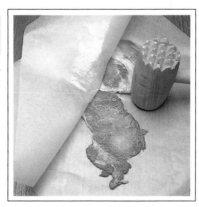

 Divide chopped onion, peppercorns and coriander between flattened cultlets.

Place between waxed paper and flatten with mallet; season lightly.

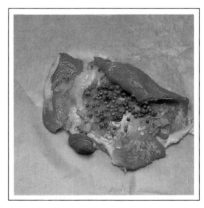 Roll and wrap each in foil; refrigerate 12 hours.

Fancy Lamb Rolls

(serves 4)

1 SERVING	380 CALORIES	5g CARBOHYDRATE
46g PROTEIN	18g FAT	trace FIBER

4	lamb kidneys, fat removed, well rinsed and ground
4 tbsp	(60 ml) breadcrumbs
1 tbsp	(15 ml) chopped parsley
4	lamb scallopini (from leg)
3 tbsp	(45 ml) melted butter
	salt and pepper

Preheat barbecue at MEDIUM.

Mix ground kidneys, breadcrumbs, parsley and pepper together. Spread over lamb, roll and secure with toothpicks.

Baste rolls with melted butter and season generously. Place on hot grill and cook 13 to 15 minutes depending on taste. Turn often and season once more.

Serve with julienne vegetables.

Rosemary Mint Lamb Chops

(serves 4)

1 SERVING	321 CALORIES	4g CARBOHYDRATE
37g PROTEIN	17g FAT	trace FIBER

½ cup	(125 ml) mint sauce
1 tsp	(5 ml) rosemary
2 tbsp	(30 ml) vegetable oil
8	lamb chops, fat trimmed
	salt and pepper

Preheat barbecue at HIGH.

Place mint sauce, rosemary and oil in deep dish; whisk together. Add lamb and mix; marinate 30 minutes.

Place chops on hot grill. Cook about 8 minutes depending on taste and size. Turn twice and season well.

Serve lamb with green beans.

Lamb Kidneys

Lamb Chops Liza

(serves 4)

1 SERVING	303 CALORIES	2g CARBOHYDRATE
29g PROTEIN	19g FAT	trace FIBER

¼ cup	(50 ml) oil
1 tbsp	(15 ml) rosemary
2 tbsp	(30 ml) chopped parsley
1 tbsp	(15 ml) ground pepper
1	garlic clove, smashed and chopped
8	lamb chops, boned
	salt

Preheat barbecue at MEDIUM.

Mix oil with seasonings, parsley and garlic; brush generously over lamb chops.

Place lamb on hot grill. Cook 12 to 15 minutes, turning and basting frequently.

Serve with vegetables.

(serves 4)

1 SERVING	189 CALORIES	5g CARBOHYDRATE
21g PROTEIN	7g FAT	trace FIBER

8	lamb kidneys
1 tbsp	(15 ml) butter
3	shallots, chopped
1 tbsp	(15 ml) chopped parsley
½ cup	(125 ml) dry white wine
1 tbsp	(15 ml) tomato paste
	salt and pepper

Preheat barbecue at HIGH.

Remove fat from kidneys, rinse in water and slice in half; set aside.

Heat butter in saucepan over medium heat. Add shallots and cook 2 minutes.

Stir in parsley and wine; bring to boil. Continue cooking 3 minutes.

Remove saucepan from stove and stir in tomato paste. Let cool slightly.

Brush mixture over kidneys and place them on hot grill. Cook 4 to 5 minutes each side, basting often. Season to taste.

Skewered Lamb Cubes

(serves 4)

1 SERVING	684 CALORIES	2g CARBOHYDRATE
72g PROTEIN	42g FAT	trace FIBER

Marinade

½ cup	(125 ml) olive oil
2	garlic cloves, smashed and chopped
1 tbsp	(15 ml) rosemary
½ tsp	(2 ml) chili powder
1 tbsp	(15 ml) curry powder

Recipe

3 lb	(1.4 kg) lamb from leg, in 2 in (5 cm) cubes
	salt and pepper

Preheat barbecue at HIGH.

Mix marinade ingredients together; pour over lamb and refrigerate 2 hours.

Thread lamb cubes on skewers. Place on hot grill and cook 8 to 10 minutes depending on taste. Turn 4 to 5 times, baste and season.

Serve with rice.

London Broil — Lamb Style

(serves 4)

1 SERVING	824 CALORIES	3g CARBOHYDRATE
70g PROTEIN	57g FAT	trace FIBER

1 lb	(500 g) ground lamb
½ lb	(250 g) lean ground pork
½ lb	(250 g) lean ground veal
1	onion, chopped and cooked
2	garlic cloves, smashed and chopped
1 tbsp	(15 ml) chopped parsley
1	egg
4	10 in (25 cm) long strips beef sirloin (to wrap around lamb steaks)
	salt and pepper

Preheat barbecue at MEDIUM.

Blend ground meats, onion, garlic, parsley and egg in mixer until well incorporated.

Shape mixture into steaks, wrap sirloin around outside and secure with toothpicks.

Place on hot grill and cook 12 to 14 minutes depending on taste. Turn at least 4 times and season twice.

If desired serve with Soya Dipping Sauce.

Soya Dipping Sauce

1 SERVING	47 CALORIES	11g CARBOHYDRATE
.7g PROTEIN	--g FAT	--g FIBER

½ cup	(125 ml) water
4 tbsp	(60 ml) granulated sugar
1 tbsp	(15 ml) honey
2 tbsp	(30 ml) soya sauce
1 tsp	(5 ml) cornstarch
2 tbsp	(30 ml) cold water

Place ½ cup (125 ml) water, sugar, honey and soya sauce in saucepan; cook 3 minutes over medium heat.

Mix cornstarch with remaining water; stir into sauce and cook 1 more minute.

Remove and serve with barbecued lamb.

Rack of Lamb

(serves 4)

1 SERVING	712 CALORIES	4g CARBOHYDRATE
50g PROTEIN	48g FAT	trace FIBER

2 tbsp	(30 ml) butter
2 tbsp	(30 ml) finely chopped parsley
2	shallots, finely chopped
1	garlic clove, smashed and chopped
2 tbsp	(30 ml) breadcrumbs
2	1 lb (500 g) racks of lamb
	salt and pepper
	oil for basting

Preheat barbecue at MEDIUM.

Mix butter, parsley and shallots together. Add garlic, breadcrumbs and season well; set aside.

Prepare lamb by removing fat from between ribs. Wrap bones in foil to prevent charring.

Baste lamb with oil and set on hot grill with bone side down. Partially cover and cook 15 minutes; turn once. Season well.

Continue barbecuing 30 minutes partially covered. Turn often and baste with more oil.

About 2 minutes before lamb is cooked, spread reserved butter mixture over meat.

Serve with potatoes.

Prepare lamb by removing fat from between ribs.

Wrap bones in foil to prevent charring.

Baste lamb with oil and place racks bone side down on hot grill.

About 2 minutes before lamb is cooked to taste, spread butter mixture over meat. Replace on grill and finish cooking.

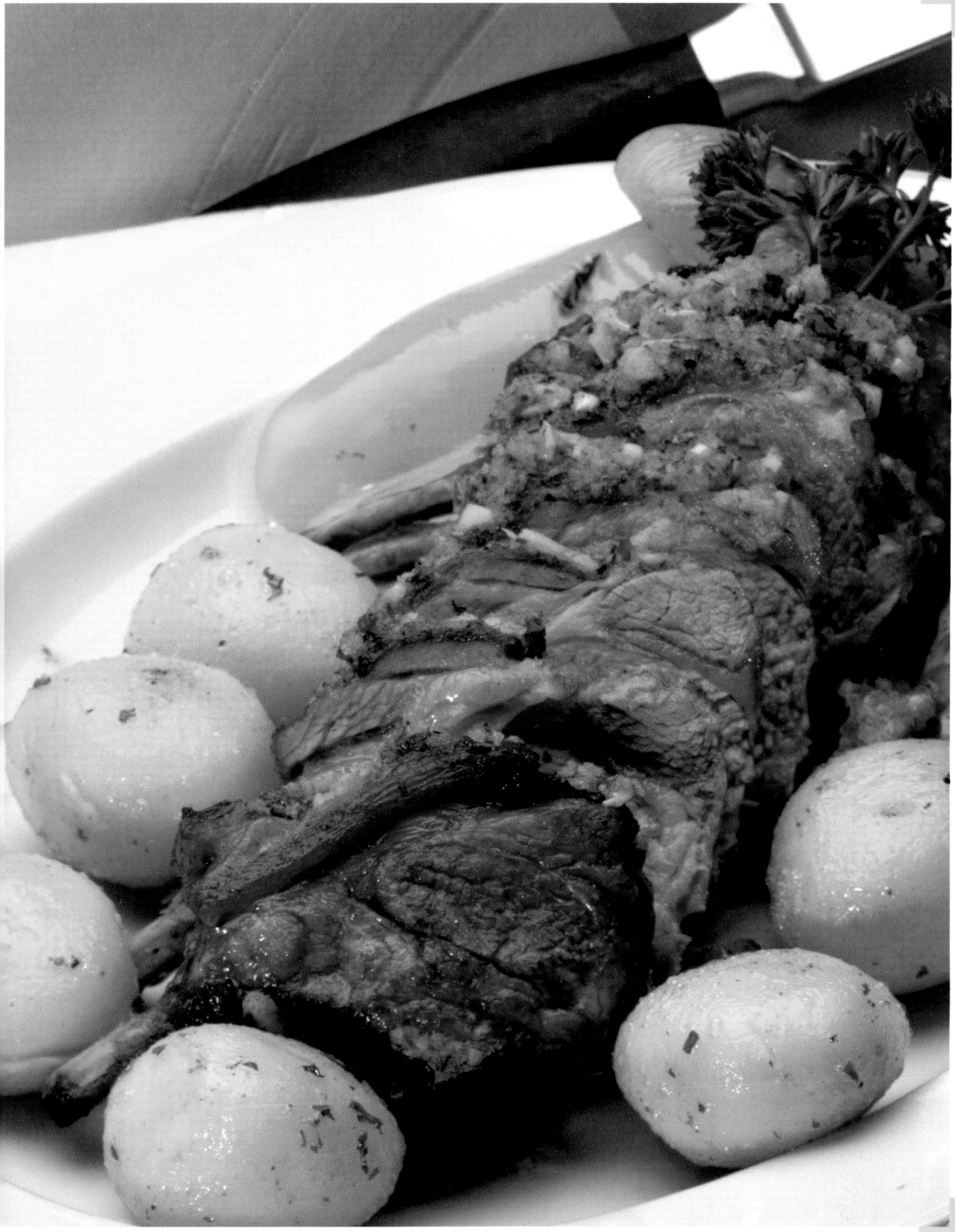

Barbecued Pork Medallions

(serves 4)

1 SERVING	642 CALORIES	17g CARBOHYDRATE
70g PROTEIN	27g FAT	trace FIBER

Marinade

¼ cup	(50 ml) soya sauce
½ cup	(125 ml) sherry wine
2 tbsp	(30 ml) honey
1 tbsp	(15 ml) brown sugar
1	garlic clove, smashed and chopped
2 tbsp	(30 ml) fresh chopped ginger
	juice ½ lemon
	salt and pepper

Recipe

2 lb	(900 g) pork tenderloin, fat removed and meat sliced in 1½ in (4 cm) medallions

Preheat barbecue at MEDIUM.

Mix marinade ingredients together, add pork and let stand 20 minutes.

Place pork medallions on hot grill. Cook 4 to 5 minutes, basting often, and turning once. Season well.

Grilled Pork Tenderloin

(serves 4)

1 SERVING	303 CALORIES	1g CARBOHYDRATE
26g PROTEIN	21g FAT	trace FIBER

2 tbsp	(30 ml) oil
2	garlic cloves, smashed and chopped
1 tbsp	(15 ml) soya sauce
1 tbsp	(15 ml) lemon juice
2	pork tenderloins, fat trimmed
	salt and pepper

Preheat barbecue at HIGH.

Mix oil with garlic, soya sauce and lemon juice; set aside.

Slice pork tenderloins open using long, thin knife. Be careful not to cut all the way through — they should remain in one piece.

Score meat on both sides, baste with lemon mixture and place on hot grill. Partially cover and cook 8 to 10 minutes each side. Turn 3 to 4 times, baste occasionally and season well.

When meat is cooked, slice and serve with wild rice and mushrooms.

Pork Meatballs

(serves 4)

1 SERVING 36g PROTEIN	651 CALORIES 52g FAT	8g CARBOHYDRATE trace FIBER

½ cup	(125 ml) chopped white bread (no crust)
1½ lb	(750 g) lean ground pork
1	onion, chopped and cooked
1 tbsp	(15 ml) chopped parsley
1 tbsp	(15 ml) chopped fresh mint
¼ tsp	(1 ml) allspice
¼ tsp	(1 ml) chili powder
1	egg
3 tbsp	(45 ml) olive oil
2	garlic cloves, smashed and chopped
	lemon juice
	salt and pepper

Preheat barbecue at LOW.

Mix bread, pork, onion, parsley, mint, seasonings and egg together in mixer until well incorporated.

Shape into small meatballs, thread on skewers and set aside.

Mix remaining ingredients together. Brush over skewers and set on hot grill. Partially cover and cook 8 minutes. Turn skewers often and baste several times.

Serve with fries.

Sweet Orange Loin of Pork

(serves 4)

1 SERVING 47g PROTEIN	693 CALORIES 38g FAT	33g CARBOHYDRATE trace FIBER

1 cup	(250 ml) dry white wine
1 tbsp	(15 ml) honey
2 lb	(900 g) boneless loin of pork, fat trimmed and meat scored
1 tbsp	(15 ml) butter
1	onion, diced
1 tbsp	(15 ml) vinegar
10 oz	(284 ml) can mandarin sections
1 cup	(250 ml) brown sauce, heated
	juice 2 oranges
	salt and pepper

Preheat barbecue at LOW.

Bring wine to boil in small saucepan; continue cooking 2 minutes.

Stir in honey and orange juice; cook 3 minutes.

Brush honey mixture over pork. Place meat on hot grill and cook, partially covered, 40 to 45 minutes depending on size. Turn frequently, baste occasionally and season once.

Before pork is done, prepare sauce. Heat butter in small saucepan. Add onion and cook 3 minutes over medium heat.

Stir in vinegar and half the juice from mandarins; cook 3 minutes.

Correct seasoning and stir in brown sauce and mandarin sections; simmer 3 to 4 minutes and serve with sliced pork.

Pork Chops Marinated in Beer

(serves 4)

1 SERVING	270 CALORIES	14g CARBOHYDRATE
24g PROTEIN	11g FAT	0.5g FIBER

Marinade

1 cup	(250 ml) beer
1 tbsp	(15 ml) teriyaki sauce
½ tsp	(2 ml) allspice
1 tbsp	(15 ml) tomato paste
	salt and pepper

Recipe

4	pork chops, ¾ in (2 cm) thick
2	apples, peeled, cored and sliced
¼ cup	(50 ml) crushed pineapple
1 tbsp	(15 ml) butter
½ tsp	(2 ml) cinnamon

Preheat barbecue at HIGH.

Mix marinade ingredients together and pour over pork; let stand 30 minutes.

Meanwhile, place apples, pineapple, butter and cinnamon on large double sheet of foil. Shape into basket and seal edges.

Drain pork and place chops along with foil basket on hot grill. Cook everything 8 to 10 minutes, depending on taste.

Turn chops over 3 to 4 times, baste occasionally and season well. Turn basket of apples over once.

Serve.

Trim excess fat from pork chops.

Add tomato paste and stir well.

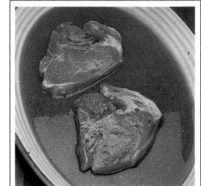
Place beer, teriyaki sauce and allspice in bowl.

Marinate pork in mixture for 30 minutes.

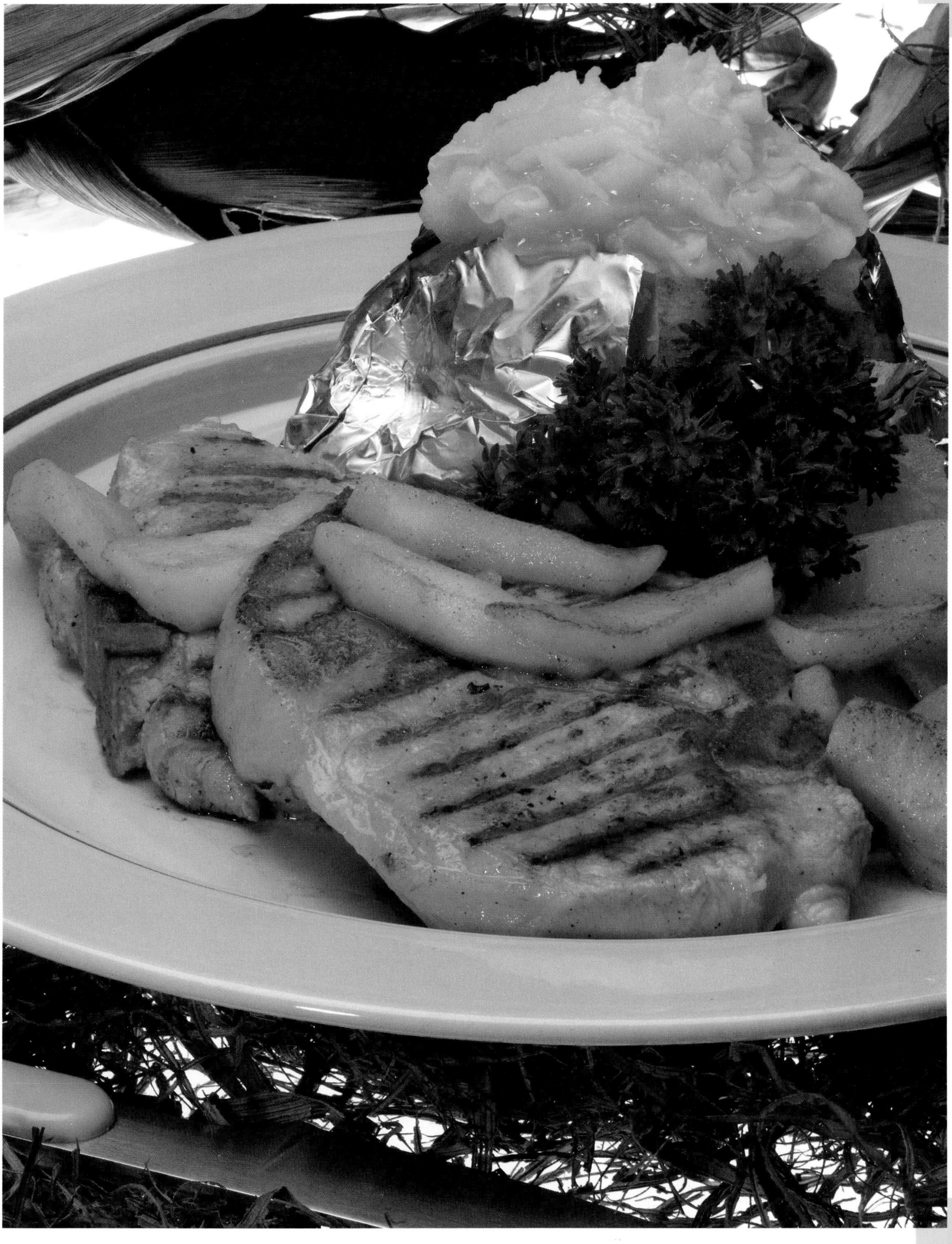

Pork Cutlets with Mango Relish

(serves 4)

1 SERVING	673 CALORIES	79g CARBOHYDRATE
49g PROTEIN	20g FAT	1.0g FIBER

1	ripe mango
½ cup	(125 ml) cider vinegar
½ cup	(125 ml) brown sugar
¼ lb	(125 g) pitted dates
½ cup	(125 ml) Smyrna raisins
1 tbsp	(15 ml) chopped ginger
1 tsp	(5 ml) chopped garlic
¼ cup	(50 ml) grated coconut
8	pork cutlets, about ¾ in (2 cm) thick
	oil
	salt and pepper

Preheat barbecue at HIGH.

Slice mango in half and remove pit. Using small knife remove fibrous middle and discard. Dice remaining flesh and set aside.

Place vinegar and sugar in small saucepan; bring to quick boil. Reduce heat and cook 4 to 5 minutes.

Add dates and mix well. Stir in raisins, ginger, garlic and mango. Sprinkle in coconut and season lightly with salt. Cook 20 minutes over low heat.

Before relish is cooked, start preparing pork by basting with oil.

Place on hot grill and cook 6 to 8 minutes depending on thickness. Turn at least twice and season several times.

Serve pork with mango relish.

Slice mango in half and remove pit.

Using small knife, remove fibrous middle and discard. Dice remaining flesh and set aside.

Place vinegar and sugar in small saucepan; bring to quick boil. Reduce heat and cook 4 to 5 minutes.

Add dates and mix well. Stir in remaining relish ingredients and finish cooking 20 minutes over low heat.

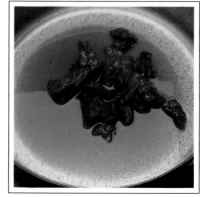

PRODUCT OF ITALY
Melini
CHIANTI
CANTINE DI GAGGIANO
DENOMINAZIONE DI ORIGINE CONTROLLATA E GARANTITA
RED WINE — VIN ROUGE
MADE IN GAGGIANO BY
CONFECTIONNÉ A GAGGIANO PAR
MELINI S.p.A.
LAZISE - ITALIE
1 l e

Sausage Skewers

(serves 4)

1 SERVING	530 CALORIES	33g CARBOHYDRATE
19g PROTEIN	36g FAT	0.5g FIBER

Marinade

½ cup	(125 ml) cider vinegar
2 tbsp	(30 ml) corn syrup
2 tbsp	(30 ml) molasses
3	cloves
½ tsp	(2 ml) cinnamon

Recipe

2 lb	(500 g) Polish sausages, sliced ¾ in (2 cm) thick
2	apples, in wedges with skin
1	red pepper, in bite-size pieces
4	small onions, cut in half
	salt and pepper

Preheat barbecue at MEDIUM.

Place marinade ingredients in saucepan; boil 3 to 4 minutes.

Meanwhile, alternate kebab ingredients on skewers and set in deep platter. Pour marinade over kebabs and season well; let stand 10 to 12 minutes.

Place kebabs on hot grill. Cover and cook 10 to 12 minutes, turning 2 to 3 times. Baste frequently and season well.

Serve with fresh vegetable sticks.

Sweet and Spicy Spareribs

(serves 4)

1 SERVING	1189 CALORIES	24g CARBOHYDRATE
53g PROTEIN	146g FAT	0.6g FIBER

Marinade

2	garlic cloves, smashed and chopped
1 tsp	(5 ml) finely chopped jalapeno pepper
1 tsp	(5 ml) dry mustard
½ tsp	(2 ml) oregano
½ tsp	(2 ml) rosemary
3 tbsp	(45 ml) honey
1 cup	(250 ml) tomato sauce
	juice 2 oranges

Recipe

3½ lb	(1.6 kg) pork spareribs, about 4-6 in (10-15 cm) long
	salt and pepper

Preheat barbecue at LOW.

Place all marinade ingredients in small saucepan and cook 15 minutes over very low heat.

Meanwhile, blanch ribs in boiling water for 15 minutes.

Drain ribs and baste with marinade sauce. Place ribs on hot grill and partly cover. Cook 30 minutes depending on size. Turn frequently, baste occasionally and season well.

If desired serve any leftover marinade as sauce.

Pork Chops and Bell Peppers

(serves 4)

1 SERVING	517 CALORIES	6g CARBOHYDRATE
60g PROTEIN	27g FAT	1.0g FIBER

1 tsp	(5 ml) oregano
1 tsp	(5 ml) rosemary
2	garlic cloves, smashed and chopped
1 tsp	(5 ml) honey
½ tsp	(2 ml) olive oil
4	large pork chops, fat trimmed
2 tbsp	(30 ml) vegetable oil
4	bell peppers, halved and seeded
	salt and pepper

Preheat barbecue at MEDIUM.

Mix seasonings, garlic, honey and olive oil together. Spread over pork chops.

Place chops on hot grill and cook 15 to 18 minutes depending on size. Season and turn occasionally.

Brush bell peppers with vegetable oil. Barbecue 3 to 4 minutes.

Serve peppers with chops.

Half Chicken Dinner

(serves 2)

1 SERVING	1311 CALORIES	14g CARBOHYDRATE
124g PROTEIN	77g FAT	trace FIBER

Marinade

½ cup	(125 ml) dry white wine
¼ cup	(50 ml) lemon juice
1	garlic clove, smashed and chopped
1 tsp	(5 ml) tarragon
¼ tsp	(1 ml) paprika
1 tbsp	(15 ml) fresh chopped ginger
2 tbsp	(30 ml) oil
1 tbsp	(15 ml) honey
	salt and pepper

Recipe

3 lb	(1.4 kg) chicken, cleaned and split in half

Preheat barbecue at LOW.

Mix all marinade ingredients together and set aside.

Prepare chicken halves as described in Technique.

Place chicken in large roasting pan and pour in marinade; refrigerate 30 minutes.

Place chicken halves (bone side down) on hot grill. Cover and cook 30 minutes. Baste and season occasionally but do not turn halves over.

Now place halves with breast side down on grill. Continue barbecuing covered for another 30 minutes. Baste occasionally and turn halves over often.

Split chicken into two halves.

Use a small knife and make a hole in skin through flesh as shown. It should be big enough for your finger to fit through.

 Push chicken leg through hole. This will help chicken maintain its shape during barbecuing.

 Marinate chicken in refrigerator for 30 minutes before cooking.

Chicken Breasts, Devil Sauce

(serves 4)

1 SERVING	321 CALORIES	12g CARBOHYDRATE
29g PROTEIN	15g FAT	0.7g FIBER

½ cup	(125 ml) dry white wine
2 tbsp	(30 ml) red wine vinegar
2	shallots, chopped
3 tbsp	(45 ml) green peppercorns
1¼ cups	(300 ml) brown sauce, heated
2	chicken breasts, skinned, halved and boned
	salt and pepper

Preheat barbecue at MEDIUM.

Cook wine, vinegar and shallots in small saucepan over high heat; bring to boil. Reduce heat to medium and continue cooking 4 to 5 minutes.

Add peppercorns and brown sauce; correct seasoning. Bring to quick boil then remove from heat.

Season chicken and baste in sauce. Place breasts on hot grill and cook 10 minutes each side. Turn at least 4 to 5 times and baste occasionally.

Serve with salad.

Grilled Chicken Anchovy

(serves 4)

1 SERVING	416 CALORIES	trace CARBOHYDRATE
30g PROTEIN	32g FAT	trace FIBER

4	anchovy filets, drained
½ cup	(125 ml) soft butter
1 tsp	(5 ml) horseradish
½ tsp	(2 ml) lemon juice
2	chicken breasts, halved and skinned
	cayenne pepper to taste

Preheat barbecue at MEDIUM.

Pat anchovy filets dry to remove any oil, then mash in mortar. Mix butter, horseradish, lemon juice and cayenne pepper with anchovy until well blended.

Force mixture through sieve using wooden spoon, then spread on both sides of chicken breasts. Wrap chicken in double sheets of foil with 2 half breasts per bundle.

Place on hot grill and cook 35 minutes with cover. Turn twice.

Remove chicken from foil and set directly on grill. Finish barbecuing 5 minutes without cover; season to taste.

Some sauce will have collected in foil packages — serve with chicken.

Spicy Chicken Legs

(serves 4)

1 SERVING	282 CALORIES	11g CARBOHYDRATE
49g PROTEIN	15g FAT	trace FIBER

4	chicken legs
½ cup	(125 ml) catsup
¼ cup	(50 ml) wine vinegar
¼ tsp	(1 ml) Tabasco sauce
½ cup	(125 ml) clam/tomato juice
2	garlic cloves, smashed and chopped
¼ tsp	(1 ml) cumin
¼ tsp	(1 ml) curry powder
½ tsp	(2 ml) fines herbes
	salt and pepper
	paprika

Preheat barbecue at HIGH.

Slash chicken legs with knife, season with paprika and set aside.

Place catsup, vinegar, Tabasco and clam/tomato juice in bowl. Add garlic and seasonings; mix well with whisk.

Place chicken on hot grill and baste with tomato mixture. Cook 5 minutes.

Turn legs over; continue cooking 10 minutes. Turn once and baste several times; season.

Turn chicken over; finish barbecuing about 27 minutes (depending on size) at LOW. Be sure to cover this time; baste often and turn legs every 4 to 5 minutes.

Slash chicken legs with knife so that basting sauce will be able to soak into meat. Season chicken with paprika.

Mix well with whisk.

Place catsup, vinegar, Tabasco and clam/tomato juice in bowl. Add garlic and seasonings.

Begin cooking legs on hot grill for 5 minutes. Baste with tomato mixture.

Cornish Hens

(serves 4)

1 SERVING	636 CALORIES	2g CARBOHYDRATE
61g PROTEIN	41g FAT	trace FIBER

3	garlic cloves, smashed and chopped
3 tbsp	(45 ml) vegetable oil
2 tbsp	(30 ml) wine vinegar
1 tbsp	(15 ml) teriyaki sauce
4	Cornish hens, cleaned and split in half
	salt and pepper

Preheat barbecue at LOW.

Place all ingredients in roasting pan and let stand 15 minutes.

Set hens on grill (bone side down) and cook 35-40 minutes with cover. Baste occasionally, turn often and season well.

Chicken Pieces with Pineapple

(serves 4)

1 SERVING	714 CALORIES	15g CARBOHYDRATE
79g PROTEIN	20g FAT	trace FIBER

1 cup	(250 ml) crushed pineapple
2 tbsp	(30 ml) brown sugar
1 cup	(250 ml) rum
2	limes, cut in half
3½ lb	(1.6 kg) chicken, cut in pieces and skinned
	salt and pepper

Preheat barbecue at LOW.

Mix pineapple, sugar and rum together in small saucepan; bring to boil over medium-high heat.

Rub limes all over chicken pieces. Pour the pineapple mixture over and refrigerate 1 hour.

Place chicken pieces on hot grill. Cook, partially covered, for the following times: white meat — 8 to 10 minutes each side; dark meat — 15 minutes each side.

Season during cooking and baste occasionally.

Chicken with Orange Marinade

(serves 4)

1 SERVING	573 CALORIES	45g CARBOHYDRATE
62g PROTEIN	15g FAT	trace FIBER

Marinade

1	onion, finely chopped
1	garlic clove, smashed and chopped
½ cup	(125 ml) catsup
1 cup	(250 ml) orange juice
½ cup	(125 ml) orange marmalade
2 tbsp	(30 ml) soya sauce

Recipe

2½ lb	(1.2 kg) chicken parts, cleaned and skinned
	salt and pepper

Preheat barbecue at MEDIUM.

Mix marinade ingredients together in small saucepan; bring to boil.

Pour over chicken parts and marinate 4 hours in refrigerator.

Place chicken parts on hot grill. Cook, partially covered, for the following times: white meat — 8 to 10 minutes each side; dark meat — 15 minutes each side.

Season during cooking and baste with any leftover orange marinade.

Half Chicken for Two

(serves 2)

1 SERVING	1325 CALORIES	40g CARBOHYDRATE
127g PROTEIN	71g FAT	0.7g FIBER

Marinade

1 cup	(250 ml) catsup
⅓ cup	(75 ml) water
1 tbsp	(15 ml) oil
1½	onions, finely chopped
2	garlic cloves, smashed and chopped
2 tbsp	(30 ml) vinegar
½ tsp	(2 ml) chili powder
½ tsp	(2 ml) ground ginger
	pinch sugar
	few drops Tabasco sauce

Recipe

3 lb	(1.4 kg) chicken, cleaned and split in half
	salt and pepper

Preheat barbecue at LOW.

Mix catsup and water together; set aside.

Heat oil in small saucepan. Add onions and garlic; cook 2 minutes over medium heat.

Stir catsup into saucepan with remaining marinade ingredients. Bring to boil and cook 2 to 3 minutes.

Place chicken halves in large roasting pan. Pour sauce over and refrigerate 30 minutes.

Place chicken halves (bone side down) on hot grill. Cover and cook 30 minutes. Baste and season occasionally but do not turn halves over.

Now place halves with breast side down on grill. Continue barbecuing covered for another 30 minutes. Baste occasionally and turn halves over often.

Marinated Chicken Wings

(serves 4)

1 SERVING	559 CALORIES	18g CARBOHYDRATE
42g PROTEIN	33g FAT	0.5g FIBER

24	chicken wings
1 tbsp	(15 ml) sunflower oil
2	pickled hot cherry peppers, seeded and finely chopped
1	green pepper, finely chopped
2	garlic cloves, smashed and chopped
½ cup	(125 ml) crushed pineapple
¼ cup	(50 ml) brown sugar
1 tbsp	(15 ml) chopped parsley
2 tbsp	(30 ml) vinegar
¼ cup	(50 ml) dry white wine
2 tbsp	(30 ml) soya sauce
¼ tsp	(1 ml) paprika
	salt and pepper

Preheat barbecue at HIGH.

Cut off wing tips and reserve for stocks or other uses. Set wings aside in deep dish.

Heat oil in saucepan over medium heat. Cook cherry peppers, green pepper and garlic 3 minutes.

Stir in pineapple and brown sugar; cook 3 to 4 minutes.

Add parsley, vinegar, wine, soya sauce and seasonings; continue cooking 3 to 4 minutes.

Pour over wings and let stand 20 minutes.

Drain wings and place on hot grill. Cover and cook 14 to 16 minutes, turning 2 to 3 times. Season generously.

Serve with pasta salad.

Cut off wing tips and reserve for stocks or other uses. Set wings aside in deep dish.

Stir in pineapple and brown sugar; cook 3 to 4 minutes.

Cook peppers and garlic in hot oil for 3 minutes.

After other ingredients have been added to marinade, pour all over chicken and let stand 20 minutes before barbecuing.

Chicken Strips

(serves 4)

1 SERVING	447 CALORIES	9g CARBOHYDRATE
62g PROTEIN	13g FAT	trace FIBER

Marinade

1 ½ cups	(375 ml) cider
2 tbsp	(30 ml) oil
2	garlic cloves, smashed and chopped
½ tsp	(2 ml) tarragon
2 tbsp	(30 ml) maple syrup

Recipe

2 lb	(900 g) chicken breast strips, about 3 in (7.5 cm) long
	salt and pepper

Preheat barbecue at MEDIUM.

Bring marinade ingredients to boil in small saucepan. Continue cooking 2 more minutes.

Pour over chicken and marinate 25 minutes.

Place chicken strips on hot grill. Cook 4 to 5 minutes each side depending on size. Baste and season twice.

Serve with potatoes.

Easy Wings

(serves 4)

1 SERVING	616 CALORIES	8g CARBOHYDRATE
42g PROTEIN	36g FAT	trace FIBER

Marinade

2 cups	(500 ml) dry red wine
2 tbsp	(30 ml) olive oil
1	garlic clove, smashed and chopped
1	small onion, thinly sliced
1	carrot, thinly sliced
1	bay leaf

Recipe

24	chicken wings, tips removed
	salt and pepper

Preheat barbecue at HIGH.

Mix marinade ingredients together; pour over wings and let stand 10 to 12 minutes.

Drain wings and place on hot grill. Cover and cook 14 to 16 minutes, turning 2 to 3 times. Season generously.

Serve with fries.

Salmon Filets with Blender Hollandaise

(serves 4)

1 SERVING	778 CALORIES	1g CARBOHYDRATE
70g PROTEIN	53g FAT	trace FIBER

2 tbsp	(30 ml) melted butter
1 tsp	(5 ml) fennel seed
4	8 oz (250 g) salmon filets
1 tbsp	(15 ml) hot water
2 tbsp	(30 ml) horseradish
3	egg yolks
½ cup	(125 ml) melted butter
	few drops Tabasco sauce
	salt and pepper
	lemon juice

Preheat barbecue at HIGH.

Brush 2 tbsp (30 ml) butter over salmon; sprinkle with fennel seed. Place fish on hot grill and cook 5 to 6 minutes each side depending on taste.

Meanwhile, mix water, horseradish, egg yolks, Tabasco, salt, pepper and lemon juice in blender for 30 seconds at high speed.

Reduce blender speed to low; very slowly incorporate second measurement of butter. Keep mixing until butter is well blended, then correct seasoning.

Serve Hollandaise with salmon.

Lobster Tails

(serves 4)

1 SERVING	413 CALORIES	4g CARBOHYDRATE
36g PROTEIN	14g FAT	trace FIBER

4	lobster tails (small if available)
8	large shrimp, shelled
8	large scallops
4 tbsp	(60 ml) melted butter
1 tbsp	(15 ml) lemon juice
1 tbsp	(15 ml) soya sauce
1	garlic clove, smashed and chopped
	salt and pepper

Preheat barbecue at HIGH.

Remove shells from lobster tails, discard and place meat in bowl; add remaining ingredients and set aside 15 minutes.

Thread ingredients on skewers in the following order; shrimp, scallop, lobster, scallop and shrimp. Repeat until full.

Place skewers on hot grill. Cook 4 minutes each side depending on size of lobster tails. Baste and season.

Salmon Tail Supreme

(serves 4)

1 SERVING	563 CALORIES	3g CARBOHYDRATE
48g PROTEIN	39g FAT	trace FIBER

2	1 lb (500 g) salmon tails
2 tbsp	(30 ml) teriyaki sauce
2	garlic cloves, smashed and chopped
3 tbsp	(45 ml) olive oil
2 tbsp	(30 ml) lemon juice
	salt and pepper

Preheat barbecue at MEDIUM.

Slide knife along backbone of salmon tail. Set outer piece of fish aside. Slice along other side of bone and set second piece of fish aside — discard piece containing bone.

Mix remaining ingredients together and pour over fish; let stand 15 minutes.

Place fish on hot grill (skin side down) and cook 14 to 16 minutes with cover. Turn pieces twice, season lightly and baste occasionally.

Slide knife along backbone of salmon tail. Set the piece without the bone aside.

Marinate fish for 15 minutes.

Repeat the same procedure on the other side of backbone — this will give you a second piece of fish. Discard middle part containing bone.

Begin barbecuing by placing salmon pieces on hot grill with skin side down.

Flounder and Vegetables

(serves 4)

1 SERVING	224 CALORIES	20g CARBOHYDRATE
26g PROTEIN	5g FAT	0.6g FIBER

1 tbsp	(15 ml) vegetable oil
2	green onions, chopped
2	small bamboo shoots, diced
1 tbsp	(15 ml) fresh chopped ginger
1	small carrot, pared and thinly sliced
1 tbsp	(15 ml) lemon rind
1¼ cups	(300 ml) hot chicken stock
2 tbsp	(30 ml) honey
2 tbsp	(30 ml) tomato paste
3 tbsp	(45 ml) wine vinegar
1 tbsp	(15 ml) cornstarch
3 tbsp	(45 ml) cold water
4	flounder filets
	salt and pepper

Preheat barbecue at HIGH.

Heat oil in saucepan. Cook onions, bamboo shoots, ginger, carrot and lemon rind 1 minute.

Season well and add chicken stock, honey, tomato paste and vinegar; bring to boil. Continue cooking 2 to 3 minutes.

Mix cornstarch with water; stir into sauce and cook 1 minute.

Spread mixture over fish and place on hot grill. Partially cover and cook 3 to 4 minutes each side according to taste.

Flounder and Tomatoes

(serves 2)

1 SERVING	306 CALORIES	6g CARBOHYDRATE
28g PROTEIN	14g FAT	2.0g FIBER

2	large flounder filets
12	cherry tomatoes, cut in half
1	onion, chopped
2 tbsp	(30 ml) soya sauce
2 tbsp	(30 ml) melted butter
1 tsp	(5 ml) lemon juice
	salt and pepper

Preheat barbecue at HIGH.

Place all ingredients on triple sheet of foil. Cover with single sheet and seal edges well.

Place on hot grill and cover. Cook 15 minutes turning once.

Seasoned Whole Trout

(serves 4)

1 SERVING	380 CALORIES	trace CARBOHYDRATE
27g PROTEIN	29g FAT	--g FIBER

4	brook trout, cleaned
⅓ cup	(75 ml) melted butter
1 tbsp	(15 ml) lemon juice
	dash paprika
	few drops Tabasco sauce
	salt and pepper

Preheat barbecue at HIGH.

It is advisable to use a fish grill.

Using scissors, cut off all fins. Slash fish on one side with sharp knife and then baste with melted butter.

Sprinkle fish with remaining ingredients and place on hot grill. Cook 6 minutes each side; season when turning.

Be sure that trout are completely gutted and cleaned. 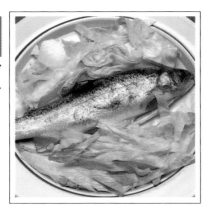 Slash fish on one side only with sharp knife.

Using scissors, cut off all fins.

 Baste with melted butter.

Double Fish Kebabs

(serves 4)

1 SERVING	220 CALORIES	7g CARBOHYDRATE
27g PROTEIN	5g FAT	trace FIBER

Marinade

1 cup	(250 ml) dry white wine
1 tbsp	(15 ml) lime juice
2 tbsp	(30 ml) fresh chopped ginger
2	garlic cloves, smashed and chopped
¼ tsp	(1 ml) crushed chillies
2 tbsp	(30 ml) soya sauce
1 tbsp	(15 ml) vegetable oil
	salt and pepper

Recipe

¾ lb	(375 g) shrimp, peeled and deveined
1	large halibut steak, cubed

Preheat barbecue at HIGH.

Mix marinade ingredients together in bowl.

Place shrimp and halibut in marinade. Let stand 30 minutes.

Thread fish on skewers. Place on hot grill and cover; cook 8 minutes. Turn twice, baste occasionally and season well.

Serve with vegetables.

Mix marinade ingredients together in bowl.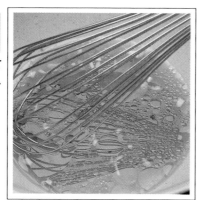

 Peel and devein shrimp.

 Place shrimp and halibut in marinade; let stand 30 minutes.

 Thread seafood on skewers. Reserve marinade for basting.

Scallops Cartagena

(serves 4)

1 SERVING	166 CALORIES	12g CARBOHYDRATE
21g PROTEIN	4g FAT	0.8g FIBER

1 lb	(500 g) fresh sea scallops
¼ cup	(50 ml) lime juice
2 tbsp	(30 ml) olive oil
1 tbsp	(15 ml) chopped fresh parsley
1 tbsp	(15 ml) chopped shallot
1 tsp	(5 ml) basil
2	large tomatoes, peeled and diced
1	red pepper, diced
	salt and pepper

Preheat barbecue at MEDIUM.

Place all ingredients on double sheet of foil. Cover with single sheet and seal edges shut.

Place foil basket on hot grill. Cover and cook 8 minutes; mix occasionally.

Serve with rice.

Scallops in Foil Basket

(serves 4)

1 SERVING	211 CALORIES	17g CARBOHYDRATE
40g PROTEIN	7g FAT	1.0g FIBER

1 lb	(500 g) sea scallops
½ cup	(125 ml) lichee nuts (optional)
2	green onions, chopped
2 tbsp	(30 ml) garlic butter (hard)
⅓ lb	(150 g) mushrooms, diced
½ cup	(125 ml) pineapple chunks
	salt and pepper

Preheat barbecue at HIGH.

Place all ingredients on double sheet of foil. Cover with single sheet and shape into basket — seal edges well.

Place on hot grill and cover; cook 8 to 10 minutes. Open foil basket during cooking to stir twice.

Serve with rice.

Halibut Steaks

(serves 4)

1 SERVING	186 CALORIES	trace CARBOHYDRATE
26g PROTEIN	8g FAT	--g FIBER

2 tbsp	(30 ml) oil
1 tsp	(5 ml) lemon juice
½ tsp	(2 ml) teriyaki sauce
¼ tsp	(1 ml) paprika
4	halibut steaks
	salt and pepper

Preheat barbecue at HIGH.

Mix oil, lemon, teriyaki and paprika together; season to taste.

Brush mixture over fish and set steaks on hot grill. Cook 10 minutes turning once or twice. Baste occasionally.

GRILLED
FISH
AND
SEAFOOD

GRILLED FISH AND COQUILLES

The seafood presented here is prepared according to two traditional cooking techniques: grilled or served in coquilles. Everybody has a favorite fish and a preferred method for cooking it, but it is hoped that you will find some exciting new concoctions among this selection that will earn their place on your top ten list. Fresh, frozen and canned fish are used in the recipes. Generally frozen and canned require little buying skill and depend more on quality control by the manufacturer. The best rule of thumb is to take note of brands and keep using those which you can depend upon. Fresh fish, however, takes a bit more scrutiny on your part. Always try to touch a whole fish before purchasing. It should feel firm and springy. Inspect the eyes, looking for clearness and fullness; avoid fish with sunken or drippy eyes. Contrary to some people's beliefs, fresh fish does not smell fishy — bad fish does. Granted, there are some species (shark for example) which do have a stronger odor. But on the whole, fish should smell clean. Cooking fish is so simple that few specialty items are needed. Aside from your regular frying pan, the only other requirement is a selection of scallop shells. These can be purchased quite inexpensively in the natural form, or you can find various replicas in porcelain. The advantage of these copy-cat versions is that they are often deeper, larger and more decorative. Now let's cast off...

Cod Steaks
and Pickles

(serves 4)

1 SERVING	350 CALORIES	24g CARBOHYDRATE
45g PROTEIN	21g FAT	0.3g FIBER

4	cod steaks
1 cup	(250 ml) seasoned flour
2 tbsp	(30 ml) vegetable oil
2 tbsp	(30 ml) melted butter
1 tbsp	(15 ml) chopped parsley
2	large pickles, diced
1	lemon, peeled, seeded and diced
	salt and pepper

Preheat oven to 150°F (70°C).

Dredge cod in flour. Heat oil in large frying pan and add fish. Cook 4 to 5 minutes each side depending on thickness. Season well when turning fish over.

Remove fish from pan and keep hot in oven.

Add butter to pan and heat. Add all remaining ingredients and cook 2 minutes over medium heat.

Season and serve pickle sauce with fish.

Sautéed Sole
Pieces

(serves 4)

1 SERVING	274 CALORIES	13g CARBOHYDRATE
22g PROTEIN	15g FAT	0.5g FIBER

4	sole filets, cut in 3 pieces
½ cup	(125 ml) seasoned flour
3 tbsp	(45 ml) melted butter
¼ lb	(125 g) mushrooms, sliced
½ cup	(125 ml) stuffed green olives
1 tbsp	(15 ml) chopped parsley
	salt and pepper
	juice 1 lemon

Dredge fish lightly in flour; set aside.

Heat half of butter in large frying pan. Add mushrooms, olives and parsley; season well. Cook 3 to 4 minutes over medium heat.

Transfer mushroom mixture to plate; set aside.

Replace frying pan on stove and add remaining butter. When hot, add fish and cook 3 to 4 minutes depending on size. Turn pieces over once and season well.

Replace mushroom mixture in pan with fish. Simmer everything 2 minutes, sprinkle with lemon juice and serve.

Grilled Sole
Parmesam

(serves 4)

1 SERVING	453 CALORIES	3g CARBOHYDRATE
48g PROTEIN	27g FAT	-- FIBER

4	large sole filets
3	beaten eggs
1½ cups	(375 ml) grated Parmesan cheese
3 tbsp	(45 ml) vegetable oil
	salt and white pepper
	dash paprika
	lemon juice

Dip sole filets in beaten eggs.

Season grated cheese with pepper and paprika; thoroughly coat filets in mixture.

Heat oil in large frying pan. Add filets and cook about 2 minutes each side, depending on size, over medium-high heat. Season during cooking.

Serve with lemon juice.

Grilled Marinated Trout

(serves 4)

1 SERVING	346 CALORIES	5g CARBOHYDRATE
27g PROTEIN	18g FAT	trace FIBER

4	brook trout, cleaned, in filets and cut in 1 in (2.5 cm) slices
1½ cups	(375 ml) dry white wine
2 tbsp	(30 ml) lemon juice
1 tbsp	(15 ml) grated orange rind
1 tbsp	(15 ml) chopped fresh ginger
1 tbsp	(15 ml) chopped chives
2 tbsp	(30 ml) olive oil
2	fennel sprigs
	salt and pepper
	lemon wedges

Place fish, wine, lemon juice, orange rind, ginger and chives in bowl. Marinate 2 hours in refrigerator.

Drain fish well.

Heat oil in large frying pan. Add fish and fennel sprigs; season well. Cook 2 to 3 minutes over high heat, stirring once or twice.

Serve fish with lemon wedges.

Grilled Trout with Tomatoes

(serves 4)

1 SERVING	514 CALORIES	32g CARBOHYDRATE
32g PROTEIN	40g FAT	3.0g FIBER

2 tbsp	(30 ml) vegetable oil
4	small brook trout, gutted and cleaned
1 cup	(250 ml) flour
1	onion, chopped
1	red pepper, diced small
½	zucchini, diced small
1	garlic clove, smashed and chopped
½ cup	(125 ml) pitted black olives
¼ tsp	(1 ml) fennel seed
1 tbsp	(15 ml) green peppercorns
1 cup	(250 ml) chopped tomatoes
	salt and pepper
	few drops lemon juice

Preheat oven to 150°F (70°C).

Heat oil in large frying pan. Dredge trout lightly in flour and place in hot oil. Cook 5 to 6 minutes each side over medium heat, depending on size. Season well.

Transfer fish to serving platter and keep hot in oven.

Add onion, red pepper, zucchini and garlic to frying pan; cook 2 minutes over medium-high heat.

Stir in olives, fennel seed, peppercorns, tomatoes, salt and pepper; cook 2 to 3 minutes over high heat.

Spoon tomato mixture over bottom of individual plates. Rest trout on top and sprinkle with lemon juice. Serve immediately.

Red Snapper Filets with Fennel

(serves 4)

1 SERVING	331 CALORIES	36g CARBOHYDRATE
28g PROTEIN	11g FAT	0.8g FIBER

4	small red snapper filets
1 cup	(250 ml) flour
1 tbsp	(15 ml) vegetable oil
2 tbsp	(30 ml) butter
1	small red pepper, halved and thinly sliced
1	zucchini, cut in half lengthwise and thinly sliced
1	green apple, cored and sliced
1 tsp	(5 ml) green peppercorns
2	fresh fennel sprigs, chopped
	salt and pepper

Dredge filets lightly in flour.

Heat oil and butter in large frying pan. Add fish and cook 3 minutes over medium-high heat.

Turn filets over, season well and continue cooking 2 to 3 minutes.

Add red pepper, zucchini and apple to pan; cook 2 to 3 minutes over medium heat.

Stir in peppercorns and fennel; season well. Cook 2 minutes and serve.

Besides choosing the best fish available, search out fresh fennel as well.

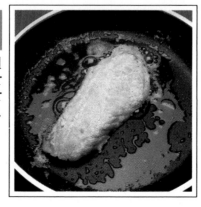

Cook lightly floured fish in hot oil and butter for 3 minutes over medium-high heat.

Turn fish over, season well and continue cooking 2 to 3 minutes.

Add vegetables and apple to pan with fish. Sauté 2 to 3 minutes over medium heat.

Snapper and Shrimp

(serves 4)

1 SERVING	446 CALORIES	27g CARBOHYDRATE
44g PROTEIN	18g FAT	0.6g FIBER

4	red snapper filets
1 cup	(250 ml) seasoned flour
2 tbsp	(30 ml) vegetable oil
2 tbsp	(30 ml) melted butter
12	medium shrimp, peeled, deveined and cut in ½ on angle
2 tbsp	(30 ml) capers
1	lemon, peeled, seeded and thinly sliced
2 tbsp	(30 ml) slivered almonds
	salt and pepper

Preheat oven to 150°F (70°C).

Dredge red snapper in flour. Heat oil in large frying pan and add filets. Cook 3 to 4 minutes each side, depending on size, over medium-high heat. Season when turning filets over.

Remove filets from pan and keep hot in oven.

Add butter and shrimp to pan. Season and add all remaining ingredients; cook 3 minutes over medium heat.

Remove red snapper from oven and serve with shrimp.

Red Snapper and Tomato

(serves 4)

1 SERVING	246 CALORIES	9g CARBOHYDRATE
27g PROTEIN	12g FAT	0.7g FIBER

4	red snapper filets
3 tbsp	(45 ml) olive oil
1	garlic clove, smashed and chopped
1	small onion, chopped
3	tomatoes, peeled, seeded and diced
¼ tsp	(1 ml) ground cloves
¼ tsp	(1 ml) sugar
	juice 1 lemon
	salt and pepper

Place filets in platter, sprinkle with few drops of oil and half of lemon juice; set aside.

Heat 1½ tbsp (25 ml) oil in large frying pan. Add garlic and onion; cook 2 to 3 minutes over medium heat.

Add tomatoes, cloves, sugar and remaining lemon juice. Season well and cook 7 to 8 minutes over medium heat.

Reduce heat to very low and let tomato mixture simmer.

Heat remaining oil in second frying pan. Cook fish 4 minutes on each side, depending on size, over medium heat. Season well when turning filets over and serve with tomatoes.

Fried Smelts

(serves 4)

1 SERVING	718 CALORIES	54g CARBOHYDRATE
38g PROTEIN	37g FAT	0.1g FIBER

24-28	smelts, cleaned and dried with paper towel
1½ cups	(375 ml) seasoned flour
1½ cups	(375 ml) milk
2	eggs
1 tsp	(5 ml) olive oil
1½ cups	(375 ml) crushed soda crackers
½ cup	(125 ml) peanut oil
	salt and pepper
	lemon juice

Dredge smelts in flour.

Place milk, eggs and olive oil in large bowl; beat together until well combined.

Dip smelts in milk mixture then roll in crushed cracker crumbs.

Heat half of oil in deep skillet until hot (about 375°F or 180°C). Carefully add half of smelts and cook 2 to 3 minutes, turning over once during cooking.

Using slotted spoon remove from oil and drain on paper towels.

Add second half of oil and repeat for remaining smelts.

Serve with lemon juice.

Herb Salmon Steaks

(serves 4)

1 SERVING	395 CALORIES	2g CARBOHYDRATE
41g PROTEIN	24g FAT	trace FIBER

2 tbsp	(30 ml) vegetable oil
4	salmon steaks, ¾ in (2 cm) thick
2 tbsp	(30 ml) butter
1 tbsp	(15 ml) chopped fresh mint
1 tbsp	(15 ml) chopped fresh chives
1 tbsp	(15 ml) chopped fresh parsley
	salt and pepper
	juice 1 lemon

Heat oil in large frying pan. Add fish and cook 3 to 4 minutes over medium heat.

Turn fish over, season and continue cooking 4 minutes.

Turn fish over again, season and cook another 7 minutes; turn fish once more during this time.

Transfer fish to heated serving platter.

Wipe frying pan clean with paper towel and add butter. Add herbs and pepper; cook 1 minute over high heat.

Add lemon juice, stir and pour over fish. Serve immediately.

Pernod Salmon

(serves 4)

1 SERVING 43g PROTEIN	516 CALORIES 32g FAT	8g CARBOHYDRATE 0.5g FIBER

1 tbsp	(15 ml) vegetable oil
2 tbsp	(30 ml) butter
4	salmon steaks, ¾ in (2 cm) thick
1	shallot, chopped
½ lb	(250 g) mushrooms, sliced
3 tbsp	(45 ml) Pernod
½ cup	(125 ml) heavy cream
1 tbsp	(15 ml) chopped parsley
	salt and pepper

Preheat oven to 150°F (70°C).

Heat oil and butter in large frying pan. When melted, add fish and season well; cover and cook 4 minutes over medium heat.

Turn fish over; continue cooking 4 to 5 minutes covered.

Remove fish from pan and keep hot in oven.

Add shallot and mushrooms to frying pan; season well. Cover and cook 3 to 4 minutes.

Pour in Pernod and bring to boil; continue cooking 2 minutes over high heat.

Correct seasoning and mix in cream and parsley. Cook sauce 2 minutes over medium heat.

Pour over fish and serve.

Heat oil and butter in large frying pan. When melted, cook fish, covered, 4 minutes over medium heat.

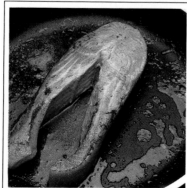

Add shallot and mushrooms to frying pan; season, cover and cook 3 to 4 minutes.

Turn fish over; continue cooking 4 to 5 minutes covered. Remove and keep hot in oven.

Pour in Pernod and bring to boil; continue cooking 2 minutes over high heat.

Salmon Steaks al Limone

(serves 4)

1 SERVING	566 CALORIES	30g CARBOHYDRATE
46g PROTEIN	29g FAT	0.3g FIBER

4	salmon steaks, ¾ in (2 cm) thick
1 cup	(250 ml) seasoned flour
¼ tsp	(1 ml) paprika
2 tbsp	(30 ml) butter
1	medium onion, chopped
1 tbsp	(15 ml) chopped chives
1 cup	(250 ml) light chicken stock, hot
¼ tsp	(1 ml) Tabasco sauce
1½ tbsp	(25 ml) cornstarch
4 tbsp	(60 ml) cold water
¼ cup	(50 ml) light cream, hot
2 tbsp	(30 ml) vegetable oil
1 tsp	(5 ml) butter
½	cucumber, seeded and sliced thick
	dash ground ginger
	salt and pepper
	juice 1 lemon

Dredge salmon in seasoned flour sprinkled with paprika; set aside.

Heat 2 tbsp (30 ml) butter in saucepan. Add onion and chives; cook 3 minutes over low heat.

Add lemon juice and continue cooking 1 minute over low heat.

Pour in chicken stock, add Tabasco, ginger and season well; bring to boil.

Mix cornstarch with water; stir into sauce and cook 1 minute over low heat.

Stir in cream and correct seasoning; bring to quick boil then remove from heat and set aside.

Heat oil in large frying pan. Add salmon and cook 4 minutes over medium-high heat.

Turn fish over and season well; continue cooking another 4 minutes.

Turn fish over again; cook another 7 minutes. Turn fish once more during this time.

Meanwhile, heat 1 tsp (5 ml) butter in second frying pan. Add cucumbers and cook 3 to 4 minutes over medium-high heat.

Simmer lemon sauce over low heat and when warmed, serve with fish and sauteed cucumbers.

Choose the freshest salmon available.

Cook onion and chives 3 minutes in hot butter.

Dredge fish in seasoned flour sprinkled with paprika; set aside.

After lemon juice and chicken stock have been added, thicken sauce with diluted cornstarch.

Grilled Fish Cakes

(serves 4)

1 SERVING	475 CALORIES	38g CARBOHYDRATE
26g PROTEIN	24g FAT	0.6g FIBER

1¾ cups	(425 ml) cooked halibut, boned and flaked
2½ cups	(625 ml) mashed potatoes, hot
1 tbsp	(15 ml) chopped parsley
3 tbsp	(45 ml) chopped cooked onions
2 tbsp	(30 ml) soft butter
1	beaten egg
1 cup	(250 ml) flour
3 tbsp	(45 ml) peanut oil
	salt and pepper

Place fish, potatoes, parsley, onions, butter and beaten egg in food processor. Season well and blend until well incorporated.

Shape mixture into small balls and flatten. Dust lightly in flour.

Heat oil in large frying pan. Add fish cakes without crowding and cook 2 to 3 minutes over medium-high heat. Turn patties over once and adjust time depending on thickness.

Serve with tartare sauce.

Halibut with Fennel Sauce

(serves 4)

1 SERVING	228 CALORIES	4g CARBOHYDRATE
24g PROTEIN	13g FAT	0.5g FIBER

1 tbsp	(15 ml) vegetable oil
2	large halibut steaks, with skin, cut in 2
5	fresh fennel sprigs
1 tbsp	(15 ml) butter
½ lb	(250 g) mushrooms, sliced
1	shallot, chopped
	salt and pepper
	juice 1 lemon

Preheat oven to 150°F (70°C).

Heat oil in large frying pan. When hot, add fish and cover; cook 3 minutes over medium-high heat.

Turn pieces over, season and drop in 2 fennel sprigs. Continue cooking 3 to 4 minutes over medium heat.

Remove fish from pan and keep hot in oven.

Add butter to frying pan. Cook remaining fennel, mushrooms and shallot 3 to 4 minutes covered; season well.

Add lemon juice, mix well and pour over fish. Serve with vegetables.

Pan-Fried Breaded Perch

(serves 4)

1 SERVING	523 CALORIES	38g CARBOHYDRATE
45g PROTEIN	19g FAT	0.1g FIBER

2 tbsp	(30 ml) olive oil
2	beaten eggs
8	ocean perch filets
1 cup	(250 ml) seasoned flour
1 cup	(250 ml) breadcrumbs
2 tbsp	(30 ml) vegetable oil
	salt and pepper
	lemon slices

Beat olive oil into eggs.

Dredge fish in flour, dip in eggs and coat with breadcrumbs.

Heat vegetable oil in large frying pan. When hot, add fish and cook 4 to 6 minutes over medium-high heat. Turn filets over twice and season once.

Serve with tartare sauce and garnish with lemon slices.

Perch Filets with Red Pepper Sauce

(serves 4)

1 SERVING	547 CALORIES	36g CARBOHYDRATE
44g PROTEIN	25g FAT	0.8g FIBER

1 tbsp	(15 ml) melted butter
1	garlic clove, smashed and chopped
1	medium onion, thinly sliced
1½	red peppers, thinly sliced
1½ cups	(375 ml) hot white sauce
¼ tsp	(1 ml) Worcestershire sauce
¼ tsp	(1 ml) Tabasco sauce
8	small perch filets
1 cup	seasoned flour
2 tbsp	(30 ml) vegetable oil
	salt and pepper
	juice ½ lemon

Heat butter in saucepan. Add garlic and onion; cover and cook 3 to 4 minutes over medium heat.

Stir in red peppers and season; continue cooking 7 to 8 minutes over medium heat, uncovered.

Pour mixture into food processor and purée. Replace in saucepan and incorporate white sauce, Worcestershire, Tabasco and lemon juice.

Simmer sauce 8 minutes over low heat. Do not cover.

Meanwhile, dredge fish in flour. Heat oil in large frying pan and add filets. Cook 3 to 4 minutes each side depending on size. Season fish well when turning.

When fish is cooked, arrange on heated serving platter and top with red pepper sauce.

Curried Grouper

(serves 4)

1 SERVING	507 CALORIES	58g CARBOHYDRATE
46g PROTEIN	9g FAT	1.0g FIBER

4 tbsp	(60 ml) curry powder
2 cups	(500 ml) flour
4	7 oz (200 g) grouper steaks
2 tbsp	(30 ml) vegetable oil
½	large cantaloupe, flesh sliced thick
1	banana, sliced thick on angle
	juice 1 tangerine
	salt and pepper

Mix curry powder with flour and season well. Dredge grouper in flour and shake off excess.

Heat oil in large frying pan. Add fish and cook 3 to 4 minutes over medium-high heat.

Turn fish over; continue cooking 2 to 3 minutes.

Season and turn fish over again; finish cooking 3 to 4 minutes depending on size. When bone can be removed easily, the fish is cooked.

Transfer fish to heated dinner plates. Quickly add remaining ingredients to frying pan and cook 2 minutes. Serve fruit with fish.

Mix curry powder with flour and season well. Dredge grouper in flour and shake off excess.

Cook fish 8 to 11 minutes depending on size. Turn steaks over twice.

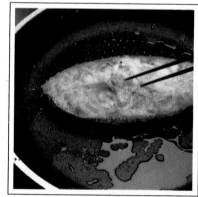

When bone can be removed easily, the fish is cooked.

Quickly cook remaining ingredients in frying pan for 2 minutes.

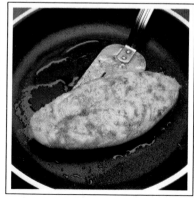

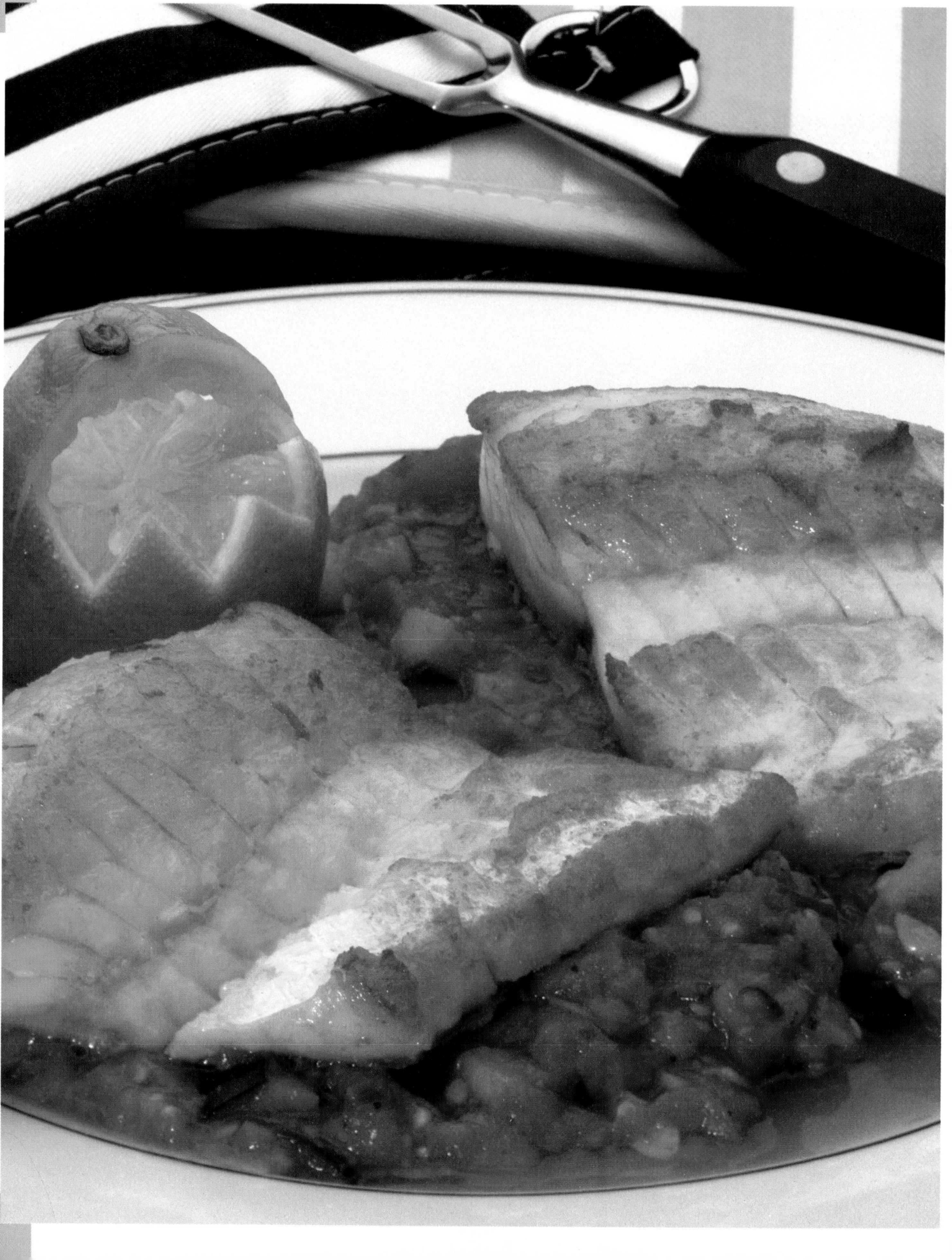

Italian Style Grouper

(serves 4)

1 SERVING	352 CALORIES	15g CARBOHYDRATE
45g PROTEIN	12g FAT	1.0g FIBER

2 tbsp	(30 ml) olive oil
2	large shallots, chopped
1	garlic clove, smashed and chopped
1	small eggplant, diced with skin
28 oz	(796 ml) can tomatoes, drained and chopped
¼ tsp	(1 ml) basil
¼ tsp	(1 ml) marjoram
½	pickled hot cherry pepper, chopped
¼ tsp	(1 ml) sugar
1 tbsp	(15 ml) vegetable oil
4	7-8 oz (200-225 g) pieces grouper
	salt and pepper

Heat olive oil in large skillet. Cook shallots and garlic 2 minutes over medium heat.

Add eggplant and cover; cook 8 to 10 minutes over medium heat stirring occasionally.

Season eggplant very well; stir in tomatoes, seasonings, chopped cherry pepper and sugar. Bring to boil and cook 8 minutes over medium-high heat.

Meanwhile, heat vegetable oil in large frying pan. Add grouper and cook 4 minutes over medium heat.

Turn pieces over, season and continue cooking 4 to 5 minutes depending on size.

Serve fish with eggplant mixture.

Heat olive oil in large skillet. Cook shallots and garlic 2 minutes over medium heat.

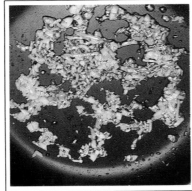

After 8 to 10 minutes of cooking, season eggplant very well.

Add eggplant and cover.

Stir in tomatoes, seasonings, cherry pepper and sugar. Bring to boil and cook 8 minutes over medium-high heat.

Grilled Shark Steaks

(serves 4)

1 SERVING	473 CALORIES	5g CARBOHYDRATE
41g PROTEIN	33g FAT	trace FIBER

2	1 lb (500 g) shark steaks
3 tbsp	(45 ml) olive oil
½ cup	(125 ml) lemon juice
2 tbsp	(30 ml) butter
1 tsp	(5 ml) chopped ginger
1	garlic clove, smashed and chopped
1 tbsp	(15 ml) chopped chives
1 tsp	(5 ml) brown sugar
1 tsp	(5 ml) lime juice
1 tsp	(5 ml) Worcestershire sauce
1 tbsp	(15 ml) vegetable oil
	salt and pepper

Place shark, olive oil and lemon juice in deep plate; marinate 20 minutes.

Drain fish well and pat dry; using heavy knife cut each shark steak into 2 pieces. A wooden mallet is useful to pound knife through bone.

Place butter, ginger, garlic, chives, sugar, lime juice and Worcestershire in small saucepan; heat until melted.

Brush butter mixture over fish.

Heat oil in large grill or frying pan. Add fish and cook 10 to 12 minutes over medium heat. Season during cooking and turn pieces over 2 to 3 times.

If desired, garnish servings with saudéed apples and steamed green beans.

A 1 lb (500 g) shark steak serves 2 people.

After fish has been marinated, use heavy knife and mallet to cut it into 2 pieces.

Place butter, ginger, garlic, chives, sugar, lime juice and Worcestershire in small saucepan; heat until melted.

Brush butter mixture over fish before cooking.

Boston Bluefish à la Nicoise

(serves 4)

1 SERVING	399 CALORIES	6g CARBOHYDRATE
42g PROTEIN	22g FAT	0.5g FIBER

1 tbsp	(15 ml) olive oil
2	shallots, chopped
1	garlic clove, smashed and chopped
1.75 oz	(50 g) tin anchovy filets, drained and chopped
2 cups	(500 ml) cherry tomatoes, halved
½ cup	(125 ml) pitted black olives
1 tbsp	(15 ml) vegetable oil
1½ lb	(750 g) Boston bluefish filets, in large pieces, lightly dredged in flour
	salt and pepper

Heat olive oil in large skillet. Cook shallots and garlic 2 to 3 minutes over medium heat.

Add anchovies and continue cooking 1 minute.

Season well, add tomatoes and olives; mix and continue cooking 1 minute over medium-high heat. Set aside.

Heat vegetable oil in large frying pan. Add fish and cook 4 to 5 minutes over medium heat.

Season and turn pieces over; continue cooking another 4 minutes.

Pour tomatoes over fish, simmer 1 minute and serve.

Add anchovies to pan and continue cooking 1 minute.

After cooking fish 4 to 5 minutes on one side, turn pieces over and continue cooking another 4 minutes. Be sure to season.

Season well, add tomatoes and olives; mix and continue cooking 1 minute over medium-high heat. Set aside.

Pour tomatoes over fish, simmer 1 minute and serve.

Sautéed Lobster Tails

(serves 4)

1 SERVING	330 CALORIES	14g CARBOHYDRATE
16g PROTEIN	2g FAT	trace FIBER

2 tbsp	(30 ml) melted butter
4	lobster tails, shelled and cut in 3
1	shallot, finely chopped
1 tbsp	(15 ml) chopped parsley
1 cup	(250 ml) tasty dill sauce
	salt and pepper
	few drops lemon juice

Heat butter in large frying pan. When hot, add lobster and cook 2 to 3 minutes over medium-high heat.

Season well and add shallot and parsley; continue cooking 1 minute.

Sprinkle with lemon juice and serve with tasty dill sauce (see following recipe).

Sweet and Sour Scampi

(serves 4)

1 SERVING	324 CALORIES	15g CARBOHYDRATE
33g PROTEIN	13g FAT	0.3g FIBER

1	green onion, chopped
3 tbsp	(45 ml) dry white wine
4 tbsp	(60 ml) white vinegar
1 tbsp	(15 ml) sugar
¼ cup	(50 ml) orange juice
1 tbsp	(15 ml) chopped fresh ginger
1 cup	(250 ml) diced pineapple
1 cup	(250 ml) hot chicken stock
1 tbsp	(15 ml) cornstarch
3 tbsp	(45 ml) cold water
1½ lb	(750 g) scampi, peeled
3 tbsp	(45 ml) melted butter
½ tsp	(2 ml) fennel seed
	salt and pepper
	lemon juice

Prepare sauce by placing green onion in saucepan. Add wine and vinegar; season well with pepper. Bring to boil and cook 3 minutes over medium heat.

Add sugar, orange juice, ginger, pineapple and chicken stock; mix well. Bring to boil again.

Mix cornstarch with water; stir into sauce and cook 2 minutes.

Correct seasoning and simmer over very low heat.

Cook scampi in two batches to avoid overcrowding the pan. Heat butter in large frying pan. Add scampi, fennel seed and lemon juice; season well. Cook 3 to 4 minutes, stirring frequently.

Serve cooked scampi with sauce.

Marinated Lobster Tails

(serves 4)

1 SERVING	293 CALORIES	4g CARBOHYDRATE
16g PROTEIN	25g FAT	0.5g FIBER

4	large lobster tails, shelled and in 1 in (2.5 cm) pieces
4 tbsp	(60 ml) olive oil
2 tbsp	(30 ml) tarragon wine vinegar
1 tbsp	(15 ml) chopped parsley
1 tbsp	(15 ml) chopped tarragon
¼ tsp	(1 ml) paprika
3 tbsp	(45 ml) melted butter
2 tbsp	(30 ml) capers
	salt and pepper
	juice ½ lemon

Place lobster, oil, vinegar, parsley, tarragon and paprika in bowl. Season well with pepper and marinate 30 minutes.

Drain lobster.

Heat butter in large frying pan. When hot, add lobster pieces and sauté 3 to 5 minutes over high heat. Stir often and turn pieces over once.

Stir in capers and lemon juice and season well. Finish cooking 1 minute.

Serve on rice.

Halibut with Fresh Fruit

(serves 4)

1 SERVING	382 CALORIES	18g CARBOHYDRATE
21g PROTEIN	26g FAT	0.2g FIBER

3 tbsp	(45 ml) butter
2	halibut steaks, cut in 2
1	mandarin, peeled and sliced in rings
2	bananas, peeled and sliced thick
½ cup	(125 ml) heavy cream
1 tsp	(5 ml) chopped fresh parsley
¼ tsp	(1 ml) paprika
	salt and pepper
	juice 1 lemon

Preheat oven to 150°F (70°C).

Heat butter in large frying pan. When partly melted, add fish and season well. Cover and cook 4 minutes over medium heat.

Squeeze in lemon juice and turn fish over; continue cooking another 4 minutes covered. Season well.

Remove fish from pan and keep hot in oven.

Add mandarin and bananas to frying pan; cook 2 minutes over high heat.

Mix in cream, parsley and paprika; season well. Cook 2 minutes, then pour over fish and serve.

Fried Shrimp with Eggs

(serves 4)

1 SERVING	280 CALORIES	5g CARBOHYDRATE
39g PROTEIN	11g FAT	-- FIBER

1½ lb	(750 g) shrimp, peeled and deveined
2 tbsp	(30 ml) soya sauce
2 tbsp	(30 ml) lemon juice
¼ tsp	(1 ml) paprika
2 tbsp	(30 ml) vegetable oil
2	beaten eggs
	salt and pepper

Place shrimp in large bowl. Add soya sauce, lemon juice and paprika; marinate 15 minutes.

Heat oil in large frying pan. Meanwhile, dip shrimp in beaten eggs and add to pan. Cook shrimp 2 minutes each side over medium heat. Season well.

When shrimp are cooked, drain on paper towels. If desired, serve with dipping sauce such as plum sauce.

Butterflied Garlic Shrimp

(serves 4)

1 SERVING	304 CALORIES	8g CARBOHYDRATE
43g PROTEIN	11g FAT	0.6g FIBER

3 tbsp	(45 ml) butter
2 lb	(900 g) medium shrimp, peeled, deveined and butterflied
3	garlic cloves, smashed and chopped
1½	green peppers, in thin strips
1	large lemon, peeled and diced
1 tbsp	(15 ml) chopped parsley
¼ tsp	(1 ml) paprika
	salt and pepper

Heat butter in large frying pan. Add shrimp and cook 2 minutes each side over medium-high heat.

Add garlic and season well; continue cooking 1 minute.

Stir in green pepper and diced lemon; cook 1 more minute.

Correct seasoning, add parsley and paprika, mix and serve.

Shrimp with Pernod Sauce

(serves 4)

1 SERVING	648 CALORIES	12g CARBOHYDRATE
44g PROTEIN	44g FAT	trace FIBER

3 tbsp	(45 ml) butter
2 lb	(900 g) medium shrimp, peeled and deveined
1 tbsp	(15 ml) chopped parsley
1	shallot, finely chopped
1 tsp	(5 ml) chopped chives
¼ cup	(50 ml) Pernod
1½ cups	(375 ml) heavy cream
¼ tsp	(1 ml) Tabasco sauce
	salt and pepper

Heat butter in large frying pan. Cook shrimp, parsley, shallot and chives 2 minutes each side over medium-high heat.

Season well and pour in Pernod; cook 2 minutes over high heat.

Remove shrimp with slotted spoon and set aside.

Replace pan over heat and pour in cream and Tabasco; cook 1½ minutes over high heat or until thickened.

Correct seasoning, replace shrimp in sauce and simmer 2 minutes.

Serve with Parisienne potatoes.

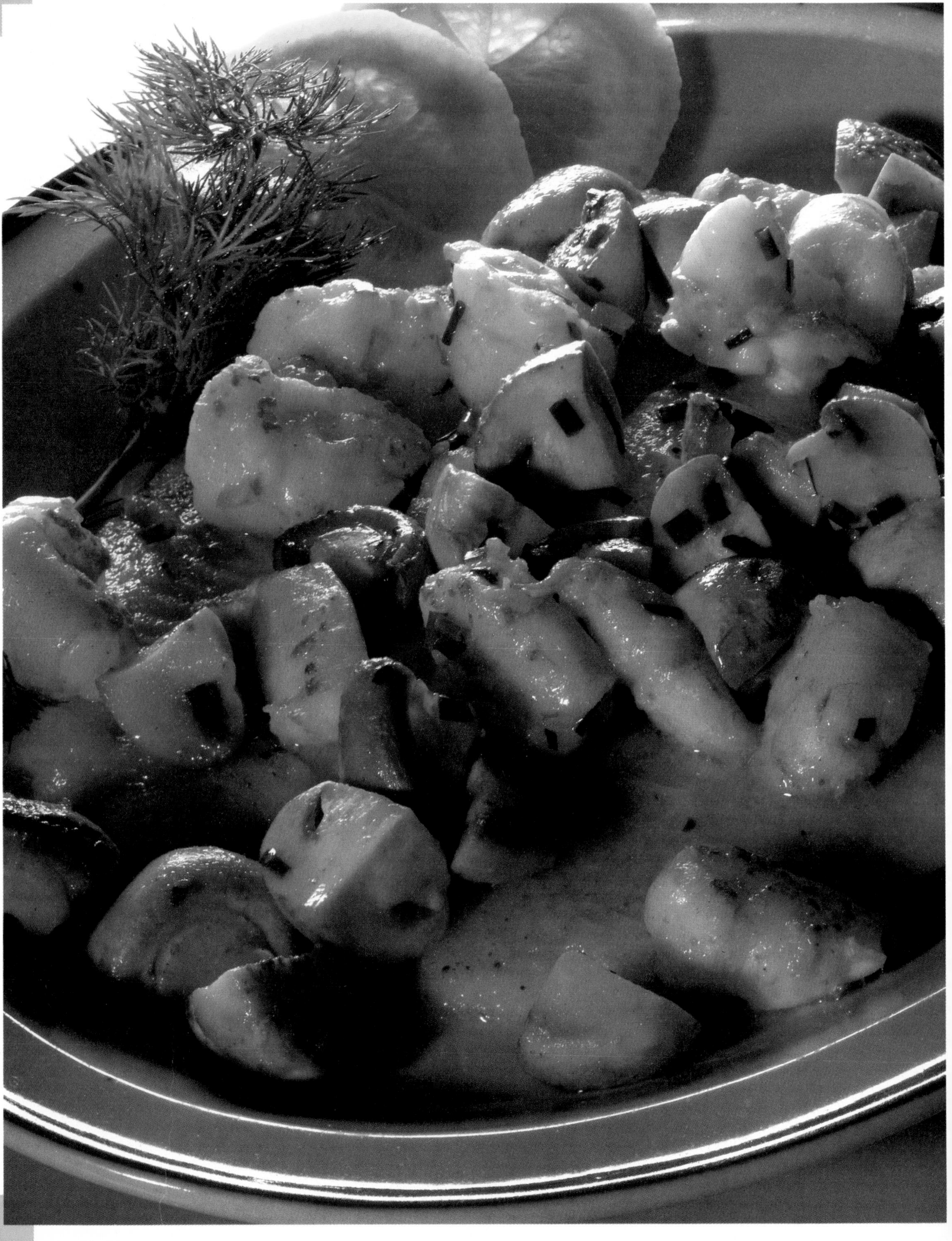

Grilled Sole and Shrimp

(serves 4)

1 SERVING	361 CALORIES	28g CARBOHYDRATE
43g PROTEIN	9g FAT	0.6g FIBER

¼ tsp	(1 ml) paprika
1 cup	(250 ml) flour
4	large sole filets
1 tbsp	(15 ml) vegetable oil
1 tbsp	(15 ml) butter
½ lb	(250 g) mushrooms, quartered
½ lb	(250 g) shrimp, peeled, deveined and cut in 3
1 tbsp	(15 ml) chopped chives
	salt and pepper
	juice 1 lemon

Preheat oven to 150°F (70°C).

Mix paprika with flour and season well. Dredge fish in flour and shake off excess.

Heat oil and butter in large frying pan. Add fish and cook 2 minutes over medium-high heat.

Turn filets over, season and continue cooking 2 minutes.

Remove fish from pan and keep hot in oven.

Place remaining ingredients in pan and cook 3 to 4 minutes over medium-high heat.

Serve with sole.

Mix paprika with flour and season well. Dredge fish in flour and shake off excess.

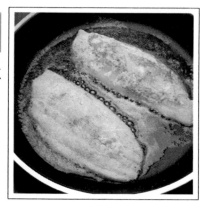

Turn filets over, season and continue cooking 2 minutes. Remove and keep hot in oven.

Add fish to hot oil and butter; cook 2 minutes over medium-high heat.

Place remaining ingredients in pan and cook 3 to 4 minutes over medium-high heat.

Fried Oysters

(serves 4)

1 SERVING	615 CALORIES	55g CARBOHYDRATE
20g PROTEIN	35g FAT	trace FIBER

2 cups	(500 ml) shucked oysters
1 cup	(250 ml) seasoned flour
2	beaten eggs
¼ cup	(50 ml) light cream
2 cups	(500 ml) crushed soda crackers
⅓ cup	(75 ml) peanut oil
	salt and pepper
	lemon juice

Dredge oysters in flour.

Mix eggs with cream; dip oysters in liquid. Coat with cracker crumbs.

Heat oil in deep skillet. When hot, add half of oysters and cook 4 minutes over high heat. Turn oysters over once.

Using slotted spoon remove cooked oysters and drain on paper towels.

Add remaining oysters to hot oil and repeat.

Serve with lemon juice and if desired with tartare sauce as well.

Quick Grilled Scallops

(serves 4)

1 SERVING	274 CALORIES	13g CARBOHYDRATE
32g PROTEIN	10g FAT	1.0g FIBER

3 tbsp	(45 ml) butter
1½ lb	(750 g) fresh scallops
1 lb	(500 g) mushrooms, quartered
1	shallot, chopped
1 tbsp	(15 ml) chopped parsley
1 tbsp	(15 ml) chopped chives
	salt and pepper
	juice 1 lemon

Heat butter in large frying pan. When hot, add scallops and season with pepper. Cover and cook 2 to 3 minutes over medium-high heat, turning scallops over once.

Add mushrooms and shallot to pan; continue cooking covered, for 1 minute.

Add remaining ingredients, mix well and correct seasoning.

Serve immediately.

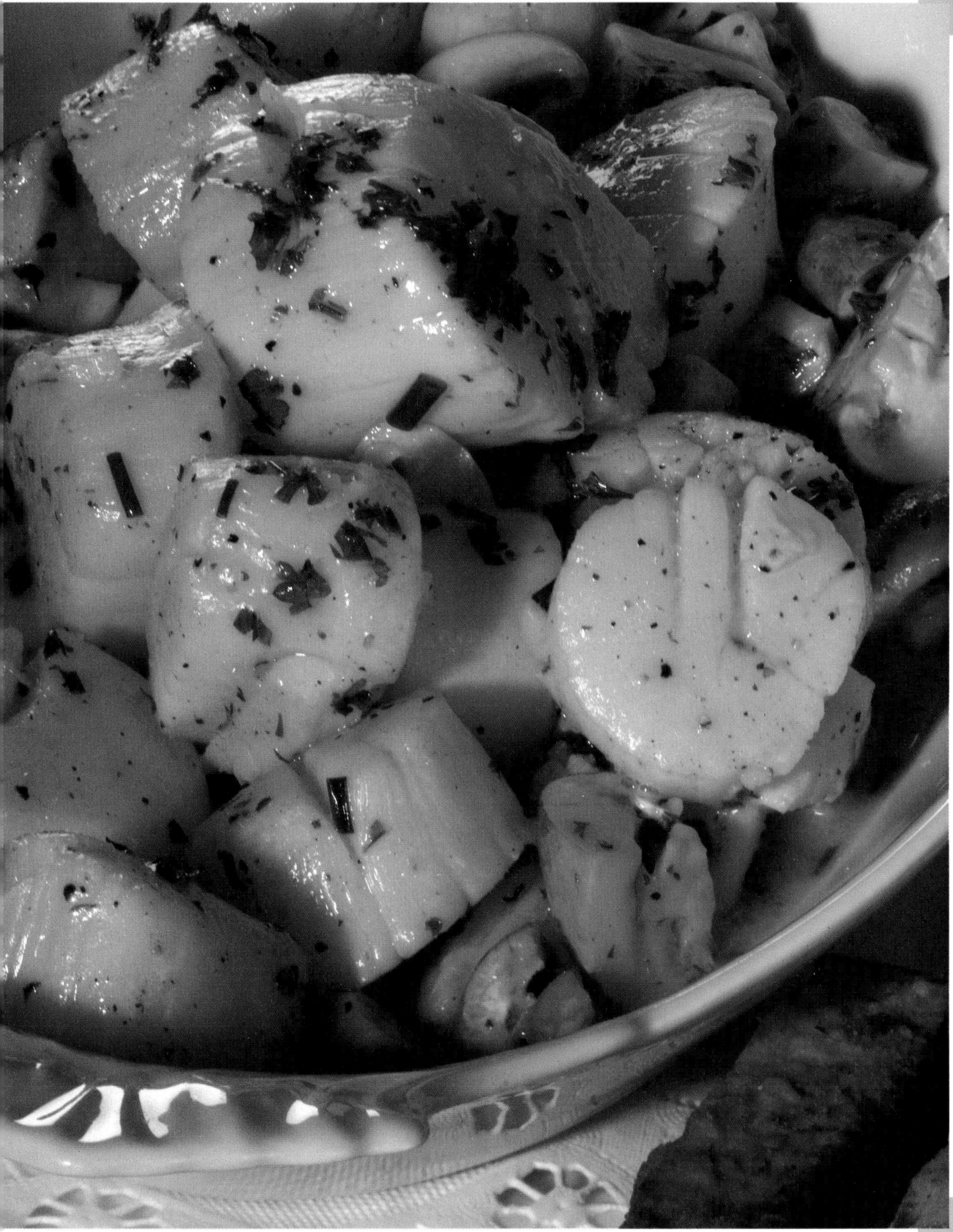

Tasty Dill Sauce

1 RECIPE	1,172 CALORIES 77g CARBOHYDRATE
6g PROTEIN	93g FAT 0.4g FIBER

4	stems watercress
1	green onion, diced
3	sprigs fresh dill
2	garlic cloves, smashed and chopped
1 tbsp	(15 ml) chopped chives
1 cup	(250 ml) mayonnaise
3 tbsp	(45 ml) Port wine
1/3 cup	(75 ml) sour cream
	juice 1 lemon
	salt and pepper
	few drops Tabasco sauce
	dash paprika

Place watercress, onion, dill, garlic and chives in food processor; blend 1 minute.

Add remaining ingredients and continue blending 30 seconds or until smooth.

Correct seasoning and serve with a variety of grilled fish.

Mornay Sauce

1 RECIPE	936 CALORIES 46g CARBOHYDRATE
31g PROTEIN	71g FAT trace FIBER

3 tbsp	(45 ml) butter
3 tbsp	(45 ml) flour
2 cups	(500 ml) hot milk
1	small onion
2	cloves
1/4 tsp	(1 ml) nutmeg
1	egg yolk
1 tbsp	(15 ml) light cream
1/4 cup	(50 ml) finely grated Gruyère Cheese
	salt and pepper

Heat butter in saucepan. When hot, add flour and cook 1 minute over low heat while mixing.

Pour in milk; mix well with whisk. Stud onion with cloves and add to saucepan along with nutmeg; season well.

Cook sauce 8 minutes over low heat. Stir occasionally.

Remove onion. Mix egg yolk with cream, then whisk into sauce. Add cheese and mix well. Serve sauce with fish.

Homemade Tartare Sauce

1 RECIPE	970 CALORIES 57g CARBOHYDRATE
2g PROTEIN	84g FAT -- FIBER

1 cup	(250 ml) mayonnaise
2 tbsp	(30 ml) light cream
1	shallot, finely chopped
1 tsp	(5 ml) chopped parsley
1 tsp	(5 ml) chopped tarragon
1 tsp	(5 ml) dry mustard
	pinch sugar
	salt and pepper
	dash paprika
	lemon juice to taste

Place all ingredients in bowl and mix together until well incorporated.

Season to taste and serve sauce with fried fish.

Seafood Mix

(serves 4)

1 SERVING	335 CALORIES	15g CARBOHYDRATE
40g PROTEIN	13g FAT	1.0g FIBER

2 tbsp	(30 ml) butter
1	garlic clove, smashed and chopped
1 cup	(250 ml) crabmeat, well drained
¾ lb	(375 g) scallops
½ lb	(250 g) shrimp, peeled and deveined
28 oz	(796 ml) can tomatoes, drained and chopped
2 tbsp	(30 ml) tomato paste
1 tbsp	(15 ml) chopped parsley
½ cup	(125 ml) grated Gruyère cheese
	salt and pepper

Heat butter in large frying pan. Add garlic, crabmeat, scallops and shrimp; season well. Cook 3 to 4 minutes over medium-low heat.

Mix in tomatoes, correct seasoning and simmer 2 to 3 minutes.

Stir in tomato paste and cook 1 minute over medium heat.

Pour mixture into large ovenproof dish. Top with parsley and cheese. Broil in oven until golden brown.

Serve in scallop shells.

Mixed Seafood Potato Coquilles

(serves 4)

1 SERVING	354 CALORIES	25g CARBOHYDRATE
31g PROTEIN	15g FAT	1.0g FIBER

2 cups	(500 ml) creamy mashed potatoes
2 tbsp	(30 ml) butter
1	garlic clove, smashed and chopped
1	green onion, chopped
1	shallot, finely chopped
⅔ lb	(300 g) mushrooms, thinly sliced
⅔ lb	(300 g) scallops, coarsely chopped
⅔ lb	(300 g) shrimp, peeled, deveined and coarsely chopped
2 tbsp	(30 ml) breadcrumbs
1 tbsp	(15 ml) chopped chives
1 tbsp	(15 ml) chopped parsley
	salt and pepper
	extra breadcrumbs
	extra butter

Force mashed potatoes through star nozzle of pastry bag and outline rims of scallop shells; set aside.

Heat 2 tbsp (30 ml) butter in large frying pan. Cook garlic, onion, shallot and mushrooms 3 to 4 minutes over medium heat. Season well.

Stir in scallops and shrimp; continue cooking 2 to 3 minutes.

Mix in breadcrumbs, chives and parsley. Fill scallop shells with mixture; top each with more breadcrumbs and dot with butter.

Broil in oven until golden brown.

Force mashed potatoes through star nozzle of pastry bag and outline rims of scallop shells; set aside.

Cook garlic, onion, shallot and mushrooms 3 to 4 minutes over medium heat; season well.

Stir in seafood and continue cooking 2 to 3 minutes.

Add breadcrumbs, chives and parsley, mix well and spoon into scallop shells. Top with more breadcrumbs and dot with butter. Broil.

Seafood on Rice

(serves 4)

1 SERVING	851 CALORIES	57g CARBOHYDRATE
39g PROTEIN	14g FAT	trace FIBER

1 lb	(500 g) scallops
½ cup	(125 ml) dry white wine
1 cup	(250 ml) water
1 tsp	(5 ml) melted butter
1 tbsp	(15 ml) chopped parsley
4	cooked lobster tails, shelled
2½ tbsp	(40 ml) butter
3 tbsp	(45 ml) flour
½ tsp	(2 ml) cumin
¼ cup	(50 ml) hot light cream
	salt and pepper
	juice 1 lemon
	cooked rice for 4

Place scallops, wine, water, melted butter, parsley, pepper and lemon juice in saucepan; bring to boil.

Add lobster. Cover saucepan and let stand 2 to 3 minutes on cold burner.

Remove scallops and lobster with slotted spoon and set aside.

Continue cooking liquid in saucepan 2 minutes over high heat. Set aside as well.

Heat 2½ tbsp (40 ml) butter in second saucepan. Add flour and cook 1 minute, stirring constantly.

Whisk in reserved cooking liquid from seafood. Add cumin and cook 1 to 2 minutes over medium heat.

Pour in cream, mix and cook 4 to 5 minutes over very low heat.

Place fish in sauce, mix and correct seasoning. Simmer 1 to 2 minutes to reheat.

Serve over rice.

Frog Legs
Frita

(serves 4)

1 SERVING	347 CALORIES	11g CARBOHYDRATE
25g PROTEIN	22g FAT	0.5g FIBER

1 tbsp	(15 ml) butter
¼ cup	(50 ml) chopped celery
1	shallot, chopped
¼ tsp	(1 ml) fennel seed
½ lb	(250 g) mushrooms, halved
16	frog legs, cleaned
1 cup	(250 ml) dry white wine
½ cup	(125 ml) water
2	parsley sprigs
1½ cups	(375 ml) hot Bercy sauce
½ cup	(125 ml) grated Emmenthal cheese
	juice ½ lemon
	salt and pepper

Grease large frying pan with butter. Add remaining ingredients except sauce and cheese.

Cook frog legs, covered, 10 to 12 minutes over low heat depending on size. Check if cooked by removing meat from the bone.

When cooked, remove all meat from bones and place in scallop shells. Using slotted spoon, add mushrooms to shells.

Replace pan containing cooking liquid on stove over high heat; cook 3 to 4 minutes.

Mix in Bercy sauce and continue cooking 2 minutes; correct seasoning.

Pour sauce over meat and mushrooms in scallop shells. Top with cheese and broil in oven until bubbly.

Coquilles Saint-Jacques

(serves 4)

1 SERVING	427 CALORIES	16g CARBOHYDRATE
37g PROTEIN	20g FAT	0.5g FIBER

4 tbsp	(60 ml) butter
½ lb	(250 g) mushrooms, quartered
2	shallots, finely chopped
¼ tsp	(1 ml) paprika
1 tsp	(5 ml) finely chopped parsley
1½ lb	(750 g) scallops
½ cup	(125 ml) dry white wine
4 tbsp	(60 ml) flour
¼ tsp	(1 ml) fennel seed
1½ cups	(375 ml) hot light chicken stock or fish stock
2 tbsp	(30 ml) heavy cream
½ cup	(125 ml) grated Gruyère cheese
	salt and pepper

Wipe ½ tsp (2 ml) of butter over surface of frying pan with paper towel. Add mushrooms, shallots, paprika and parsley.

Add scallops and wine; season well with pepper. Cover and bring to boil over medium-high heat.

Turn scallops over and remove pan from heat. Let stand 30 seconds.

Remove scallops from frying pan using slotted spoon and set aside. Pour remaining contents in pan into bowl; set aside as well.

Heat remaining butter in saucepan until melted. Add flour and mix well; cook 1 minute over low heat while stirring constantly.

Pour mushrooms and liquid from bowl into saucepan. Add fennel seed and mix well to incorporate.

Pour in chicken stock, mix and season. Add cream and bring to boil. Cook 8 minutes over low heat.

Place scallops in sauce and simmer 1 minute to reheat. Spoon mixture into scallop shells set on ovenproof tray.

Top with cheese and broil in oven until melted.

If desired serve with a light fruit dessert.

Wipe ½ tsp (2 ml) of butter over surface of frying pan with paper towel. Add mushrooms, shallots, paprika and parsley.

Add scallops and wine; season well with pepper. Cover and bring to boil over medium-high heat.

After scallops have been cooked, remove from pan with slotted spoon and set aside. Pour remaining contents in pan into bowl for later use.

After flour mixture has cooked, add reserved mushrooms and liquid. Add fennel seed and mix well to incorporate.

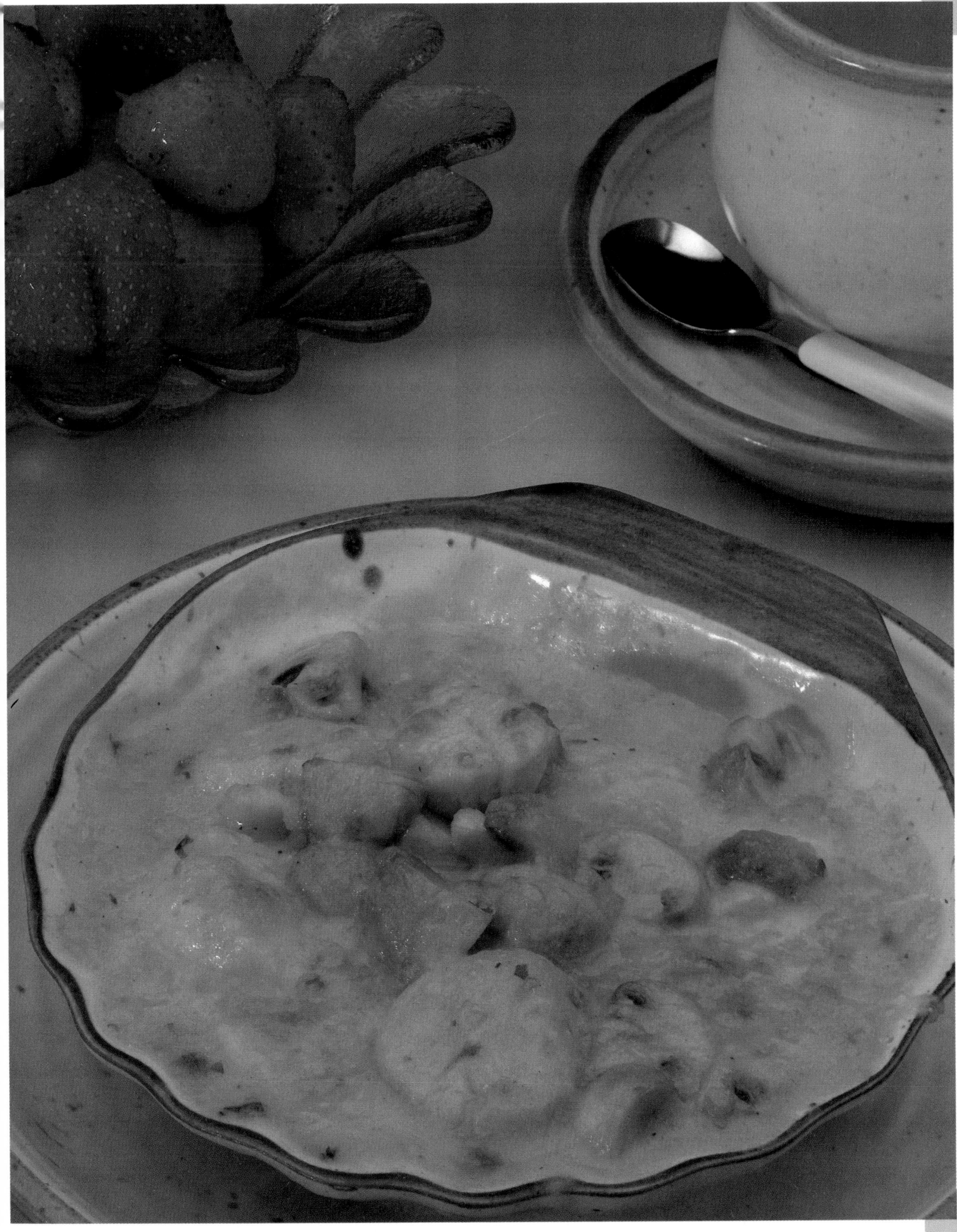

Scallops Emmenthal

(serves 4)

1 SERVING	327 CALORIES	15g CARBOHYDRATE
30g PROTEIN	17g FAT	2.0g FIBER

2 tbsp	(30 ml) vegetable oil
1	medium onion, chopped
1	eggplant, diced small with skin
½ tsp	(2 ml) oregano
1 tbsp	(15 ml) chopped fresh ginger
1 lb	(500 g) scallops
1 cup	(250 ml) grated Emmenthal cheese
1 tsp	(5 ml) chopped parsley
	dash paprika
	salt and pepper
	lime slices

Heat oil in large frying pan. Cook onion, covered, 2 to 3 minutes over medium-low heat.

Add eggplant and seasonings; continue cooking 6 to 7 minutes, covered, over medium heat.

Stir in scallops and season well. Cook 3 to 4 minutes, covered, over low heat; stir occasionally.

Mix in half of cheese and cook 1 minute over low heat uncovered.

Spoon mixture into scallop shells, top with remaining cheese and broil in oven until lightly browned. Garnish with lime slices and sprinkle with chopped parsley.

Scallops in Garlic-Cream Sauce

(serves 4)

1 SERVING	371 CALORIES	16g CARBOHYDRATE
31g PROTEIN	19g FAT	0.6g FIBER

4 tbsp	(60 ml) butter
2	garlic cloves, smashed and chopped
1 tsp	(5 ml) chopped chives
¼ tsp	(1 ml) fennel seed
2	small zucchini, diced
3½ tbsp	(55 ml) flour
2½ cups	(625 ml) light chicken stock, hot
1¼ lb	(625 g) cooked scallops, cut in ½
3 tbsp	(45 ml) heavy cream
¼ cup	(50 ml) grated Parmesan cheese
	salt and pepper
	few drops lemon juice

Heat butter in saucepan. Add garlic, chives, fennel and zucchini; season well. Cook 4 to 5 minutes over medium heat, stirring several times.

Mix in flour and cook 1 minute over low heat.

Add chicken stock and mix well; bring to boiling point. Season and continue cooking 6 to 8 minutes over low heat.

Mix in scallops, cream and lemon juice; cook 1 minute.

Pour into scallop shells, top with cheese and serve.

Fish and Vegetable Coquilles

(serves 4)

1 SERVING	517 CALORIES	25g CARBOHYDRATE
30g PROTEIN	33g FAT	1.0g FIBER

4	large carrots, pared
1	potato, peeled
1 tbsp	(15 ml) butter
2-3 tbsp	(30-45 ml) hot light cream
2 cups	(500 ml) cooked boned salmon
1½ cups	(375 ml) hot white sauce
2 tbsp	(30 ml) coarse breadcrumbs
	salt and pepper
	few drops melted butter

Cook carrots and potato in saucepan of salted boiling water. When cooked, drain well and purée vegetables through food mill into bowl.

Add butter and cream; season well. Mix until well blended.

Border scallop shells with vegetable purée. Be sure to leave enough space in middle for the salmon. Set shells aside.

In another bowl, mix salmon with white sauce; season well. Spoon into scallop shells.

Sprinkle with breadcrumbs and few drops melted butter. Broil in oven until lightly browned.

Shrimp and Tomato in Shells

(serves 4)

1 SERVING	261 CALORIES	12g CARBOHYDRATE
35g PROTEIN	8g FAT	1.0g FIBER

2 tbsp	(30 ml) olive oil
1 ½ lb	(750 g) shrimp, peeled and deveined
2	garlic cloves, smashed and chopped
28 oz	(796 ml) can tomatoes, drained and chopped
1 tsp	(5 ml) chopped parsley
¼ tsp	(1 ml) fennel seed
½ tsp	(2 ml) lime juice
	salt and pepper
	pinch sugar

Heat oil in large frying pan. Add shrimp and garlic; season and cook 3 to 4 minutes over high heat. Stir occasionally.

Remove shrimp from pan and set aside.

Add tomatoes and parsley to pan. Season with salt, pepper and fennel seed; cook 4 to 5 minutes over high heat, stirring occasionally.

Stir in lime juice and sugar and replace shrimp in pan. Simmer 1 minute to reheat, then spoon into scallops shells and serve with vegetables.

Peel and devein shrimp.

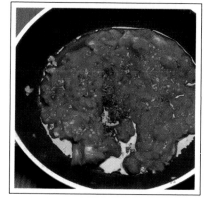

Remove shrimp from pan and set aside.

Cook shrimp and garlic in hot oil for 3 to 4 minutes over high heat.

Add tomatoes and parsley to pan. Season with salt, pepper and fennel seed; cook 4 to 5 minutes over high heat.

Coastal Shrimp Coquilles

(serves 4)

1 SERVING	627 CALORIES	49g CARBOHYDRATE
48g PROTEIN	26g FAT	1.0g FIBER

3 tbsp	(45 ml) butter
1	small onion, chopped
1 cup	(250 ml) long grain rice, rinsed
1½ cups	(375 ml) light chicken stock, hot
¾ cup	(175 ml) grated Gruyère cheese
1½ lb	(750 g) small shrimp, peeled and deveined
1½ cups	(375 ml) hot paprika sauce
3 tbsp	(45 ml) coarse breadcrumbs
	salt and pepper

Preheat oven to 350°F (180°C).

Heat 1 tbsp (15 ml) butter in ovenproof casserole. Add onion and cook 2 minutes over medium heat.

Stir in rice and cook 2 minutes over high heat.

Pour in chicken stock, mix well and season. Cover and cook 18 minutes in oven.

Four minutes before end of cooking time, mix in cheese and continue cooking.

Remove cooked rice from oven, fluff with fork and set aside.

Heat remaining butter in frying pan. Cook shrimp 3 minutes over medium-high heat, stirring once and seasoning.

Spoon layer of rice in bottom of scallop shells. Add shrimp and cover with paprika sauce.

Top with breadcrumbs and broil in oven for several minutes.

Zucchini-Shrimp Coquilles

(serves 4)

1 SERVING	381 CALORIES	24g CARBOHYDRATE
30g PROTEIN	18g FAT	1.0g FIBER

1 tbsp	(5 ml) butter
1 lb	(500 g) shrimp, peeled and deveined
2	zucchini, sliced ½ in (1.2 cm) thick
¼ cup	(50 ml) dry white wine
1 cup	(250 ml) water
½ tsp	(2 ml) fennel seed
1½ cups	(375 ml) thick white sauce, hot
3 tbsp	(45 ml) breadcrumbs
	juice 1 lemon
	salt and pepper
	few drops Tabasco sauce

Grease bottom of deep skillet with butter. Add shrimp, zucchini, wine, water, fennel seed and lemon juice. Cover and bring to boiling point over medium heat.

Turn shrimp over and continue cooking 1 minute over medium heat, covered.

Using slotted spoon, remove shrimp and zucchini from skillet; set aside.

Bring liquid in skillet to boil; do not cover. Continue cooking 5 minutes over high heat to reduce by ¾.

Mix in white sauce, salt, pepper and Tabasco. Cook 1 to 2 minutes over medium heat.

Replace shrimp and zucchini in sauce and mix well.

Spoon mixture into scallop shells and top with breadcrumbs. Broil in oven several minutes or until hot.

Shrimp Provençale

(serves 4)

1 SERVING	292 CALORIES	7g CARBOHYDRATE
35g PROTEIN	13g FAT	0.5g FIBER

3 tbsp	(45 ml) olive oil
1½ lb	(750 g) shrimp, peeled and deveined
3	garlic cloves, smashed and chopped
1	red pepper, halved and thinly sliced
½	zucchini, halved lengthwise and thinly sliced
1 tbsp	(15 ml) coarsely chopped fresh oregano
1 tbsp	(15 ml) chopped parsley
3 tbsp	(45 ml) grated Parmesan cheese
	salt and pepper
	juice ½ lemon

Heat 2 tbsp (30 ml) oil in large frying pan. Add shrimp and garlic; season well. Cook 2 to 3 minutes each side over high heat; stir occasionally.

Remove shrimp from pan and set aside.

Add remaining oil to pan. Cook vegetables, oregano and parsley 2 to 3 minutes over medium-high heat. Season well and sprinkle with lemon juice.

Replace shrimp in pan, stir and cook 1 minute.

Spoon mixture into scallop shells, sprinkle with cheese and broil in oven until lightly browned.

Lobster and Leek Coquilles

(serves 4)

1 SERVING	334 CALORIES	10g CARBOHYDRATE
20g PROTEIN	24g FAT	trace FIBER

2 tbsp	(30 ml) melted butter
2 tbsp	(30 ml) chopped shallots
2	leeks, white part only, well washed and finely chopped
¼ tsp	(2 ml) fennel seed
1½ cups	(375 ml) cooked chopped lobster meat
1½ cups	(375 ml) hot white sauce
½ cup	(125 ml) grated Gruyère cheese
	salt and pepper

Heat butter in saucepan. Add shallots and cook 1 minute over medium heat.

Add leeks and fennel; season well. Cover and cook 8 to 10 minutes over medium-low heat.

Stir in lobster meat, then add white sauce; mix again. Season and simmer 3 minutes over low heat, uncovered.

Spoon into scallop shells and top with cheese. Broil in oven until bubbly.

Coquille Supreme

(serves 4)

1 SERVING	444 CALORIES	13g CARBOHYDRATE
57g PROTEIN	16g FAT	trace FIBER

1 tbsp	(15 ml) butter
4½ lb	(2 kg) mussels, cooked*, shelled and chopped
11.3 oz	(320 g) can lobster meat, chopped
1 tbsp	(15 ml) capers
2 tbsp	(30 ml) cornstarch
4 tbsp	(60 ml) cold water
¾ cup	(175 ml) grated Gruyère cheese
	salt and pepper
	chopped parsley

* Strain cooking liquid from mussels through cheesecloth and reserve for later use in recipe.

Heat butter in large frying pan. Add mussels, lobster and capers; cook 2 to 3 minutes over medium heat.

Season well with pepper and pour in reserved cooking liquid from mussels; bring to boil.

Mix cornstarch with water; stir into sauce and cook 1 minute over medium heat.

Add ⅓ cup (75 ml) cheese and continue cooking 1 minute.

Pour into large ovenproof dish, top with remaining cheese and parsley; broil in oven until golden brown. Serve in scallop shells.

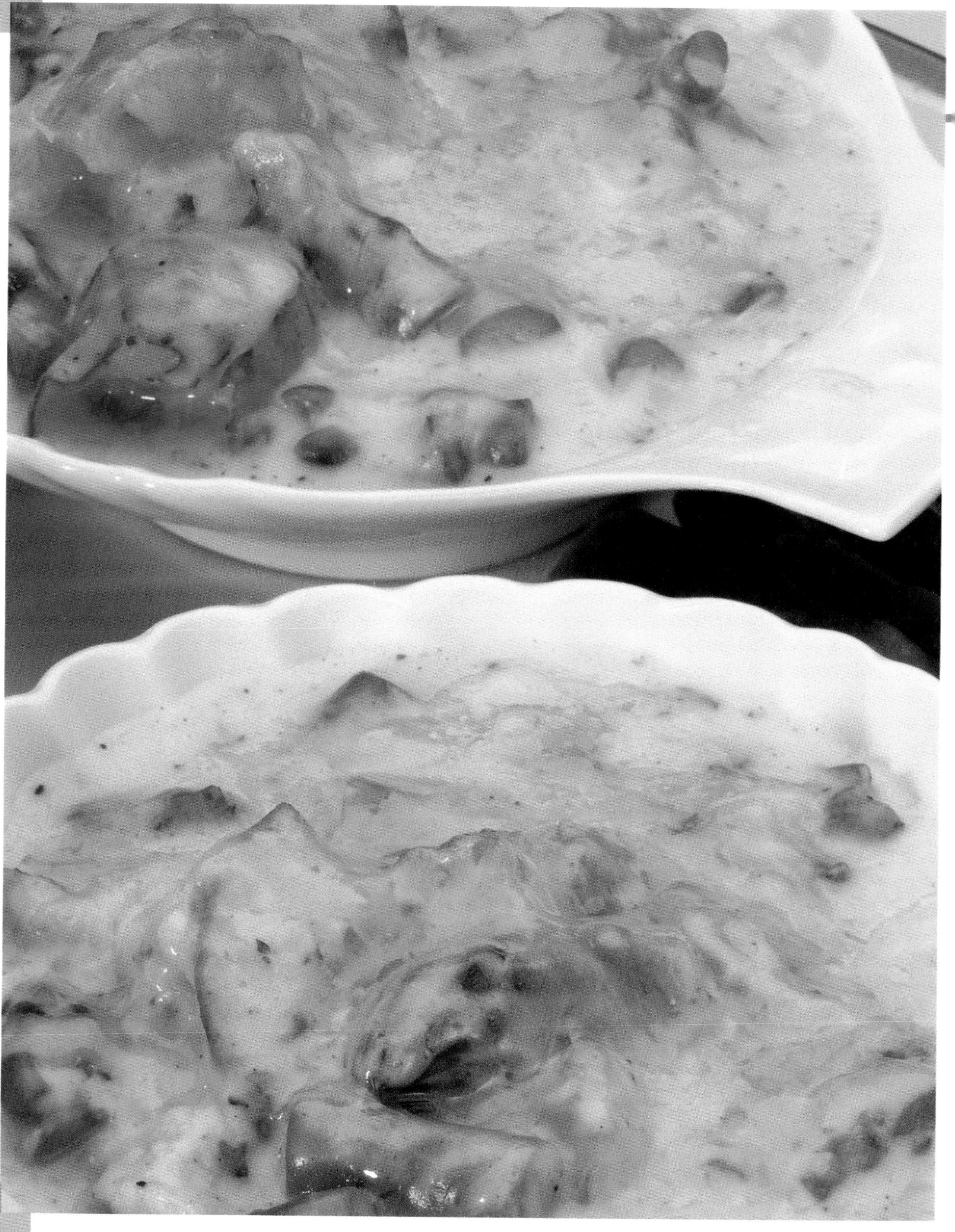

Lobster and Asparagus Coquilles

(serves 4)

1 SERVING	426 CALORIES	11g CARBOHYDRATE
35g PROTEIN	27g FAT	trace FIBER

3½ tbsp	(55 ml) butter
1	shallot, finely chopped
1 lb	(500 g) frozen lobster meat, thawed, drained and diced
1	bunch fresh asparagus, cooked and diced
¼ tsp	(1 ml) lemon juice
3 tbsp	(45 ml) flour
2 cups	(500 ml) hot milk
¼ tsp	(1 ml) nutmeg
1 cup	(250 ml) grated Emmenthal cheese
	salt and pepper
	pinch ground cloves

Heat 1 tsp (5 ml) butter in saucepan. Add shallot and cook 1 minute over medium heat.

Stir in lobster, asparagus and lemon juice; cover and simmer 6 to 7 minutes over very low heat.

Heat remaining butter in second saucepan. Mix in flour and cook 2 minutes over low heat, stirring constantly.

Pour in milk and season with nutmeg and cloves; blend well with whisk. Correct seasoning and cook sauce 6 to 7 minutes over low heat.

Transfer lobster and asparagus to saucepan containing sauce. Mix in half of cheese and simmer 1 to 2 minutes.

Spoon into scallop shells, top with remaining cheese and broil until golden brown.

Seaside Mussel Coquilles

(serves 4)

1 SERVING	252 CALORIES	12g CARBOHYDRATE
21g PROTEIN	11g FAT	0.7g FIBER

1 tbsp	(15 ml) melted butter
5	stems fresh basil, leaves chopped
3	large tomatoes, peeled, seeded and chopped
1	garlic clove, smashed and chopped
¼ cup	(50 ml) heavy cream
2 cups	(500 ml) cooked shucked mussels
½ cup	(125 ml) grated mozzarella cheese
	few drops lemon juice
	few drops Tabasco sauce
	salt and pepper

Heat butter in sauce pan. Add basil and cover; cook 3 to 4 minutes over medium-low heat. Stir twice during cooking.

Add tomatoes and garlic; season well and cook 5 to 6 minutes over high heat, uncovered.

Mix in cream and cook 2 minutes over high heat.

Add mussels, lemon juice and Tabasco; mix well.

Spoon into scallop shells, top with cheese and broil several minutes in oven.

Mussel Coquilles

(serves 4)

1 SERVING	575 CALORIES	17g CARBOHYDRATE
39g PROTEIN	36g FAT	-- FIBER

3 lb	(1.6 kg) fresh mussels, cleaned
4 tbsp	(60 ml) butter
½ cup	(125 ml) dry white wine
½ cup	(125 ml) cold water
1	shallot, chopped
1¼ cups	(300 ml) thick white sauce, hot
¼ tsp	(1 ml) paprika
¾ cup	(175 ml) grated Gruyère cheese
	salt and pepper

Place mussels, butter and wine in large saucepan.

Add water and shallot. Cover and bring to boil; cook until shells open.

Remove saucepan from heat. Separate mussels from shells, pouring juices back into saucepan. Set mussels aside and discard shells.

Strain cooking liquid from mussels through cheesecloth into clean saucepan. Bring to boil and continue cooking 4 to 5 minutes.

Mix in white sauce and paprika; season well. Cook 3 to 4 minutes over low heat.

Stir in ½ cup (125 ml) cheese; continue cooking sauce 1 minute over low heat.

Remove saucepan from heat and add mussels; mix well. Spoon into scallop shells and top with remaining cheese. Broil in oven until golden brown.

Before cooking mussels check for any opened shells and discard them.

As soon as the shells open, remove saucepan from heat.

Cook mussels in butter with wine, water and shallot. Cover pan.

Separate mussels from shells, pouring juices back into saucepan.

Crabmeat Coquilles

(serves 4)

1 SERVING	330 CALORIES	8g CARBOHYDRATE
34g PROTEIN	18g FAT	0.8g FIBER

2 tbsp	(30 ml) vegetable oil
1	yellow pepper, thinly sliced
1	shallot, finely chopped
½ lb	(250 g) mushrooms, finely chopped
2 tbsp	(30 ml) tomato paste
12	shrimp, peeled, deveined and cut in 3
7 oz	(200 g) can crabmeat, chopped
¼ tsp	(1 ml) fennel seed
1 tsp	(5 ml) chopped chives
1 cup	(250 ml) grated cheddar cheese
	salt and pepper

Heat oil in large frying pan. Add yellow pepper, shallot and mushrooms; season and cook 5 to 6 minutes over medium heat, covered. Stir mixture once.

Stir in tomato paste, shrimp, crabmeat, fennel seed and chives. Cover and cook 3 minutes over medium heat.

Mix in half of cheese and cook 1 minute uncovered.

Correct seasoning and spoon mixture into scallop shells. Top with remaining cheese and broil in oven until melted.

Crabmeat au Gratin

(serves 4)

1 SERVING	461 CALORIES	12g CARBOHYDRATE
33g PROTEIN	31g FAT	trace FIBER

1 tbsp	(15 ml) butter
½	small onion, chopped
¼	celery stalk, chopped
2	hard-boiled eggs, sliced
2 cups	(500 ml) cooked crabmeat, diced or chopped
2 cups	(500 ml) hot cheese sauce
½ cup	(125 ml) grated mozzarella cheese
	few drops lime juice
	salt and pepper

Heat butter in saucepan. Add onion and celery; cover and cook 3 minutes over medium heat.

Add eggs, crabmeat, lime juice and cheese sauce; mix carefully. Season well and simmer 2 to 3 minutes.

Spoon mixture into scallop shells and top with grated cheese. Broil in oven until melted.

Tasty Oyster Coquilles

(serves 4)

1 SERVING	264 CALORIES	12g CARBOHYDRATE
17g PROTEIN	16g FAT	trace FIBER

3 tbsp	(45 ml) butter
1	small onion, chopped
1	small carrot, pared and diced small
¼	celery stalk, diced
3½ tbsp	(55 ml) flour
2½ cups	(625 ml) hot chicken stock
½ tsp	(2 ml) basil
1¾ cups	(425 ml) cooked shucked oysters
½ cup	(125 ml) grated Gruyère cheese
	few drops Tabasco sauce
	salt and pepper

Heat butter in saucepan. Add onion, carrot and celery; cover and cook 5 minutes over medium heat.

Add flour and mix well; cook 1 minute over low heat.

Pour in chicken stock and mix well. Add basil, Tabasco sauce and season well. Cook 7 to 8 minutes over low heat uncovered.

Stir in oysters and simmer 2 to 3 minutes.

Spoon into scallop shells, top with cheese and broil several minutes in oven.

Hawaiian Coquilles

(serves 4)

1 SERVING	295 CALORIES	10g CARBOHYDRATE
32g PROTEIN	13g FAT	trace FIBER

4	small halibut steaks
4	thick rings fresh pineapple
1 tbsp	(15 ml) chopped parsley
1 tbsp	(15 ml) melted butter
2 cups	(500 ml) water
2 tbsp	(30 ml) cornstarch
4 tbsp	(60 ml) cold water
¼ cup	(50 ml) hot light cream
¼ tsp	(1 ml) paprika
¼ tsp	(1 ml) Tabasco sauce
4-6	small squares mozzarella cheese
	salt and pepper

Place fish, pineapple, parsley, butter and 2 cups (500 ml) water in frying pan. Cover and bring to boil.

Turn fish over; cover and continue cooking 3 minutes over low heat, depending on size.

When bone can be removed easily, the halibut is cooked. Remove from pan and set aside.

Replace pan on stove and bring to boil. Mix cornstarch with water; stir into liquid and cook 2 to 3 minutes over high heat.

Pour cream into frying pan, season and add paprika and Tabasco. Cook 2 minutes over medium-high heat.

Bone and flake fish; add to sauce with mozzarella. Cook 2 minutes over low heat.

Serve in scallop shells or on heated plates.

Fresh pineapple, if in season, is the best choice for this particular recipe, as it adds more flavor.

Place fish, pineapple, parsley, butter and water in large frying pan. Cover and bring to boil.

Turn fish over; cover and continue cooking 3 minutes over low heat, depending on size.

When bone can be removed easily, the fish is cooked.

Sole au Gratin

(serves 4)

1 SERVING	337 CALORIES	9g CARBOHYDRATE
29g PROTEIN	18g FAT	trace FIBER

4	sole filets
¼ tsp	(1 ml) fennel seed
3-4	fresh mint leaves
¼ lb	(125 g) mushrooms, sliced thick
½ cup	(125 ml) dry white wine
1 cup	(250 ml) water
3 tbsp	(45 ml) butter
3½ tbsp	(55 ml) flour
¾ cup	(175 ml) grated cheddar cheese
	extra butter
	juice 1 lemon
	salt and pepper

Lightly grease frying pan with a bit of butter. Add fish, fennel seed, mint, mushrooms and lemon juice; season well.

Pour in wine and water; cover and bring to boil.

Turn filets over, shut off heat and let stand 1 minute.

Remove fish and set aside.

Replace frying pan on stove and cook liquid 2 to 3 minutes over high heat; set aside.

Heat 3 tbsp (45 ml) butter in saucepan. Add flour and cook 1 minute, stirring constantly.

Add cooking liquid with mushrooms to saucepan; mix well and season. Cook 8 minutes over low heat.

Break fish into smaller pieces and place in scallop shells. Pour mushroom sauce over and top with cheese. Broil in oven until melted.

Place fish, fennel seed, mint, mushrooms and lemon juice in lightly buttered frying pan; season well.

Pour in wine and water; cover and bring to boil.

After fish is cooked, remove from pan and set aside.

Add cooking liquid with mushrooms to flour mixture in saucepan; mix well and season. Cook 8 minutes over low heat.

Place 3 tbsp (45 ml) butter and chopped mint in saucepan. Melt over medium heat.

Add shallot and curry powder; cook 1 minute over medium heat.

Mix in flour with wooden spoon and cook 2 minutes over low heat.

Pour in milk and whisk until well incorporated; season to taste. Cook sauce 7 to 8 minutes over low heat.

Almond Sole
with Mint Sauce

(serves 4)

1 SERVING	377 CALORIES	16g CARBOHYDRATE
29g PROTEIN	22g FAT	trace FIBER

3 tbsp	(45 ml) butter
3	stems fresh mint, leaves coarsely chopped
1	shallot, chopped
1 tbsp	(15 ml) curry powder
3½ tbsp	(55 ml) flour
2 cups	(500 ml) hot milk
4	sole filets
1½ cups	(375 ml) water
1 tbsp	(15 ml) melted butter
1	onion, thinly sliced
1 tbsp	(15 ml) chopped parsley
4 tbsp	(60 ml) slivered almonds
	salt and pepper
	juice ½ lemon

Place 3 tbsp (45 ml) butter and mint in saucepan. Melt over medium heat.

Add shallot and curry powder; cook 1 minute over medium heat.

Mix in flour with wooden spoon and cook 2 minutes over low heat.

Pour in milk and whisk until well incorporated; season to taste. Cook sauce 7 to 8 minutes over low heat.

Meanwhile, roll filets (do not tie) and set in large frying pan. Add water, melted butter, onion, parsley, lemon juice, salt and pepper. Cover and bring to boil.

Turn fish rolls over; continue cooking 2 to 3 minutes over low heat, covered.

Transfer fish rolls to scallop shells. Top with mint sauce, sprinkle with slivered almonds and broil in oven until lightly browned.

Spinach Sole
Coquilles

(serves 4)

1 SERVING	303 CALORIES	21g CARBOHYDRATE
24g PROTEIN	14g FAT	1.0g FIBER

1 tbsp	(15 ml) vegetable oil
4	thick slices tomato
½ cup	(125 ml) breadcrumbs
1½ cups	(375 ml) cooked spinach, well drained and chopped
3	cooked sole filets, in 1½ in (4 cm) pieces
1½ cups	(375 ml) hot curry sauce
4 tbsp	(60 ml) grated coconut
	salt and pepper

Heat oil in frying pan. Meanwhile, dredge tomato slices in breadcrumbs. Fry in hot oil until browned on both sides. Remove and drain on paper towels.

Arrange layer of spinach in bottom of large scallop shells. Add slice of tomato.

Spoon fish over tomato slices and spinach; cover with curry sauce. Season well.

Sprinkle with coconut and broil several minutes in oven.

Layered Coquilles

(serves 4)

1 SERVING	350 CALORIES	15g CARBOHYDRATE
30g PROTEIN	19g FAT	0.8g FIBER

2	10 oz (284 g) packages spinach, cooked
4	small turbot filets
½	zucchini, sliced
1	large parsley sprig
¼ tsp	(1 ml) celery seed
1-2	slices lemon
1½ cups	(375 ml) hot white sauce
½ cup	(125 ml) grated Gruyère cheese
¼ tsp	(1 ml) paprika
	salt and pepper
	melted butter

Shape cooked spinach into balls and squeeze out excess water. Chop and place in bottom of ovenproof dish; set aside.

Place fish, zucchini, parsley, celery seed, lemon, salt and pepper in large frying pan. Pour in just enough water to cover. Cover and bring to boil.

Remove cooked fish from pan and rest on spinach in baking dish. Discard remaining contents in pan.

Cover fish with white sauce and top with cheese and paprika. Moisten with a bit of melted butter and broil in oven until golden brown.

Serve in scallop shells.

Place chopped spinach in bottom of ovenproof dish; set aside.

Remove cooked fish from pan and rest on spinach.

Place fish, zucchini, parsley, lemon and seasonings in frying pan with just enough water to cover. Bring to boil, covered.

Cover fish with white sauce and top with cheese and paprika; broil in oven.

Turbot Coquilles Mornay

(serves 4)

1 SERVING	467 CALORIES	15g CARBOHYDRATE
44g PROTEIN	26g FAT	trace FIBER

1½ cups	(375 ml) water
1	small onion, quartered
1	clove
½	celery stalk, thinly sliced
2 lb	(900 g) fresh turbot filets, cut in 1 in (2.5 cm) pieces
2 tbsp	(30 ml) butter
¼ lb	(125 g) mushrooms, diced
1 tsp	(5 ml) chopped chives
1¾ cups	(425 ml) Mornay sauce, hot
½ cup	(125 ml) grated mozzarella cheese
	juice 1 lemon
	salt and pepper

Pour water into skillet. Stud one quarter of onion with clove and place all in pan. Add celery, lemon juice and salt; bring to boil.

Add fish and cook over low heat for 3 to 4 minutes.

Remove fish and drain well; set aside.

Heat butter in saucepan. Add mushrooms and chives; cook 3 minutes over low heat.

Stir in Mornay sauce and season well. Simmer 3 minutes.

Place fish in Mornay sauce mixture and stir well; simmer 1 minute.

Pour into scallop shells, top with cheese and broil in oven until golden.

Coquille of Turbot au Feta

(serves 4)

1 SERVING	167 CALORIES	12g CARBOHYDRATE
15g PROTEIN	5g FAT	1.0g FIBER

1 tbsp	(15 ml) butter
2	turbot filets, cut in 1 in (2.5 cm) pieces
2	shallots, chopped
½ lb	(250 g) mushrooms, sliced
1 tbsp	(15 ml) fresh tarragon, finely chopped
½ cup	(125 ml) dry white wine
1¾ cups	(425 ml) spicy tomato sauce, hot
3 tbsp	(45 ml) feta cheese
	salt and pepper

Grease large frying pan with butter. Add fish, shallots, mushrooms, tarragon and wine. Cover with sheet of buttered waxed paper and bring to boiling point over medium heat.

As soon as liquid starts to boil, remove pan from heat and let stand 1 minute.

Remove fish from pan and set aside.

Replace pan on stove; cook 2 to 3 minutes at high heat. Add tomato sauce, mix well and season; bring to boil. Continue cooking 2 to 3 minutes over high heat.

Correct seasoning, replace fish in sauce and mix. Spoon into scallop shells and top with cheese; broil in oven several minutes.

Cold Coquilles

(serves 4)

1 SERVING	254 CALORIES	9g CARBOHYDRATE
21g PROTEIN	15g FAT	trace FIBER

3 oz	(90 g) blue cheese, mashed
1 tbsp	(15 ml) Dijon mustard
4-5 tbsp	(60-75 ml) lemon juice
¾ cup	(175 ml) light cream
1	garlic clove, smashed and chopped
¾ lb	(375 g) scallops, cooked and cooled
¼ lb	(125 g) mushrooms, well cleaned and sliced
1 tbsp	(15 ml) chopped parsley
	few drops Worcestershire sauce
	few drops Tabasco sauce
	salt and pepper
	green onions for decoration

In large bowl, mix together cheese and mustard.

Blend in lemon juice to taste. Add cream, garlic, Worcestershire, Tabasco, salt and pepper; mix until well incorporated.

Place scallops, mushrooms and parsley in second bowl. Pour in dressing and toss until evenly coated.

Serve in scallop shells with green onions as decoration. If desired, garnish with fruit and lettuce leaves.

Bercy Sauce

1 RECIPE	626 CALORIES	26g CARBOHYDRATE
14g PROTEIN	52g FAT	trace FIBER

4 tbsp	(60 ml) butter
1 tbsp	(15 ml) chopped parsley
1 tbsp	(15 ml) chopped chives
2	garlic cloves, smashed and chopped
1 tbsp	(15 ml) chopped fresh tarragon
3½ tbsp	(55 ml) flour
2 cups	(500 ml) light chicken stock, hot
	salt and pepper
	few drops Tabasco sauce

Heat butter in saucepan. Add parsley, chives, garlic and tarragon; cook 3 minutes over low heat.

Mix in flour and continue cooking 2 minutes.

Add chicken stock and season well with salt, pepper and Tabasco sauce. Mix and cook sauce 10 to 12 minutes over low heat, stirring twice.

Use in a variety of coquille recipes.

Paprika Sauce

1 RECIPE	942 CALORIES	75g CARBOHYDRATE
24g PROTEIN	65g FAT	5.0g FIBER

4 tbsp	(60 ml) butter
2	medium onions, thinly sliced
2 tbsp	(30 ml) paprika
4 tbsp	(60 ml) flour
1	large apple, peeled, cored and chopped
3 cups	(750 ml) light chicken stock, hot
3 tbsp	(45 ml) hot light cream
	salt and pepper

Heat butter in saucepan. Add onions and cook 4 minutes over low heat.

Stir in paprika and flour; mix well and cook 1 minute over low heat.

Add apple and chicken stock; mix well and season. Cook sauce 8 to 10 minutes over medium heat.

Remove sauce from heat and pour into food processor; blend until smooth.

Incorporate hot cream and serve.

Curry Sauce

1 RECIPE	672 CALORIES	39g CARBOHYDRATE
20g PROTEIN	52g FAT	3.0g FIBER

3 tbsp	(45 ml) butter
1	onion, finely chopped
1	small garlic clove, smashed and finely chopped
2 tbsp	(30 ml) curry powder
1 tsp	(5 ml) cumin
3 tbsp	(45 ml) flour
2½ cups	(625 ml) light chicken stock, hot
3 tbsp	(45 ml) hot light cream
	salt and pepper

Heat butter in saucepan. Add onion and garlic; cook 3 minutes over medium heat.

Mix in curry powder, cumin and flour; cook 4 to 5 minutes over low heat, stirring often.

Pour in chicken stock and season well. Mix and cook sauce 7 to 9 minutes over medium heat.

Incorporate cream, correct seasoning and serve.

SALADS

SALADS

Mmmm... salads, is there any other combination of foods that is so fresh and crisp, so bursting with color and seemingly with the power to make you feel as though you are getting healthier with each and every bite? Salads are a wonderful way to balance out a heavy dinner, or start or finish a light meal, and just as wonderful served on their own as the star attraction. Their versatility is unlimited — only your preferences and produce availability will set any restrictions. Preparing the perfect salad is quite simple but begins long before you start the recipe — a fact that is often forgotten. First, you must search out the freshest vegetables you can find, inspecting items carefully for hidden blemishes or just plain poor quality. Secondly, it is essential that all vegetables be thoroughly washed in plenty of cold water — tomatoes, cucumbers, everything! Thirdly, they must also be thoroughly dried (especially greens), otherwise the dressing you so carefully blended will not adhere properly, causing the whole salad to taste watery. And lastly, they should be trimmed, pared, cut as suggested in the recipe and assembled in a large serving bowl for tossing. Even if the salad is small it should be tossed with the dressing in a large bowl to make sure everything is evenly coated. Enjoy.

Summer Salad

(serves 4)

1 SERVING	571 CALORIES	20g CARBOHYDRATE
5g PROTEIN	55g FAT	2.8g FIBER

1 tbsp	(15 ml) strong mustard
1 tsp	(5 ml) chopped chives
1 tsp	(5 ml) chopped parsley
1 tbsp	(15 ml) green peppercorns, mashed
¼ cup	(50 ml) wine vinegar
1 cup	(250 ml) olive oil
1	head Romaine lettuce, leaves in bite-size pieces
1 cup	(250 ml) cooked green beans
1 cup	(250 ml) cooked yellow beans
1 cup	(250 ml) cooked green peas
2	carrots, pared and in fine julienne
	salt and pepper
	few drops lemon juice

Place mustard, chives, parsley, peppercorns, salt and lemon juice in bowl. Whisk in vinegar.

Incorporate oil in thin stream, whisking constantly. Correct seasoning.

Place remaining ingredients in large salad bowl. Pour on vinaigrette to taste, toss and serve.

Vegetable Salad with Cheese Dressing

(serves 4)

1 SERVING	403 CALORIES	36g CARBOHYDRATE
25g PROTEIN	22g FAT	2.1g FIBER

1	Boston lettuce
1	small Romaine lettuce
1	celery stalk, thinly sliced
2 cups	(500 ml) cooked cauliflower
3	canned beets, in julienne
½ cup	(125 ml) well-cooked bacon, chopped
1 cup	(250 ml) garlic croutons
3 oz	(90 g) blue cheese
4 tbsp	(60 ml) sour cream
3 tbsp	(45 ml) lemon juice
1 tbsp	(15 ml) cider vinegar
3 tbsp	(45 ml) heavy cream
	salt and pepper

Wash and dry both lettuces. Tear leaves into smaller pieces and place in large bowl.

Add celery, cauliflower, beets, bacon and croutons.

Mix blue cheese, sour cream and remaining ingredients in food processor until smooth.

Correct seasoning, pour dressing over salad and toss well. Serve.

Mixed Vegetable Side Salad

(serves 4)

1 SERVING	165 CALORIES	7g CARBOHYDRATE
7g PROTEIN	12g FAT	2.9g FIBER

1	English cucumber
1	head broccoli, in flowerets, cooked
1	carrot, pared and grated
3 oz	(90 g) cheddar cheese, in julienne
	salt and pepper
	vinaigrette of your choice

Do not peel cucumber. Cut in half lengthwise, remove seeds and slice.

Place cucumber in bowl with cooked broccoli, carrot and cheese. Season and toss.

Pour in vinaigrette, toss again and serve.

Eggplant Salad

(serves 4)

1 SERVING	637 CALORIES	48g CARBOHYDRATE
12g PROTEIN	48g FAT	1.0g FIBER

2	garlic cloves, smashed and chopped
¼ cup	(50 ml) wine vinegar
¾ cup	(175 ml) olive oil
1 tbsp	(15 ml) lemon juice
1	small eggplant
4	potatoes, cooked in jackets and still hot
4	large tomatoes, skinned, cut in half and sliced
2	bunches asparagus, tips cooked and cut in half
1 cup	(250 ml) cubed pineapple, drained
4 tbsp	(60 ml) toasted slivered almonds
	salt and pepper
	vegetable oil

Preheat ovent to 400°F (200°C).

Place garlic, vinegar, olive oil, lemon juice, salt and pepper in small bowl; whisk together and set aside.

Cut eggplant lengthwise into slices ½ in (1.2 cm) thick. Cut into long strips and dice. Place eggplant on cookie sheet and brush generously with vegetable oil.

Cook 15 minutes in oven, turning pieces over often.

Transfer eggplant to large salad bowl.

Peel hot potatoes, cut in half and slice; add to salad bowl.

Add tomatoes, asparagus, pineapple and almonds to bowl. Pour in vinaigrette to taste, toss well, season and serve.

Lettuce and Fruit Salad

(serves 4)

1 SERVING	447 CALORIES	12g CARBOHYDRATE
3g PROTEIN	45g FAT	1.4g FIBER

4 tbsp	(60 ml) wine vinegar
⅔ cup	(150 ml) olive oil
1 tsp	(5 ml) sugar
1 tbsp	(15 ml) lemon juice
2	endives, separated, leaves cut in ½
1	small bunch watercress
1	Boston lettuce, in leaves
1	yellow pepper, cut in thin strips
2 cups	(500 ml) ripe strawberries, hulled
	salt and pepper

Using whisk, mix vinegar with oil, sugar and lemon juice; season well and set dressing aside.

Place endives and watercress in salad bowl. Tear lettuce leaves into smaller pieces and add to bowl with yellow pepper and strawberries.

Whisk dressing and pour over salad. Toss and serve.

The Best Bean Salad

(serves 4-6)

1 SERVING	420 CALORIES	35g CARBOHYDRATE
19g PROTEIN	26g FAT	2.0g FIBER

1½ cups	(375 ml) white beans, soaked in cold water overnight
1	carrot, sliced
1	onion, chopped
1 tsp	(5 ml) celery seed
2	bay leaves
1 tsp	(5 ml) basil
1 tsp	(5 ml) chopped parsley
1 cup	(250 ml) cooked red kidney beans
1 cup	(250 ml) black-eyed peas (ready to serve)

1 tsp	(5 ml) vegetable oil
4	slices back bacon, ¼ in (0.65 cm) thick, diced
1	medium onion, chopped
1	garlic clove, smashed and chopped
1 tbsp	(15 ml) strong mustard
¼ cup	(50 ml) raspberry wine vinegar
½ cup	(125 ml) olive oil
	salt and pepper

Drain beans and place in large saucepan. Add carrot, 1 chopped onion, celery seed, bay leaves, basil and parsley.

Pour in enough water to cover by 2 in (5 cm). Partially cover and cook 1½ hours, skimming as necessary during cooking.

Drain beans and vegetables; transfer to salad bowl.

Add kidney beans and peas; toss and set aside.

Heat vegetable oil in small frying pan. Cook bacon, remaining onion and garlic 3 to 4 minutes over medium-high heat or until browned.

Stir this into salad mixture.

Mix mustard, vinegar and oil together in small bowl; season well and whisk. Pour over beans, toss and serve warm or slightly chilled.

Drain beans and place in large saucepan with carrot, 1 chopped onion and seasonings. Cover with water and cook 1½ hours partially covered; skim as necessary.

Cook bacon with remaining onion and garlic in hot oil, then add to salad bowl.

Add kidney beans and peas to drained white beans and vegetables; toss and set aside.

Pour dressing over beans, toss and serve warm or cold.

Tomato Mustard Salad

(serves 4)

1 SERVING	553 CALORIES	8g CARBOHYDRATE
5g PROTEIN	67g FAT	0.8g FIBER

4	ripe tomatoes, cut in ½ and sliced
2	shallots, finely chopped
1 tsp	(5 ml) chopped parsley
1 tsp	(5 ml) chopped chives
2	hard-boiled eggs, sliced
1 tbsp	(15 ml) Dijon mustard
¼ cup	(50 ml) wine vinegar
1 cup	(250 ml) olive oil
	salt and pepper

Place tomatoes, shallots, parsley, chives and eggs in bowl; season well.

Place mustard, vinegar and oil in another bowl. Mix together with whisk and season well.

Pour vinaigrette over tomatoes to taste, toss and serve.

Light Side Salad

(serves 4)

1 SERVING	184 CALORIES	28g CARBOHYDRATE
4g PROTEIN	8g FAT	1.4g FIBER

3	bananas, peeled and sliced
2	celery stalks, thinly sliced
12	cherry tomatoes, halved
1 tbsp	(15 ml) lemon juice
4 tbsp	(60 ml) sour cream
¼ cup	(50 ml) chopped walnuts
	salt and pepper
	Boston lettuce leaves

Place bananas, celery and tomatoes in bowl. Mix in lemon juice and sour cream; season well.

Arrange lettuce leaves on side plates, add salad and sprinkle servings with chopped walnuts.

Cucumber Salad with Sour Cream Dressing

(serves 4)

1 SERVING	79 CALORIES	12g CARBOHYDRATE
3g PROTEIN	3g FAT	1.1g FIBER

1	cucumber, peeled, seeded and sliced
2	celery stalks, sliced
12	cherry tomatoes, halved
3	hearts of palm, sliced
1 tbsp	(15 ml) chopped parsley
4 tbsp	(60 ml) sour cream
¼ tsp	(1 ml) dry mustard
1 tsp	(5 ml) red wine vinegar
	juice 1 lemon
	pinch sugar
	salt and pepper
	alfalfa sprouts for decoration
	pinch paprika

Place cucumber, celery, tomatoes, hearts of palm and parsley in salad bowl. Toss gently.

Mix together remaining ingredients with the exception of alfalfa sprouts and paprika.

Pour dressing over salad and toss to coat evenly. Arrange servings on small bed of alfalfa sprouts and sprinkle with a dash of paprika.

Watercress Salad

(serves 4)

1 SERVING	614 CALORIES	12g CARBOHYDRATE
18g PROTEIN	57g FAT	1.7g FIBER

¼ cup	(50 ml) wine vinegar
½ cup	(125 ml) olive oil
½	zucchini, in julienne and blanched
¼ lb	(125 g) green beans, pared and cooked
2	endives, leaves separated
1	small bunch watercress
6 oz	(170 g) cheddar cheese, in julienne
2	hard-boiled eggs, sliced
½ cup	(125 ml) chopped walnuts
½	ripe avocado, sliced thick
	salt and pepper
	juice 1 lemon

Mix vinegar, salt, pepper and lemon juice together in small bowl. Very slowly incorporate oil while mixing constantly with whisk. Set dressing aside.

Arrange remaining ingredients in large salad bowl. Pour in dressing, toss and serve.

Endive Salad Robert

(serves 4)

1 SERVING	429 CALORIES	33g CARBOHYDRATE
22g PROTEIN	21g FAT	2.7g FIBER

6	artichoke bottoms, cut in 3
5	endives, leaves well washed
1	cooked chicken breast, skinned and in julienne
1	Boston lettuce
2	tomatoes, cored and in wedges
½	cucumber, peeled, seeded and sliced
1	onion, finely chopped
¼ cup	(50 ml) wine vinegar
1 cup	(250 ml) dry white wine
⅔ cup	(150 ml) brown sauce, heated
	salt and pepper
	your favorite vinaigrette

Place artichoke bottoms, endives and chicken in salad bowl.

Tear washed lettuce leaves into smaller pieces; add to bowl along with tomatoes and cucumber.

Place onion in small saucepan. Add vinegar and wine and season with pepper. Cook 4 minutes over medium-high heat.

Mix in brown sauce and season; continue cooking 2 minutes.

Mix this sauce to taste with your favorite vinaigrette, then pour over salad, toss and serve.

Refrigerate remaining brown sauce for other uses.

Endives with Cucumber Mayonnaise

(serves 4)

1 SERVING	576 CALORIES	24g CARBOHYDRATE
42g PROTEIN	35g FAT	0.7g FIBER

½	cucumber, peeled and seeded
1¼ cups	(300 ml) mayonnaise
¼ tsp	(1 ml) paprika
¼ tsp	(1 ml) Tabasco sauce
1 tsp	(5 ml) lemon juice
3	endives, separated, leaves cut in ½
1	apple, peeled, cored and sliced
4	slices Black Forest ham, in julienne
2 tbsp	(30 ml) pine nuts
	salt and pepper

Place cucumber in food processor and purée.

Add mayonnaise, paprika, Tabasco sauce, lemon juice, salt and pepper; blend 30 seconds. Set aside.

Arrange endives, apple and ham in large salad bowl. Add cucumber mayonnaise to taste, mix well and serve.

Garnish individual portions with pine nuts.

Potato Bacon Salad

(serves 4)

1 SERVING	263 CALORIES	31g CARBOHYDRATE
10g PROTEIN	22g FAT	0.8g FIBER

2	green onions, chopped
1	shallot, chopped
6	potatoes, cooked in jackets and still hot, peeled and cubed
1 tbsp	(15 ml) chopped parsley
4	slices crisp bacon, chopped
3 tbsp	(45 ml) wine vinegar
⅓ cup	(75 ml) olive oil
3 tbsp	(45 ml) dry white wine
	salt and pepper

Place onions, shallot, potatoes and parsley in large bowl; toss and season.

Add bacon and remaining ingredients; toss gently but well.

Cool before serving.

Warm Potato Salad

(serves 4)

1 SERVING	236 CALORIES	18g CARBOHYDRATE
5g PROTEIN	16g FAT	0.5g FIBER

4	medium potatoes
2	hard-boiled eggs, chopped
2 tbsp	(30 ml) wine vinegar
4 tbsp	(60 ml) olive oil
1 tbsp	(15 ml) chopped chives
	salt and pepper
	few sprigs fresh watercress

Cook potatoes in jackets in salted boiling water.

When cooked, drain well and let stand 5 minutes in saucepan.

Peel potatoes, cut in ½ and slice; place in bowl.

Add eggs and toss gently. Add remaining ingredients, except watercress, and toss well.

Serve salad decorated with watercress.

Potato Salad with Mussels

(serves 4)

1 SERVING	470 CALORIES	27g CARBOHYDRATE
20g PROTEIN	32g FAT	1.3g FIBER

1 tsp	(5 ml) curry powder
1 tsp	(5 ml) sugar
4 tbsp	(60 ml) wine vinegar
½ cup	(125 ml) olive oil
½ tsp	(2 ml) lemon juice
1 tbsp	(15 ml) chopped parsley
1	garlic clove, smashed and chopped
1	bunch asparagus tips, cooked
4	potatoes, cooked in jackets and still hot
2	hard-boiled eggs, quartered
1½ cups	(375 ml) marinated mussels, drained
2 tbsp	(30 ml) chopped sweet pimento
	few blanched snow pea pods
	salt and pepper

Mix curry, sugar, wine vinegar, oil, salt and pepper together in bowl. Whisk until completely incorporated.

Blend in lemon juice, parsley and garlic; set dressing aside.

Place cooked asparagus in large salad bowl.

Peel hot potatoes and cut into large cubes. Add to bowl along with remaining ingredients.

Whisk dressing again and pour over salad. Toss and serve.

Hot Veggie Side Salad

(serves 4)

1 SERVING	187 CALORIES	14g CARBOHYDRATE
3g PROTEIN	10g FAT	1.5g FIBER

½	red pepper, diced large
½	yellow pepper, diced large
1	onion, diced large
1 cup	(250 ml) dry white wine
1	celery stalk, sliced thick
3	green onion, in 1 in (2.5 cm) lengths
¼	head broccoli, in flowerets
⅓	cucumber, peeled, halved, seeded and sliced thick
⅓	zucchini, sliced thick
¼	Chinese cabbage, sliced thick
2	garlic cloves, smashed and chopped
1 tbsp	(15 ml) chopped parsley
2	bay leaves
1 tsp	(5 ml) basil
3 tbsp	(45 ml) olive oil
3 tbsp	(45 ml) wine vinegar
	salt and pepper
	fresh mint to taste
	fresh dill to taste
	juice ½ lime

Place peppers, diced onion, wine, celery and green onions in skillet. Season, cover and cook 3 minutes over high heat.

Add all remaining ingredients, except lime juice, and cook 6 minutes covered over medium-high heat.

Sprinkle in lime juice and serve immediately.

Cut and trim the vegetables as neatly as possible to further enhance the finished product.

Place peppers, diced onion, wine, celery and green onions in skillet. Season, cover and cook 3 minutes over high heat.

Add all remaining ingredients, except lime juice, and cook 6 minutes covered over medium-high heat.

Sprinkle in lime juice and serve immediately.

Marinated Mushrooms

(serves 4)

1 SERVING	335 CALORIES	14g CARBOHYDRATE
6g PROTEIN	31g FAT	1.8g FIBER

2 lb	(900 g) fresh mushrooms, well cleaned
1 tbsp	(15 ml) butter
1 tbsp	(15 ml) chopped parsley
1	lemon, cut in ½
1 cup	(250 ml) dry red wine
¼ cup	(50 ml) wine vinegar
½ cup	(125 ml) olive oil
1 tsp	(5 ml) tarragon
¼ tsp	(1 ml) ground cloves
1	shallot, chopped
	salt and pepper

Place mushrooms, butter and parsley in saucepan. Squeeze juice from lemon halves, add to saucepan and season well.

Pour in wine, vinegar and olive oil. Mix well.

Add remaining ingredients, season and cook 8 to 10 minutes over high heat with cover. Stir once or twice during cooking.

Cool mushrooms before serving.

Arrange on fresh lettuce leaves with slices of lemon if desired.

Place mushrooms, butter and parsley in saucepan. Squeeze juice from lemon halves, add to saucepan and season well.

Pour in wine.

Pour in vinegar.

Pour in olive oil.

Rice Salad with Lemon Dressing

(serves 4)

1 SERVING	622 CALORIES	33g CARBOHYDRATE
27g PROTEIN	43g FAT	1.3g FIBER

4 tbsp	(60 ml) lemon juice
1	egg yolk
¾ cup	(175 ml) sunflower oil
2 cups	(500 ml) cooked rice
1	red pepper, diced small
1	celery stalk, sliced
16	cooked shrimp, cut in 3
1	bunch asparagus, tips cooked and cut in 1 in (2.5 cm) lengths
¼ lb	(125 g) cooked green beans, cut in 2
1 tbsp	(15 ml) chopped parsley
	pinch sugar
	dash paprika
	salt and pepper

Place lemon juice, egg yolk, sugar, paprika, salt and pepper in small bowl. Whisk together until well incorporated.

Incorporate oil in thin stream while whisking constantly. Season very well.

Place remaining ingredients in large salad bowl. Pour in dressing, season and toss well. Serve.

Chick Pea Salad

(serves 4)

1 SERVING	521 CALORIES	50g CARBOHYDRATE
17g PROTEIN	6g FAT	3.3g FIBER

19 oz	(540 ml) can chick peas, drained
¼ lb	(250 g) cooked green beans
1½ cups	(375 ml) marinated cauliflower, drained
1 tbsp	(15 ml) chopped parsley
1	yellow pepper, diced
1 tbsp	(15 ml) tarragon
¼ cup	(50 ml) cider vinegar
½ tsp	(2 ml) sugar
½ cup	(125 ml) olive oil
1 tsp	(5 ml) fresh chopped mint
	salt and pepper
	few drops lemon juice
	Tabasco sauce to taste

Place chick peas, beans, cauliflower, parsley and yellow pepper in large salad bowl.

In separate bowl, mix together remaining ingredients, whisking until well incorporated.

Pour dressing over salad, toss and serve.

Hearty Pasta Salad

(serves 4)

1 SERVING	395 CALORIES	40g CARBOHYDRATE
13g PROTEIN	21g FAT	1.9g FIBER

1	garlic clove, smashed and chopped
1 tbsp	(15 ml) Dijon mustard
1	egg yolk
1	hard-boiled egg
¼ tsp	(1 ml) paprika
⅓ cup	(75 ml) olive oil
1½ cups	(375 ml) cooked medium pasta bows
1 cup	(250 ml) cooked red kidney beans
½ cup	(125 ml) cooked green peas

½ cup	(125 ml) blanched diced carrots
1	green onion, chopped
2	artichoke bottoms, sliced
1	celery stalk, sliced
1	leaf Chinese lettuce, sliced
	salt and pepper
	grated Parmesan cheese to taste
	juice 1 lemon

Place garlic, mustard and egg yolk in small bowl; whisk together.

Add hard-boiled egg by forcing through sieve. Whisk in paprika, salt, pepper, dash of Parmesan cheese and lemon juice.

Incorporate oil in thin stream while whisking constantly. Set dressing aside.

Place remaining ingredients in large salad bowl and pour in dressing. Toss, correct seasoning and serve.

Add hard-boiled egg to dressing ingredients by forcing through sieve.

Whisk in paprika, salt, pepper, dash of Parmesan cheese and lemon juice.

 Incorporate oil in thin stream while whisking constantly.

 Pour dressing over salad ingredients, toss, correct seasoning and serve.

Chicken Salad

(serves 4)

1 SERVING	286 CALORIES	18g CARBOHYDRATE
32g PROTEIN	10g FAT	1.0g FIBER

2	chicken breasts, skinned and halved
1	celery stalk, sliced thick on angle
1	parsley sprig
4	lemon slices
1	onion, diced large
¼ tsp	(1 ml) celery seed
1	green onion, chopped
1	celery stalk, sliced
2	hard-boiled eggs, sliced
¼ tsp	(1 ml) paprika

6	water chestnuts, sliced
½ cup	(125 ml) seedless green grapes
2 tbsp	(30 ml) diced pimento
3 tbsp	(45 ml) mayonnaise
1 tsp	(5 ml) curry powder
	salt and pepper
	several cherry tomatoes, halved
	juice 1 lemon

Place chicken, first celery stalk, parsley sprig, lemon slices, diced onion, celery seed, salt and pepper in saucepan. Pour in enough water to cover. Cover and cook about 18 minutes over medium heat, depending on size of breasts.

When chicken is cooked, drain and discard other ingredients. Bone chicken and cut meat in large slices.

Place green onion, other celery stalk, eggs and paprika in bowl. Add chicken and season well.

Mix in water chestnuts, grapes, pimento and tomatoes; toss slightly.

Mix in remaining ingredients until well incorporated and serve salad on lettuce leaves.

Place chicken, first celery stalk, parsley sprig, lemon slices, diced onion, celery seed, salt and pepper in saucepan. Add water to cover and cook, covered, about 18 minutes over medium heat depending on size of breasts.

Place green onion, other celery stalk, eggs and paprika in bowl.

Add cooked chicken and season.

Add remaining ingredients, mix until well incorporated and correct seasoning.

Chicken and Beef Salad

(serves 4)

1 SERVING	621 CALORIES	7g CARBOHYDRATE
38g PROTEIN	49g FAT	0.9g FIBER

1 tbsp	(15 ml) Dijon mustard
1 tsp	(5 ml) chopped fresh tarragon
1	garlic clove, smashed and chopped
3 tbsp	(45 ml) wine vinegar
2 tbsp	(30 ml) lemon juice
¾ cup	(175 ml) olive oil
1	head Chinese lettuce
1	cooked chicken breast, skinned and boned
1 cup	(250 ml) leftover cooked steak, in strips
2	tomatoes, cut in half, then in wedges
1	celery stalk, sliced
2	hard-boiled eggs, sliced
	salt and pepper

Place mustard, tarragon, garlic, vinegar and lemon juice in small bowl; whisk together.

Incorporate oil in thin stream while whisking constantly. Correct seasoning and set aside.

Wash and dry lettuce; tear leaves into smaller pieces. Cut cooked chicken breast into strips; place in salad bowl with lettuce.

Add steak, tomatoes, celery and eggs to salad bowl. Toss everything well.

Whisk vinaigrette and pour over salad to taste. Toss well, season and serve.

Chinatown Salad

(serves 4)

1 SERVING	263 CALORIES	27g CARBOHYDRATE
19g PROTEIN	2g FAT	1.9g FIBER

1	cooked chicken breast, skinned, boned and sliced thick
1 tbsp	(15 ml) chopped fresh ginger
2	garlic cloves, smashed and chopped
1 tbsp	(15 ml) soya sauce
1½ cups	(375 ml) shredded radicchio
1 cup	(250 ml) cooked green peas
1 cup	(250 ml) bean sprouts
1	yellow pepper, thinly sliced
2	green onions, chopped
3 tbsp	(45 ml) red wine vinegar
¼ cup	(50 ml) sesame oil
	salt and pepper

Place chicken, ginger, garlic, soya sauce, radicchio and green peas in bowl. Season well.

Add bean sprouts, yellow pepper and green onions. Pour in wine vinegar and oil. Toss everything to incorporate well, correct seasoning and serve.

Place chicken,  ginger, garlic and soya sauce in bowl.

Add bean  sprouts, yellow pepper and green onions. Pour in wine vinegar.

Add radicchio  and green peas; season well.

Pour in oil, toss  and correct seasoning.

Elegant Strawberry and Shrimp Salad

(serves 4)

1 SERVING	459 CALORIES	70g CARBOHYDRATE
31g PROTEIN	6g FAT	1.8g FIBER

¾ lb	(375 g) cooked shrimp
12	canned baby corn on the cob
1	pear, peeled and sliced
½ lb	(250 g) ripe strawberries, hulled and halved
4 tbsp	(60 ml) sour cream
1 tsp	(5 ml) dry mustard
1 tbsp	(15 ml) apple cider
1 tsp	(5 ml) ground ginger
	juice 1 lemon
	pinch sugar
	few drops Tabasco sauce

Place shrimp, corn, pear and strawberries in salad bowl.

Mix sour cream with mustard; add lemon juice.

Whisk in cider, sugar, ginger and Tabasco sauce.

Pour over salad and mix well. Serve on lettuce leaves if desired.

Shrimp and Pepper Salad

(serves 4)

1 SERVING	412 CALORIES	9g CARBOHYDRATE
17g PROTEIN	35g FAT	1.5g FIBER

2 tbsp	(30 ml) vegetable oil
1	onion, thinly sliced
2	yellow peppers, thinly sliced
2	garlic cloves, smashed and chopped
1½ cups	(375 ml) thinly sliced eggplant
½ lb	(250 g) cooked shrimp
3 tbsp	(45 ml) wine vinegar
½ cup	(125 ml) olive oil
	salt and pepper

Heat vegetable oil in large frying pan. Cook onion, peppers, garlic and eggplant 7 minutes over medium heat with cover. Stir 2 to 3 times during cooking and season well.

Remove vegetables from pan and transfer to salad bowl; set aside.

Add shrimp, vinegar and olive oil to frying pan; season well. Cook 1 to 2 minutes over medium-high heat.

Drain most of the oil off, then add shrimp to salad bowl. Toss and cool slightly before serving.

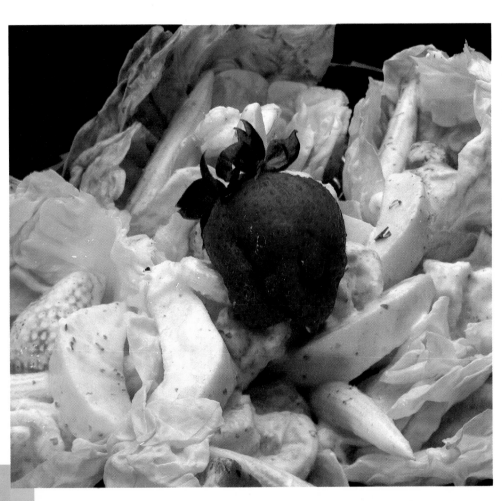

Scallop Salad

(serves 4)

1 SERVING	309 CALORIES	28g CARBOHYDRATE
35g PROTEIN	6g FAT	1.6g FIBER

3	large potatoes, peeled and cut into balls
1 lb	(500 g) large mushrooms, quartered
1 tbsp	(15 ml) lemon juice
1 tbsp	(15 ml) oil
¼ tsp	(1 ml) fennel seed
1 lb	(500 g) scallops
1 tbsp	(15 ml) chopped parsley
3 tbsp	(45 ml) sour cream
1 tbsp	(15 ml) Dijon mustard
1 tbsp	(15 ml) chopped pimento
	juice 1 lemon
	salt and pepper

Place potato balls in saucepan, season with salt and pour in enough cold water to cover. Bring to boil. Continue cooking 5 minutes over medium heat.

Add mushrooms, 1 tbsp (15 ml) lemon juice, oil and fennel seed; continue cooking 2 minutes.

Drop in scallops and finish cooking 1 minute.

Drain well and transfer boiled ingredients to salad bowl; sprinkle with parsley.

Squeeze in juice of 1 lemon and season well. Mix in sour cream, mustard and pimento; toss until all is evenly coated.

Serve.

Fish and Vegetable Salad

(serves 4)

1 SERVING	431 CALORIES	18g CARBOHYDRATE
15g PROTEIN	35g FAT	2.1g FIBER

3 tbsp	(45 ml) wine vinegar
2	garlic cloves, smashed and chopped
1 tbsp	(15 ml) soya sauce
½ tsp	(2 ml) sugar
½ cup	(125 ml) olive oil
2 tbsp	(30 ml) vegetable oil
2	sole filets, cut in 1 in (2.5 cm) pieces
2 cups	(500 ml) broccoli flowerets, blanched
¼ lb	(125 g) snow peas, blanched
6	cooked asparagus, cut in 2.5 cm (1 in) lengths
6	cherry tomatoes, halved
2 tbsp	(30 ml) chopped fresh chives
6	water chestnuts, sliced
¼ tsp	(1 ml) ground ginger
½ tsp	(2 ml) ground cumin
	juice 1 lemon
	salt and pepper

Whisk vinegar, garlic, soya, sugar, olive oil and lemon juice together until well incorporated; set aside.

Heat remaining oil in large frying pan. Cook fish 2 minutes each side over high heat.

Add broccoli and pea pods; mix well.

Add remaining ingredients, season to taste and cook 3 to 4 minutes over high heat.

Transfer mixture to large salad bowl. Whisk dressing and pour over ingredients; toss well and serve immediately.

Cook fish in hot oil for 2 minutes on each side over high heat.

Add broccoli and pea pods; mix well.

Add remaining ingredients, season to taste and cook 3 to 4 minutes over high heat.

Pour prepared dressing over salad, toss and serve.

Penne with Crab *(serves 4)*

1 SERVING	494 CALORIES	40g CARBOHYDRATE
14g PROTEIN	30g FAT	0.6g FIBER

¼ cup	(50 ml) wine vinegar
1 tbsp	(15 ml) chopped parsley
½ cup	(125 ml) olive oil
1 tbsp	(15 ml) Dijon mustard
1 tsp	(5 ml) sugar
1 tsp	(5 ml) tarragon
¼ cup	(50 ml) grated Parmesan cheese
1	shallot, finely chopped
2	garlic cloves, smashed and chopped
¼ tsp	(1 ml) Tabasco sauce
3 cups	(750 ml) cooked penne
5	cooked asparagus, diced
2	hearts of palm, sliced
4.25 oz	(120 g) can crabmeat, well drained
2 tbsp	(30 ml) chopped pickled sweet pimento
	salt and pepper
	lettuce leaves for serving

Whisk together vinegar, parsley and oil until well incorporated.

Add mustard, sugar, tarragon, cheese, shallot, garlic, Tabasco, salt and pepper; continue whisking until vinaigrette has thickened.

Place remaining ingredients in salad bowl. Pour in vinaigrette, season and toss. Serve on lettuce leaves.

Whisk together vinegar, parsley and oil until well incorporated.

Add mustard, sugar, tarragon, cheese, shallot, garlic, Tabasco, salt and pepper; continue whisking until thickened.

Place salad ingredients in bowl.

Pour in vinaigrette, season and toss.

Fancy Meal Salad

(serves 4)

1 SERVING	306 CALORIES	41g CARBOHYDRATE
13g PROTEIN	13g FAT	4.2g FIBER

3	pears, peeled and cut in wedges
½ lb	(250 g) white mushrooms, in julienne
3 cups	(750 ml) cooked green beans
1	yellow pepper, thinly sliced
1 cup	(250 ml) seedless green grapes
5 oz	(142 g) can crabmeat, drained
1 tbsp	(15 ml) curry powder
3 tbsp	(45 ml) lemon juice
1 tbsp	(15 ml) horseradish
1 cup	(250 ml) sour cream
1 tbsp	(15 ml) chopped chives
	salt and pepper

Place pears, mushrooms, beans, yellow pepper, grapes and crabmeat in salad bowl.

Place curry powder, lemon juice and horseradish in small bowl; whisk together very well and season generously.

Add sour cream and chives; whisk again until incorporated. Season again to taste and pour over salad; toss and serve.

Herring Salad

(serves 4)

1 SERVING	595 CALORIES	29g CARBOHYDRATE
13g PROTEIN	49g FAT	1.0g FIBER

1	hard-boiled egg
1 tbsp	(15 ml) Dijon mustard
4 tbsp	(60 ml) wine vinegar
¾ cup	(175 ml) olive oil
1 tbsp	(15 ml) lemon juice
3	cooked marinated herring filets, cubed
3	apples, peeled, cored and sliced
3	cooked potatoes, peeled and sliced
2	pickles, in julienne
3	canned beets, sliced
	salt and pepper

Cut hard-boiled egg in half and force yolk and white through sieve into bowl.

Add mustard and vinegar; whisk well.

Incorporate oil in thin stream while whisking constantly. Mix in lemon juice and correct seasoning.

Place herring, apples, potatoes, pickles and beets in large salad bowl.

Pour in vinaigrette to taste, toss well and correct seasoning.

APPETIZERS

APPETIZERS

Appetizers, in their countless shapes and sizes, come to our tables in hopes of awakening sleepy palates by tantalizing our senses with a sampling of flavors and textures that are married to perfection. Whether served hot or cold, appetizers are meant to be eaten for the pure pleasure of eating, so they should never be to filling or so complicated that they prevent the diner from enjoying the fleeting moments with ease. From the simplest open-faced canapé to servings of fancy Lobster Liza, appetizers encourage spontaneity not just with ingredients but with the way in which they are presented. If you are serving an assortment of buffet-style appetizers, try arranging the platters on different levels surrounded by attractive plates, cutlery and napkins. Although hot appetizers require a little more care and planning (so they can be served promptly), take a few extra minutes to decorate portions with fresh herbs or condiments such as pickles and olives. The following recipes offer you an interesting selection of hot and cold dishes to choose from. Remember that an appetizer doesn't necessarily have to reflect what the main meal is about — so make your choice by what strikes your fancy and have fun with it!

Lobster Liza

(serves 4-6)

1 SERVING	326 CALORIES	27g CARBOHYDRATE
25g PROTEIN	11g FAT	0.9g FIBER

2 tbsp	(30 ml) butter
2	shallots, chopped
1	green pepper, chopped
1 lb	(500 g) chopped lobster meat, cooked
1¼ cups	(300 ml) thick tomato sauce, heated
1 tbsp	(15 ml) lemon juice
½ cup	(125 ml) grated Parmesan cheese
	salt and pepper
	toasted white bread

Heat butter in sauce pan. Cook shallots and green pepper 3 minutes over low heat.

Mix in lobster meat and tomato sauce; season well and add lemon juice. Cook over low heat 2 to 3 minutes.

Correct seasoning and spoon mixture over toast. Top with cheese and broil 2 to 3 minutes in oven.

Deep-Fried Fish

(serves 4-6)

1 SERVING	460 CALORIES	53g CARBOHYDRATE
29g PROTEIN	14g FAT	trace FIBER

2 cups	(500 ml) crushed soda crackers
1	garlic clove, smashed and chopped
1 tbsp	(15 ml) curry powder
1 tbsp	(15 ml) celery seed
4	large sole filets
1½ cups	(375 ml) seasoned flour
3	beaten eggs
	pepper
	peanut oil

Mix crackers with garlic, curry powder and celery seed; set aside in bowl.

Cut fish into strips ½ in (1.2 cm) wide. Throughly coat in flour.

Dip fish strips in beaten eggs, then in soda cracker crumbs. Season well with pepper.

Deep-fry in hot oil for 2 minutes.

Pat dry with paper towels and serve with lemon wedges.

Hot Shrimp Kebabs

(serves 4)

1 SERVING	422 CALORIES	20g CARBOHYDRATE
32g PROTEIN	24g FAT	0.7g FIBER

24	shrimp, peeled and deveined
3 tbsp	(45 ml) sesame oil
1 tbsp	(15 ml) lemon juice
¼ tsp	(1 ml) Tabasco sauce
24	large cubes fresh pineapple
24	wedges red apple
	salt and pepper
	melted butter seasoned with lemon juice

Place shrimp, oil, lemon juice and Tabasco sauce in bowl. Marinate 30 minutes.

Alternate shrimp, pineapple and apple on short wooden skewers. Baste with melted lemon butter and season very well.

Place skewers on ovenproof platter and broil 3 minutes each side in oven. Baste frequently.

Smoked Salmon Canapés

(serves 4-6)

1 SERVING	658 CALORIES	47g CARBOHYDRATE
34g PROTEIN	36g FAT	-- FIBER

1 lb	(500 g) sliced smoked salmon
½ cup	(125 ml) soft butter
1 tbsp	(15 ml) lemon juice
¼ tsp	(1 ml) Tabasco sauce
1	loaf French bread, sliced
3 tbsp	(45 ml) capers
	pepper
	sliced hard-boiled eggs

Place 4 slices of salmon in food processor. Add butter, lemon juice, Tabasco sauce and pepper; blend 30 seconds.

Butter bread with mixture and top with remaining smoked salmon. Sprinkle canapés with capers and decorate platter with sliced boiled eggs.

Rice Canapés

(serves 6-8)

1 SERVING	336 CALORIES	49g CARBOHYDRATE
12g PROTEIN	10g FAT	trace FIBER

5	hard-boiled eggs, chopped
1 cup	(250 ml) cooked saffron rice
½	celery stalk, diced small
2	green onions, finely chopped
1 tsp	(5 ml) chopped chives
3 tbsp	(45 ml) mayonnaise
2 tbsp	(30 ml) sour cream
1 tsp	(5 ml) Worcestershire sauce
	juice ½ lemon
	salt and pepper
	sliced Italian bread

Place eggs, rice, celery, onions and chives in bowl; mix well.

Add mayonnaise, sour cream, Worcestershire sauce, lemon juice, salt and pepper; mix again until incorporated.

Spread over sliced Italian bread and serve.

Party Canapés

(serves 6)

1 SERVING	289 CALORIES	39g CARBOHYDRATE
7g PROTEIN	10g FAT	1.0g FIBER

4	stems watercress, finely chopped
1	celery stalk, chopped
1	red apple, peeled, cored, quartered and chopped
1 tbsp	(15 ml) pine nuts
1 tbsp	(15 ml) chopped parsley
1 tsp	(5 ml) curry powder
2 tbsp	(30 ml) mayonnaise
1 tbsp	(15 ml) sour cream
1 tsp	(5 ml) lemon juice
10-12	slices "party" light rye bread with caraway seeds
	salt and pepper
	halved cherry tomatoes for garnish

Mix all ingredients together except bread and tomatoes.

Season to taste, spread mixture over bread slices and garnish with halved cherry tomatoes. If desired serve with blanched broccoli.

Cold Beef Appetizer

(serves 4)

1 SERVING	866 CALORIES	60g CARBOHYDRATE
31g PROTEIN	56g FAT	0.5g FIBER

½ lb	(250 g) soft butter
1	medium onion, finely chopped
1	garlic clove, smashed and chopped
1 tbsp	(15 ml) paprika
1	loaf French bread
½ lb	(250 g) thin slices cooked roast beef
	few drops lemon juice
	salt and pepper

Heat 1 tbsp (15 ml) butter in small saucepan. Cook onion and garlic 3 minutes over medium heat.

Mix in paprika and continue cooking 1 minute. Remove and purée in food processor; set aside to cool.

Mix onion mixture, remaining butter, lemon juice, salt and pepper together until well incorporated.

Slice bread and toast in oven. Spread butter over pieces of bread and top with roast beef.

Serve cold with pickles.

Fancy Pastrami Canapés

(serves 4)

1 SERVING	569 CALORIES	17g CARBOHYDRATE
31g PROTEIN	41g FAT	trace FIBER

10	thin slices deli bread
4 tbsp	(60 ml) butter
1 tbsp	(15 ml) mustard
1 tsp	(5 ml) horseradish
10	slices pastrami
1 cup	(250 ml) fine herb pâté
2 tbsp	(30 ml) sour cream
	shredded lettuce for garnish

Place slices of bread on cutting board.

Mix butter with mustard and horseradish; spread evenly over bread.

Place slice of pastrami on each slice of bread, trim crusts and cut into two triangles.

Arrange canapés on shredded lettuce.

Mix pâté with sour cream until well blended. Place in pastry bag and decorate canapés with mixture.

Cheesy Crab Bread

(serves 6)

1 SERVING	335 CALORIES	26g CARBOHYDRATE
13g PROTEIN	20g FAT	trace FIBER

3 tbsp	(45 ml) butter
1	onion, chopped
¼ lb	(125 g) mushrooms, chopped
5 oz	(142 g) can crabmeat, drained
1¼ cups	(300 ml) white sauce, heated
8-10	slices white bread, toasted
½ cup	(125 ml) grated Emmenthal cheese
	salt and pepper
	few drops Tabasco sauce

Heat butter in saucepan. Cook onion and mushrooms 2 to 3 minutes over medium-high heat; season well and add Tabasco sauce.

Mix in crabmeat, season and pour in white sauce. Cook 2 minutes over medium heat.

Spoon mixture over toast, top with cheese and broil 2 minutes in oven.

Camembert Treat

(serves 6-8)

1 SERVING	243 CALORIES	26g CARBOHYDRATE
11g PROTEIN	10g FAT	trace FIBER

1 cup	(250 ml) fine breadcrumbs
3	garlic cloves, smashed and finely chopped
1 tbsp	(15 ml) chopped parsley
1 tsp	(5 ml) celery seed
1 tsp	(5 ml) sesame seed
¼ tsp	(1 ml) paprika
1	small round of Camembert cheese, chilled
½	French baguette, sliced and toasted on both sides
	dash cayenne pepper

Mix breadcrumbs with garlic, parsley and seasonings; set aside.

Remove soft crust from sides of cheese. Lightly scrape top and bottom with knife.

Place cheese in bowl with breadcrumbs and coat. Remove cheese and set on cutting board; flatten with rolling pin.

Turn cheese over, sprinkle with more breadcrumbs and roll again.

Repeat procedure using all breadcrumbs and rolling until cheese is ¼ in (0.65 cm) thick.

Using cookie cutter about the same size as the bread slices, cut out pieces of cheese and set on bread.

Broil 2 minutes in oven.

Serve cold.

Beef Strips

(serves 8-10)

1 SERVING	314 CALORIES	26g CARBOHYDRATE
19g PROTEIN	15g FAT	trace FIBER

1 tbsp	(15 ml) vegetable oil
1½ lb	(750 g) strip loin steaks, 1 in (2.5 cm) thick, fat trimmed
1	shallot, chopped
1 tbsp	(15 ml) chopped parsley
1 tsp	(5 ml) lemon juice
1 tsp	(5 ml) Worcestershire sauce
1 tbsp	(15 ml) red wine vinegar
2 tbsp	(30 ml) olive oil

3 tbsp	(45 ml) butter
1 tsp	(5 ml) strong mustard
	salt and pepper
	sliced French baguette
	endive leaves for garnish

Heat oil in large frying pan or on nonstick grill. When very hot, add meat and sear 3 minutes over medium-high heat.

Turn meat over, season well and continue searing another 3 to 4 minutes.

Turn meat over again; finish cooking 3 minutes for rare meat.

Remove meat from pan and slice thinly on an angle; place pieces on plate.

Cover meat with shallot, parsley, lemon juice, Worcestershire sauce, vinegar, oil and pepper. Cover loosely with plastic wrap and refrigerate 2 hours.

Drain meat if necessary and set aside.

Mix butter with mustard, spread over bread and toast in oven.

Remove and top with marinated meat. Serve with endive leaves as garnish.

Trim excess fat from meat.

Sear meat a total of 9 to 10 minutes for rare.

Remove meat from pan and thinly slice on an angle; place pieces on plate.

Cover meat with shallot, parsley, lemon juice, Worcestershire sauce, vinegar, oil and pepper. Cover loosely with plastic wrap and refrigerate 2 hours.

Cheesy Muffin Starter

(serves 4)

1 SERVING	413 CALORIES	25g CARBOHYDRATE
15g PROTEIN	29g FAT	2.0g FIBER

1 cup	(250 ml) stuffed green olives, sliced
4	green onions, chopped
1	celery stalk, chopped
2	slices processed Gruyère cheese, diced
¼ tsp	(1 ml) celery seed
¼ tsp	(1 ml) paprika
3 tbsp	(45 ml) mayonnaise
1 tbsp	(15 ml) Dijon mustard
1 tsp	(5 ml) lemon juice
¼ tsp	(1 ml) Worcestershire sauce
2	English muffins, halved
4	squares mozzarella cheese
	salt and pepper
	more paprika to taste

Place olives, onions, celery, Gruyère cheese, seasonings and mayonnaise in bowl; mix well.

Add mustard, lemon juice and Worcestershire sauce; mix again and correct seasoning.

Set muffin halves on ovenproof platter and top with olive mixture. Cover with mozzarella and dash of paprika.

Broil in oven until melted.

Place olives, onions and celery in bowl.

Add Gruyère cheese, seasonings and mayonnaise; mix well.

Add mustard, lemon juice and Worcestershire sauce; mix again and correct seasoning.

Set muffin halves on ovenproof platter and top with olive mixture. Cover with mozzarella and dash of paprika. Broil in oven until melted.

Ricotta Tomato Bread

(serves 4-6)

1 SERVING	429 CALORIES	58g CARBOHYDRATE
16g PROTEIN	14g FAT	1.0g FIBER

2 tbsp	(30 ml) vegetable oil
1	celery stalk, diced
½	green pepper, chopped
1	onion, chopped
2	garlic cloves, smashed and chopped
¼ tsp	(1 ml) paprika
¼ tsp	(1 ml) chili powder
28 oz	(796 ml) can tomatoes, drained and chopped

3 tbsp	(45 ml) tomato paste
⅓ cup	(75 ml) grated Parmesan cheese
1	French baguette, cut in half lengthwise
½ cup	(125 ml) ricotta cheese
	salt and pepper

Heat oil in large skillet. Cook celery, green pepper, onion, garlic, paprika and chili powder 4 to 5 minutes over low heat.

Mix in tomatoes and tomato paste; season well. Continue cooking 15 minutes.

Add Parmesan cheese and finish cooking 5 minutes.

Slice each bread half into 3 pieces and toast in oven.

Place bread on cookie sheet or ovenproof platter. Spoon tomato mixture over and top with ricotta cheese.

Broil 3 to 4 minutes or until melted.

Serve immediately.

Cook celery, green pepper, onion, garlic, paprika and chili powder in hot oil for 4 to 5 minutes over low heat.

Add Parmesan cheese and finish cooking 5 minutes.

Mix in tomatoes and tomato paste; season well. Continue cooking 15 minutes.

Place toasted bread on cookie sheet and add tomato mixture; top with ricotta cheese and broil in oven.

Vegetable Sandwich Loaf

(serves 6-8)

1 SERVING	323 CALORIES	42g CARBOHYDRATE
9g PROTEIN	13g FAT	trace FIBER

6 oz	(170 g) pepper cream cheese
3 tbsp	(45 ml) sour cream
1 tsp	(5 ml) chopped parsley
¼ tsp	(1 ml) paprika
1	loaf white bread, unsliced
½	English cucumber, thinly sliced
6	radishes, thinly sliced
1	small bunch asparagus, cooked
	salt and pepper

Mix cheese, sour cream, parsley, paprika, salt and pepper together in food processor until smooth.

Using long bread knife, slice off top and bottom crusts of loaf. Continue cutting loaf to obtain 4 slices. See Technique for visual help.

Spread first slice of bread with cheese mixture. Set on large sheet of aluminum foil and layer with cucumbers; season well.

Butter second slice of bread with cheese mixture on both sides and set over cucumbers. Layer radishes on bread and season well.

Butter third slice of bread with cheese mixture on both sides; place on sandwich. Arrange asparagus on bread, trimming to size; season well.

Butter last slice of bread with cheese mixture on one side only. Place, face down, over asparagus and cover sandwich loaf in foil. Use another sheet if needed.

Refrigerate overnight, then slice and serve. If desired trim off crusts before serving.

Mix cheese, sour cream, parsley, paprika, salt and pepper together in food processor until smooth.

Using long bread knife, slice off top and bottom crusts.

Continue cutting loaf to obtain 4 slices.

Add the last vegetable layer of the sandwich.

Crêpes with Spinach

(serves 4)

1 SERVING	579 CALORIES	35g CARBOHYDRATE
22g PROTEIN	36g FAT	1.0g FIBER

1 cup	(250 ml) all-purpose flour
¼ tsp	(1 ml) salt
¼ tsp	(1 ml) paprika
¼ tsp	(1 ml) ground ginger
½ tsp	(2 ml) celery seed
3	whole eggs
1 cup	(250 ml) beer
3 tbsp	(45 ml) melted butter
½ cup	(125 ml) milk
2	10 oz (284 g) packages spinach, well washed and drained
½ cup	(125 ml) grated Parmesan cheese
¼ cup	(50 ml) olive oil
¼ tsp	(1 ml) nutmeg
½ cup	(125 ml) grated Romano cheese
1 tbsp	(15 ml) melted butter
	extra butter
	salt and pepper

Mix flour, salt, paprika, ginger and celery seed together in bowl.

Whisk in eggs until throughly blended. Add beer and whisk again. Stir in 3 tbsp (45 ml) melted butter.

Pass batter through medium-fine sieve (holes must be large enough for celery seed) into clean bowl.

Pour in milk and mix well. Refrigerate 2 hours uncovered.

Remove batter from refrigerator and mix well. If too thick, add a bit of milk.

Spread small amount of butter on crêpe pan with paper towel. Place pan over medium-high heat and when butter heats wipe off excess with paper towel.

Pour small ladle of batter on tilted crêpe pan and rotate to completely coat bottom. Allow excess batter to drip back into bowl.

Cook crêpe over medium-high heat until brown — about 1 minute. Then using long spatula knife turn crêpe over and cook other side about the same time.

After each crêpe, wipe pan with lightly buttered paper towel. Adjust heat as necessary to maintain an even temperature for all the crêpes.

Set cooked crêpes aside.

Steam spinach 3 minutes. Squeeze out excess liquid by pressing with spoon. Blend 2 minutes in food processor.

Add Parmesan cheese and blend 1 minute; season well.

Add olive oil through top in food processor while it is mixing. Correct seasoning and add nutmeg.

Lay desired amount of crêpes flat on cutting board. Spread puréed spinach over each crêpe but keep some filling for decoration.

Roll crêpes and place on cookie sheet. Sprinkle with Romano cheese and 1 tbsp (15 ml) melted butter. Broil several minutes in oven.

Decorate crêpes with reserved spinach filling.

Mix flour, salt, paprika, ginger and celery seed together in bowl.

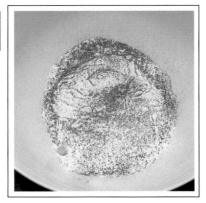

Whisk in eggs until thoroughly blended.

Cook crêpe over medium-high heat until brown — about 1 minute. Then using long spatula knife turn crêpe over.

Cook other side of crêpe about the same length of time.

Crab Vol-au-Vent

(serves 4-6)

1 SERVING	537 CALORIES	26g CARBOHYDRATE
16g PROTEIN	41g FAT	trace FIBER

3 tbsp	(45 ml) butter
1	shallot, chopped
½	celery stalk, chopped
8	large mushrooms, chopped
¼ tsp	(1 ml) anise
¼ tsp	(1 ml) paprika
2 tbsp	(30 ml) flour
1½ cups	(375 ml) hot milk
1 tsp	(5 ml) cumin
5 oz	(142 g) can snow crabmeat, drained
12	small vol-au-vent, cooked
1 cup	(250 ml) grated cheddar cheese
	salt and pepper

Heat butter in large skillet. Cook shallot 1 minute.

Add celery, mushrooms, anise, paprika and season well. Continue cooking 2 to 3 minutes over medium heat.

Mix in flour and cook 2 minutes over medium-low heat.

Add milk, mix well and bring to boil. Add cumin and continue cooking 4 to 5 minutes over low heat.

Stir in crab and finish cooking 2 minutes over low heat.

Spoon crab mixture into vol-au-vent set on ovenproof platter. Top with cheese and broil in oven until melted.

Decorate with olives if desired.

Add celery mushrooms, anise, paprika, salt and pepper to shallot in skillet. Continue cooking 2 to 3 minutes.

Add milk, mix well and bring to boil. Add cumin and continue cooking 4 to 5 minutes over low heat.

Mix in flour and cook 2 minutes over medium-low heat.

Stir in crab and finish cooking 2 minutes over low heat.

Scallops in Pastry Shells

(serves 4-6)

1 SERVING	514 CALORIES	27g CARBOHYDRATE
15g PROTEIN	34g FAT	trace FIBER

1 tbsp	(15 ml) butter
½ lb	(250 g) mushrooms, quartered
½ cup	(125 ml) dry white wine
1 tbsp	(15 ml) chopped shallot
1 tbsp	(15 ml) chopped parsley
½ lb	(250 g) scallops, halved
¾ cup	(175 ml) thick white sauce, hot
12	small vol-au-vent or tartlets, cooked and cooled
½ cup	(125 ml) grated Parmesan cheese
	salt and pepper

Heat butter in skillet. Add mushrooms, wine, shallot and parsley; cook 3 to 4 minutes over medium-high heat.

Stir in scallops and continue cooking 2 minutes over medium heat.

Pour in white sauce, season and cook 1 minute.

Place pastry shells on ovenproof platter and fill with scallop mixture. Top with cheese and broil 2 to 3 minutes in oven.

Serve on lettuce leaves if desired.

Mushroom Vol-au-Vent

(serves 4)

1 SERVING	692 CALORIES	27g CARBOHYDRATE
16g PROTEIN	57g FAT	0.5g FIBER

10 oz	(284 g) fine liver pâté
2 tbsp	(30 ml) sour cream
1 tbsp	(15 ml) Dijon mustard
2 tbsp	(30 ml) butter
1	shallot, chopped
1	garlic clove, smashed and chopped
½ lb	(250 g) mushrooms, finely chopped
3 tbsp	(45 ml) ricotta cheese
12	small vol-au-vent, cooked
	dash paprika
	salt and pepper

Blend pâté, sour cream and mustard together in food processor; set aside.

Heat butter in saucepan. Cook shallot and garlic 2 minutes over medium heat.

Add mushrooms and paprika; season well. Continue cooking 4 to 5 minutes.

Stir in cheese, correct seasoning and cook 2 minutes over low heat. Remove saucepan from heat and set aside to cool.

Fill vol-au-vent with cold mushroom mixture and arrange on serving platter.

Spoon pâté mixture into pastry bag fitted with plain nozzle. Decorate the tops of vol-au-vent. Keep leftover pâté for spreading on crackers.

Garnish with watercress and quartered black olives if desired.

Asparagus Pastry Bites

(serves 8-10)

1 SERVING	558 CALORIES	46g CARBOHYDRATE
9g PROTEIN	38g FAT	0.7g FIBER

3 tbsp	(45 ml) butter
1 tbsp	(15 ml) green peppercorns, mashed
1	red pepper, diced
1	green onion, sliced
1 tsp	(5 ml) chopped jalapeno pepper
3 tbsp	(45 ml) flour
1½ cups	(375 ml) hot milk
1 tsp	(5 ml) fennel seed
2	bunches asparagus, tips cooked and diced
24	tartlets, cooked and cooled
½ cup	(125 ml) grated cheddar cheese
	salt and pepper

Heat butter in skillet. Cook mashed peppercorns, red pepper, green onion and jalapeno pepper 3 minutes over medium heat.

Mix in flour and continue cooking 2 minutes over low heat.

Pour in milk, add fennel seed and season well. Mix and continue cooking 5 to 6 minutes over low heat.

Stir in asparagus, season and simmer 2 minutes.

Place tartlets on ovenproof platter and fill with asparagus mixture. Top with cheese and broil in oven until melted.

Serve on a bed of alfalfa sprouts if desired.

Vegetable Tartlets

(serves 4)

1 SERVING	569 CALORIES	40g CARBOHYDRATE
10g PROTEIN	40g FAT	0.6g FIBER

2 tbsp	(30 ml) butter
2	shallots, finely chopped
1	garlic clove, smashed and chopped
½ lb	(250 g) mushrooms, chopped
1 cup	(250 ml) white sauce, heated
8	tartlets, cooked
¼ cup	(50 ml) grated Parmesan cheese
	salt and pepper
	dash nutmeg

Heat butter in saucepan. Cook shallots and garlic 2 minutes over low heat.

Season and add mushrooms and nutmeg; cook 4 to 5 minutes over medium-high heat.

Pour in white sauce and continue cooking 2 to 3 minutes over medium heat.

Spoon mixture into tartlets set on cookie sheet. Add cheese and broil 3 minutes in oven.

Shrimp and Mushroom Tartlets

(serves 4)

1 SERVING	713 CALORIES	43g CARBOHYDRATE
31g PROTEIN	47g FAT	0.7g FIBER

2 tbsp	(30 ml) butter
18	mushrooms, diced
1	shallot, chopped
1 tbsp	(15 ml) curry powder
¾ lb	(375 g) cooked shrimp, diced
1½ cups	(375 ml) white sauce, heated
8	tartlets, cooked
½ cup	(125 ml) grated Gruyère cheese
	salt and pepper

Heat butter in frying pan over medium heat. Cook mushrooms and shallot 4 minutes.

Season and add curry powder and shrimp; continue cooking 1 minute.

Pour in sauce, mix well and cook 1 minute.

Fill tartlets with mixture and top with cheese. Broil 2 to 3 minutes in oven and serve.

Spinach-Stuffed Mushrooms

(serves 6-8)

1 SERVING	233 CALORIES	14g CARBOHYDRATE
12g PROTEIN	16g FAT	1.0g FIBER

3 tbsp	(45 ml) butter
1 lb	(500 g) spinach, cooked, chopped and well drained
2	garlic cloves, smashed and chopped
3 tbsp	(45 ml) flour
1½ cups	(375 ml) hot milk
¼ tsp	(1 ml) nutmeg
1¼ cups	(300 ml) grated mozzarella cheese
2 lb	(900 g) mushroom caps, cleaned
2 tbsp	(30 ml) melted butter
	salt and pepper
	juice ½ lemon
	dash paprika

Place 3 tbsp (45 ml) butter in large skillet and heat. When melted, add spinach and garlic; cook 3 to 4 minutes over medium-high heat.

Mix in flour and continue cooking 2 to 3 minutes over low heat while mixing constantly.

Pour in milk and season with nutmeg, salt and pepper; mix well. Add ½ cup (125 ml) cheese, mix and cook 2 to 3 minutes over medium heat.

Set mushroom caps on ovenproof serving platter; sprinkle with lemon juice, paprika and 2 tbsp (30 ml) melted butter. Broil 5 minutes in oven.

Fill mushroom caps with spinach stuffing and top with remaining cheese. Finish broiling about 5 minutes or until cheese starts to brown.

Vegetable Artichoke Bottoms

(serves 4)

1 SERVING	223 CALORIES	20g CARBOHYDRATE
5g PROTEIN	15g FAT	.4g FIBER

8	artichoke bottoms
1 tbsp	(15 ml) lemon juice
2 tbsp	(30 ml) olive oil
¼ tsp	(1 ml) Tabasco sauce
1	green pepper, diced small
1	carrot, pared and diced small
1	yellow pepper, diced small
⅓	celery stalk, diced small
3 tbsp	(45 ml) mayonnaise
¼ tsp	(1 ml) Worcestershire sauce
	salt and pepper

Place artichoke bottoms in bowl; sprinkle with lemon juice, oil, Tabasco sauce, salt and pepper. Marinate 30 minutes.

Place remaining vegetables in another bowl. Add mayonnaise, Worcestershire sauce, salt and pepper; mix well.

Fill artichoke bottoms with vegetable mixture and serve.

Fancy Artichoke Bottoms

(serves 4)

1 SERVING	378 CALORIES	25g CARBOHYDRATE
18g PROTEIN	26g FAT	5.0g FIBER

12	stuffed green olives, chopped
12	pitted black olives, chopped
4 oz	(113 g) can small shrimp, drained and rinsed
1 tsp	(5 ml) chopped parsley
1	celery stalk, chopped
½	pickled banana pepper, chopped
3 tbsp	(45 ml) mayonnaise
¼ cup	(50 ml) water
1 tbsp	(15 ml) butter
10	artichoke bottoms
10	small squares mozzarella cheese
	salt and pepper
	juice ½ lemon

Mix both olives, shrimp, parsley, celery, banana pepper and mayonnaise together. Correct seasoning and add extra mayonnaise if desired.

Place water, butter, artichoke bottoms and lemon juice in saucepan; bring to boil. Remove saucepan from heat and let stand 2 to 3 minutes on counter.

Remove artichoke bottoms from pan and transfer to ovenproof serving platter. Fill each with shrimp stuffing and top with squares of mozzarella cheese.

Broil about 2 to 3 minutes in oven or until cheese melts. If desired sprinkle with paprika for decoration.

Shrimp-Stuffed Eggs

(serves 6)

1 SERVING	280 CALORIES	1g CARBOHYDRATE
16g PROTEIN	23g FAT	-- FIBER

6	large eggs
4 oz	(113 g) can small shrimp, drained and rinsed
1 tsp	(5 ml) chopped parsley
2 tbsp	(30 ml) soft butter
3 tbsp	(45 ml) mayonnaise
¼ tsp	(1 ml) paprika
	few drops lemon juice
	few drops Worcestershire sauce
	salt and pepper
	extra chopped parsley
	extra mayonnaise

Cook eggs 10 minutes in gently boiling water. When cooked, drain and cool under running water for at least 3 to 4 minutes.

Peel eggs and cut in half, either lengthwise or widthwise.

Carefully remove yolks and place in sieve set over bowl. Force through with pestle and be sure to scrape the bottom of sieve to gather all the yolks. Set aside in bowl.

Pat shrimp dry with paper towel. Place in food processor along with parsley; purée.

Transfer shrimp to bowl containing sieved yolks. Add butter and mix well.

Stir in mayonnaise until well incorporated. Season with paprika, lemon juice, Worcestershire sauce, salt and pepper. Mix well with spatula.

Arrange the egg white halves on plate. Decorate several by coating tops in mayonnaise then dipping in chopped parsley.

Spoon shrimp filling into pastry bag fitted with large star nozzle. Force into egg white halves and, if desired, decorate with a bit of caviar.

After eggs have cooled for at least 3 to 4 minutes in cold water, peel away shells.

With pestle, force egg yolks through sieve into bowl.

Cut eggs in half, either lengthwise or widthwise.

Purée shrimp with parsley in food processor.

Vegetables with Cheese Dip

(serves 6-8)

1 SERVING	255 CALORIES	29g CARBOHYDRATE
16g PROTEIN	12g FAT	4.0g FIBER

6 oz	(170 g) blue cheese, in chuncks
1 tsp	(5 ml) Worcestershire sauce
½ cup	(125 ml) sour cream
¼ tsp	(1 ml) paprika
2 tbsp	(30 ml) caviar
1	head broccoli, flowerets blanched

2	carrots, pared, cut in sticks, and blanched if desired
6	green onion sticks
1	zucchini, peeled and in sticks
1	apple, cored and in wedges
1	celery stalk, in sticks
1	green pepper, sliced
	salt and pepper
	few leaves Boston lettuce

Place cheese and Worcestershire sauce in food processor; blend until puréed.

Add sour cream and paprika; continue blending until very smooth. Use spatula several times to clean sides of bowl.

Add caviar and blend another 30 seconds. Season with some salt and plenty of pepper.

Arrange lettuce leaves in middle of large serving platter. Spoon cheese dip over leaves and surround with vegetable and apple sticks.

Although the broccoli should be blanched it is a matter of taste as to whether or not you blanch the carrots.

Place cheese and Worcestershire sauce in food processor; blend until puréed.

Add sour cream and paprika; continue blending until very smooth. Use spatula several times to clean sides of bowl.

Add caviar and blend another 30 seconds. Season with some salt and plenty of pepper.

Spicy Dip for Vegetables

(serves 4)

1 RECIPE	948 CALORIES	13g CARBOHYDRATE
21g PROTEIN	92g FAT	1.0g FIBER

1 tsp	(5 ml) strong mustard
½ lb	(250 g) cream cheese
½ cup	(125 ml) finely chopped red pepper
½ tsp	(2 ml) cumin
1	garlic clove, smashed and chopped
1 tbsp	(15 ml) sour cream
1 tsp	(5 ml) finely chopped chives
¼ tsp	(1 ml) paprika
¼ tsp	(1 ml) celery seed
	few drops lemon juice
	salt and pepper
	assorted vegetable sticks

Blend mustard and cream cheese in food processor until smooth.

Add red pepper, cumin, garlic and sour cream; mix well.

Stir in chives, paprika, celery seed, lemon juice; season very well and blend together.

Serve with assorted vegetable sticks.

Versatile Cheese Dip

(serves 4)

1 RECIPE	1997 CALORIES	6g CARBOHYDRATE
65g PROTEIN	192g FAT	-- FIBER

½ lb	(250 g) strong cheddar cheese
¼ cup	(50 ml) sour cream
¼ lb	(125 g) soft butter
1 tbsp	(15 ml) finely chopped chives
1 tbsp	(15 ml) finely chopped parsley
	salt and pepper
	few drops Tabasco sauce
	few drops Worcestershire sauce
	assorted crackers

Blend cheese in food processor until quite smooth.

Add sour cream and butter; mix again until incorporated.

Add chives, parsley, salt, pepper, Tabasco and Worcestershire; blend again.

Serve dip on crackers.

Chicken Liver Appetizer

(serves 4)

1 SERVING	312 CALORIES	9g CARBOHYDRATE
34g PROTEIN	14g FAT	0.6g FIBER

1	head Boston lettuce
2 tbsp	(30 ml) olive oil
1 lb	(500 g) fresh chicken livers, cleaned, halved and fat trimmed
2	garlic cloves, smashed and chopped
1	onion, thinly sliced
3	anchovy filets, chopped
2 tbsp	(30 ml) capers
¼ tsp	(1 ml) sage
1½ cups	(375 ml) chicken stock, heated
1 tbsp	(15 ml) cornstarch
3 tbsp	(45 ml) cold water
	salt and pepper

Wash and dry lettuce; arrange leaves like baskets on four individual plates. Set aside.

Heat oil in frying pan. Cook livers, garlic and onion 3 to 4 minutes over medium heat; season well.

Stir in anchovies, capers and sage; continue cooking 1 minute.

Pour in chicken stock and bring to boil. Mix cornstarch with water; incorporate into sauce and cook 1 minute over low heat.

Spoon mixture into lettuce baskets and serve immediately.

DESSERTS

Desserts

«If I had to live the rest of my life as a food, I would choose to be a lone strawberry, covered ever so delicately in smooth chocolate sauce, set atop the highest mound of swirled vanilla ice cream surrounded by a tiny sea of colored sprinkles.»

Anonymous

It's a fact that no matter how hard we try to resist the temptation, desserts in their many forms and disguises win the tug-of-war almost every time!

For some it may be the cool elegance of a parfait, assembled so neatly in a tall, frosty glass that makes their eyes sparkle. For others, a generous portion of rich chocolate cake smothered in fluffy, cognac-laced whipped cream might be the ultimate reward. Whatever your enthusiasm, this collection of fruit and dessert recipes will surpass anything your palate has experienced before. You will discover the natural goodness of exotic fruit in recipes such as Mango Mousse and Passion Fruit Cream Dessert, and devour such favorites as Shortbread Cookies and Almond Brownies. And for those who relish a mysterious tinge to their cookery, you can try Apple Galette and Cherry Clafoutis.

Before reading on, remember one thing: desserts are not just another course — they are extra-special and need your complete concentration. So put your whole heart into the preparation of these recipes and no cutting corners — they will turn out every bit as sumptuous as you imagined!

Chocolate Frosting

¼ cup (50 ml)	248 CALORIES	35g CARBOHYDRATE
2g PROTEIN	10g FAT	0.2g FIBER

4 oz	(125 g) unsweetened chocolate
2¼ cups	(550 ml) icing sugar
3 tbsp	(45 ml) hot rum
2	egg yolks
¼ cup	(50 ml) softened unsalted butter

Place chocolate in stainless steel bowl, set over saucepan half-filled with boiling water. Melt.

Remove bowl from heat and add icing sugar. Incorporate using electric beater.

Add hot rum and mix well with spatula.

Add egg yolks, one at a time, mixing well between each.

Add butter and mix very well with spatula or electric beater if necessary. Consistency should be smooth.

When cool, spread frosting over almost any type of cake.

Chocolate Sundae

(serves 4)

1 SERVING	598 CALORIES	55g CARBOHYDRATE
10g PROTEIN	37g FAT	0.9g FIBER

4 oz	(125 g) unsweetened chocolate
½ cup	(125 ml) granulated sugar
1 tbsp	(15 ml) maple syrup
¼ cup	(50 ml) water
2 tbsp	(30 ml) rum
½ cup	(125 ml) heavy cream
	vanilla ice cream
	chopped walnuts

Place chocolate in stainless steel bowl set over saucepan half-filled with boiling water and melt.

Remove bowl from heat and set aside.

Place sugar, maple syrup and water in saucepan. Bring to boil and continue cooking 2-3 minutes over medium heat.

Remove saucepan from heat and let cool slightly.

When sugar-syrup mixture is lukewarm, add rum and mix well.

Add melted chocolate and mix well. Slowly pour in cream while whisking constantly.

Pour chocolate sauce into bowl and refrigerate until cold.

Serve with vanilla ice cream and decorate with chopped walnuts.

Chocolate Layer Cake

(serves 8-10)

1 SERVING	479 CALORIES	57g CARBOHYDRATE
7g PROTEIN	25g FAT	0.4g FIBER

2 cups	(500 ml) pastry flour
1¾ cups	(425 ml) granulated sugar
⅔ cup	(150 ml) unsweetened cocoa
1 tsp	(5 ml) baking soda
1 tbsp	(15 ml) baking powder
¾ cup	(175 ml) all-vegetable shortening
1 cup	(250 ml) milk
3	eggs
	pinch salt
	whipped cream
	shaved chocolate

Preheat oven to 325°F (160°C). Butter 9 inch (23 cm) spring-form cake pan.

Sift flour, sugar, cocoa, baking soda, baking powder and salt into large bowl.

Add shortening and incorporate with pastry blender.

Pour in milk and beat well with electric beater until batter is smooth.

Add eggs, one at a time, beating 30 seconds after each addition.

Pour batter into prepared cake pan and bake 65 minutes or until toothpick inserted comes out clean.

When cake is cooked, remove from oven and let cool 10-15 minutes in pan.

Carefully unmold and let cool completely on wire rack at room temperature.

Slice cake into two or three layers and ice with whipped cream. Decorate with shaved chocolate.

Chocolate Mousse

(serves 4-6)

1 SERVING	376 CALORIES	9g CARBOHYDRATE
9g PROTEIN	34g FAT	0.5g FIBER

6 oz	(170 g) semi-sweet chocolate
3 tbsp	(45 ml) unsalted butter
¼ cup	(50 ml) water
4	egg yolks
2 tbsp	(30 ml) Tia Maria liqueur
4	egg whites, beaten stiff
½ cup	(125 ml) heavy cream, whipped
	shaved chocolate for decoration

Place chocolate, butter and water in saucepan and cook over low heat to melt. Mix constantly with wooden spoon.

Remove from heat and transfer chocolate to bowl.

Add egg yolks, one at a time, mixing between additions with whisk.

Add Tia Maria and continue whisking several seconds.

Incorporate egg whites using spatula, being careful not to overmix.

Add whipped cream and incorporate with spatula.

Mix well with whisk for several seconds.

Pour into glass bowls and refrigerate 4 hours before serving. Decorate with shaved chocolate.

Chocolate Berry Mousse

(serves 4-6)

1 SERVING	321 CALORIES	24g CARBOHYDRATE
3g PROTEIN	24g FAT	0.5g FIBER

3	squares semi-sweet chocolate
1	egg
½ cup	(125 ml) puréed strawberries
1 cup	(250 ml) hot heavy cream
3	egg whites
½ cup	(125 ml) sugar

Melt chocolate in stainless steel bowl set over saucepan half-filled with hot water, placed over medium heat.

Remove bowl from pan; mix in whole egg with whisk.

Add puréed strawberries and mix well. Pour into food processor and blend 1 minute.

Blend in hot cream and continue processing until well incorporated. Refrigerate to cool.

Beat egg whites until stiff. Slowly add sugar while beating until incorporated.

Fold egg whites into chilled mousse batter and spoon into glass dishes.

Refrigerate before serving.

Strawberry and Raspberry Mousse

(serves 6-8)

1 SERVING	226 CALORIES	28g CARBOHYDRATE
4g PROTEIN	11g FAT	1.6g FIBER

1½	small envelopes unflavored gelatine
¼ cup	(50 ml) hot water
⅔ cup	(150 ml) granulated sugar
3 tbsp	(45 ml) maple syrup
½ cup	(125 ml) boiling water
2 cups	(500 ml) fresh strawberries, hulled
1 cup	(250 ml) fresh raspberries
1 tbsp	(15 ml) grated lemon rind
5	egg whites
1 cup	(250 ml) heavy cream, whipped

Grease 8 cup (2 L) soufflé mold with oil.

Sprinkle gelatine over ¼ cup (50 ml) hot water placed in small bowl; set aside.

Place half of sugar, maple syrup and boiling water in saucepan. Bring to boil and continue cooking 2 minutes over medium heat.

Stir in both fruits and lemon rind; continue cooking 3 minutes.

Transfer contents to food processor and purée.

Replace mixture in saucepan and mix in gelatine; cook 1 minute.

Pour fruit mixture into bowl and refrigerate.

When fruit mixture starts to set, begin preparing egg whites by placing them in bowl.

Beat with electric beater until they peak. Add remaining sugar and continue beating 30 seconds.

Fold into fruit mixture using spatula.

Incorporate whipped cream and pour mixture into prepared mold. Refrigerate 8 hours.

Unmold and serve with a fruit sauce.

Strawberry Omelet

(serves 4)

1 SERVING	369 CALORIES	28g CARBOHYDRATE
13g PROTEIN	23g FAT	1.8g FIBER

2 cups	(500 ml) strawberries, hulled and sliced in 3
4 tbsp	(60 ml) butter
3 tbsp	(45 ml) sugar
1 cup	(250 ml) orange juice
2 tsp	(10 ml) cornstarch
3 tbsp	(45 ml) cold water
8	eggs, well beaten

Set strawberries aside in bowl.

Heat half of butter in frying pan. Add 2 tbsp (30 ml) sugar and cook 2 minutes over high heat while stirring constantly.

Continue stirring, pour in orange juice and bring to boil. Cook 2 more minutes over high heat.

Mix cornstarch with water; stir into sauce. Cook 1 minute over high heat, stirring occasionally.

Pour over strawberries and let stand 15 minutes.

Heat remaining butter in large nonstick frying pan or omelet pan. When hot, pour in eggs and cook 30 seconds over high heat while mixing with fork.

Continue cooking another 30 seconds or until top is set.

Add half of strawberries and cook another 20 seconds.

Carefully roll omelet while tilting pan, then turn onto ovenproof serving platter.

Sprinkle with remaining sugar and broil several minutes in oven.

Meanwhile, heat remaining strawberries in small saucepan.

When ready to serve, pour strawberries over omelet and garnish with shredded coconut if desired.

Using spatula, cream together the butter and brown sugar. **1**

Add first **2** egg and beat well with electric beater.

Add second egg and 2 tbsp (30 ml) of flour to bowl; beat well with electric beater. **3**

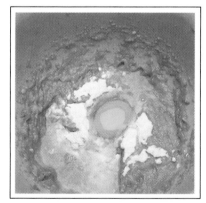

Add last **4** egg, flour and beat again. Pour in coffee and rum; beat well. Pour in cream, beat and add cherries.

Cherry Clafoutis

(serves 4-6)

1 SERVING	362 CALORIES	42g CARBOHYDRATE
6g PROTEIN	19g FAT	0.1g FIBER

¼ cup	(50 ml) softened butter
½ cup	(125 ml) brown sugar
3	eggs
½ cup	(125 ml) all-purpose flour
1 tsp	(5 ml) baking powder
¼ cup	(50 ml) strong black coffee
2 tbsp	(30 ml) rum
1 cup	(250 ml) light cream
14 oz	(398 ml) can pitted Bing cherries, well drained
1 tbsp	(15 ml) granulated sugar
	whipped cream

Preheat oven to 350°F (180°C). Butter 10 inch (25 cm) glass pie plate.

Place butter and brown sugar in bowl; using spatula cream together.

Add first egg and beat well with electric beater.

Sift flour and baking powder together.

Add second egg and 2 tbsp (30 ml) of flour to bowl; beat well with electric beater.

Add last egg and rest of flour; beat again.

Pour in coffee and rum; beat well. Pour in cream, beat and add cherries.

Pour batter into prepared pie plate; bake 45-50 minutes or until toothpick inserted comes out clean.

About 5 minutes before clafoutis is cooked, sprinkle with a bit of granulated sugar and resume cooking.

Serve warm with whipped cream.

Bavarian Cream with Cherries

(serves 6-8)

1 SERVING	260 CALORIES	22g CARBOHYDRATE
5g PROTEIN	17g FAT	0.3g FIBER

6	egg yolks
½ cup	(125 ml) sugar
2 cups	(500 ml) hot milk
1 tbsp	(15 ml) vanilla
2 tbsp	(30 ml) gelatine
¼ cup	(50 ml) cold water
1 cup	(250 ml) heavy cream
2 cups	(500 ml) pitted cherries

Place egg yolks and sugar in stainless steel bowl. Mix together with electric beater for 2 minutes.

Add hot milk and vanilla; mix well to incorporate.

Have ready a saucepan filled with hot water placed over medium heat. Set bowl over saucepan and cook cream until it coats the back of a spoon. Stir constantly.

Remove bowl from saucepan and set aside. Dilute gelatine in cold water; let stand 2 minutes.

Incorporate diluted gelatine into cooked cream. Set bowl over larger bowl filled with ice water.

As soon as the cream mixture starts to set, whip the heavy cream.

Incorporate cherries, then whipping cream into gelling mixture. Pour into oiled mold and refrigerate overnight.

Cottage Sundaes

(serves 4)

1 SERVING	305 CALORIES	38g CARBOHYDRATE
20g PROTEIN	8g FAT	0.9g FIBER

¾ lb	(375 g) pitted cherries
¼ cup	(50 ml) sugar
¼ cup	(50 ml) water
1 tbsp	(15 ml) grated lemon rind
1 tsp	(5 ml) cornstarch
2 tbsp	(30 ml) cold water
2½ cups	(625 ml) cottage cheese
	whipped cream for topping
	maraschino cherries for decoration

Place cherries, sugar, ¼ cup (50 ml) water and lemon rind in saucepan. Cover and cook 2 to 3 minutes over medium heat, stirring occasionally.

Mix cornstarch with 2 tbsp (30 ml) water; stir into cherry sauce and continue cooking 1 minute. Remove pan from heat and let cool.

To build sundaes, alternate cherry sauce and cottage cheese in tall dessert glasses.

Top with whipped cream and decorate with maraschino cherries if desired.

Pastry Cream

¼ cup (50 ml)	81 CALORIES	8g CARBOHYDRATE
3g PROTEIN	4g FAT	0g FIBER

4	egg yolks
¼ cup	(50 ml) granulated sugar
4 tbsp	(60 ml) flour
2 cups	(500 ml) hot milk
2 tbsp	(30 ml) slivered almonds

Place egg yolks in bowl. Add sugar and beat well with whisk.

Add flour, mix with whisk, and pour in milk. Continue mixing until well incorporated.

Stir in almonds and pour mixture into saucepan. Cook over medium heat, stirring constantly, until mixture reaches boiling point.

Continue cooking 2 minutes or until cream starts to thicken.

Pour cream into bowl and let cool slightly. Cover with plastic wrap (it must touch surface of cream) and refrigerate until cold.

Use this pastry cream recipe in a variety of dessert dishes.

Pears with Pastry Cream

(serves 6)

1 SERVING	179 CALORIES	36g CARBOHYDRATE
6g PROTEIN	1g FAT	4.8g FIBER

4 cups	(1 L) water
1½ cups	(375 ml) granulated sugar
1 tbsp	(15 ml) lemon juice
2 tbsp	(30 ml) light rum
6	pears, cored and peeled
1½ cups	(375 ml) pastry cream
4	egg whites, beaten stiff
¼ cup	(50 ml) hot rum

Place water, sugar, lemon juice and light rum in saucepan; bring to boil and continue cooking 4 minutes over medium heat.

Add whole pears and reduce heat. Cook 6 to 7 minutes over low heat.

Remove saucepan from heat and let pears cool in syrup.

Pour pastry cream into ovenproof baking dish. Arrange pears in cream and decorate sides of dish with beaten egg whites. It is best to use pastry bag and nozzle for this.

Broil 2 minutes or until lightly browned.

Remove from oven, pour in hot rum and flambé. Serve immediately.

Sugared Pears

(serves 4)

1 SERVING	514 CALORIES	87g CARBOHYDRATE
3g PROTEIN	17g FAT	7.2g FIBER

½ cup	(125 ml) sugar
2 cups	(500 ml) water
½ cup	(125 ml) orange juice
4	large pears, cored, peeled and halved
1 tbsp	(15 ml) cornstarch
3 tbsp	(45 ml) cold water
3 tbsp	(45 ml) shredded coconut
1 cup	(250 ml) crushed macaroons
1 tbsp	(15 ml) butter

Place sugar, 2 cups (500 ml) water and orange juice in saucepan. Bring to boil over medium heat and continue cooking 3 to 4 minutes.

Add pears and cook 3 minutes over low heat.

Remove saucepan from heat and let pears stand in syrup 5 to 6 minutes.

Remove pears from saucepan and place in baking dish; set aside.

Replace saucepan of syrup on stove; cook 4 to 5 minutes over high heat.

Mix cornstarch with 3 tbsp (45 ml) cold water; stir into syrup and continue cooking 1 minute over low heat.

Pour half of syrup over pears. Top with coconut and macaroons; dot with butter. Broil 3 minutes in oven.

Orange Pears

(serves 4)

1 SERVING	181 CALORIES	42g CARBOHYDRATE
0g PROTEIN	0g FAT	4.7g FIBER

½ cup	(125 ml) sugar
2½ cups	(625 ml) water
1 tsp	(5 ml) vanilla
4	Bartlett pears
½ cup	(125 ml) orange juice
2 tbsp	(30 ml) grated orange rind
1 tsp	(5 ml) cornstarch
2 tbsp	(30 ml) cold water
2 tbsp	(30 ml) orange liqueur

Place sugar, 2½ cups (625 ml) water and vanilla in saucepan. Bring to boil.

Meanwhile, carefully core pears without removing stem. Peel and place pears in syrup mixture in saucepan.

Cook 4 to 5 minutes over low heat. Remove saucepan from heat and let pears cool in syrup.

Remove pears and set on serving platter; set aside.

Remove 1 cup (250 ml) of syrup and transfer to clean saucepan. Bring to boil.

Add orange juice and rind; bring to boil again and continue cooking 3 minutes over high heat.

Mix cornstarch with 2 tbsp (30 ml) water; stir into orange syrup and cook 1 minute.

Mix in liqueur and pour sauce over pears. Cool before serving.

Buckwheat Crêpes with Peaches

(serves 6-8)

1 SERVING	264 CALORIES	32g CARBOHYDRATE
5g PROTEIN	13g FAT	1.1g FIBER

1 cup	(250 ml) buckwheat flour
¼ cup	(50 ml) all-purpose flour
½ tsp	(2 ml) salt
1½ cups	(375 ml) milk
3	beaten eggs
2 tbsp	(30 ml) melted butter
4 tbsp	(60 ml) butter
4 tbsp	(60 ml) brown sugar
5	large peaches, blanched, peeled and sliced
3 tbsp	(45 ml) rum
	icing sugar

Stir both flours and salt together in large bowl. Mix in milk until well incorporated, then add eggs; mix vigorously with whisk. Pass through sieve.

Stir in melted butter and refrigerate batter 1 hour.

Lightly butter crêpe pan and place over medium-high heat. Whisk batter well.

As butter melts, wipe off excess with paper towel. When pan is hot, pour in small ladle of batter and rotate pan to completely coat bottom.

Replace pan over heat and cook crêpe 1 minute until lightly browned.

Turn crêpe over (use long spatula rather than flipping) and continue cooking 1 minute.

Repeat for rest of batter, stacking cooked crêpes on large plate. During cooking wipe pan with butter as needed and monitor heat to keep it at medium-high.

For crêpe filling, heat 4 tbsp (60 ml) butter in saucepan. Add brown sugar and peaches; cook 2 minutes over medium-high heat.

Mix in rum and spoon peaches on middle of flat crêpes (keep some peaches for garnish). Fold crêpes into 4 and place on ovenproof platter.

Sprinkle with icing sugar and broil several minutes.

Serve with remaining peach slices.

Delicious Fruit Trifle

(serves 10-12)

1 SERVING	305 CALORIES	43g CARBOHYDRATE
5g PROTEIN	11g FAT	2.1g FIBER

4	egg yolks
½ cup	(125 ml) sugar
1 cup	(250 ml) boiled milk, tepid
1 tbsp	(15 ml) dark rum
1 cup	(250 ml) mixed berries
2 cups	(500 ml) blueberries
2 cups	(500 ml) diced watermelon
1	small angel or sponge cake, sliced into 3 layers
⅓ cup	(75 ml) light rum
3 cups	(750 ml) strawberries, hulled and halved
2½ cups	(625 ml) whipped cream

Place egg yolks and sugar in stainless steel bowl; beat together with electric beater until mixture forms ribbons.

Mix in milk until well incorporated. Stir in dark rum and set bowl over saucepan half-filled with hot water. Cook over medium heat while stirring constantly with wooden spoon. Do not boil.

When cream coats the back of the spoon, remove bowl from saucepan and set aside to cool.

Toss mixed berries, blueberries and watermelon together in small bowl.

When custard cream has cooled, begin building trifle in large glass bowl or substitute. Set one layer of cake in bottom followed by sprinkling of rum.

Continue with layer of strawberries, whipped cream, custard cream and mixed fruit.

Repeat layers until ingredients are used, ending with a generous topping of whipped cream.

If desired decorate trifle with glaze.

Fruit in the Shell

(serves 2)

1 SERVING	390 CALORIES	79g CARBOHYDRATE
2g PROTEIN	7g FAT	8.5g FIBER

1	small pear, peeled and diced
1	nectarine, diced
1	slice watermelon, seeded and diced
12	strawberries, hulled and halved
1	kiwi fruit, peeled and sliced
6-8	blackberries
¼ cup	(50 ml) blueberries
1 tbsp	(15 ml) soft butter
2 tbsp	(30 ml) sugar
3 tbsp	(45 ml) rum
1	pineapple
	juice 1 orange
	juice 1 lemon
	several pitted cherries
	few whole strawberries for decoration

Place pear, nectarine, watermelon, halved strawberries, kiwi fruit, blackberries and blueberries in mixing bowl; set aside.

Heat butter in frying pan over medium heat. Add sugar and cook 3 minutes over high heat while stirring constantly — mixture should become golden in color.

Add orange and lemon juices; mix well. Stir in rum and cook 3 minutes.

Pour syrup over fruit in bowl, toss and marinate 30 minutes.

Slice pineapple in half, lengthwise. Using sharp knife and spoon, cut and scoop out insides from shells. Reserve pineapple flesh for other recipes.

When fruit is ready, spoon into hollowed shells and decorate with cherries and whole strawberries.

Fruit à la Mode

(serves 4)

1 SERVING	398 CALORIES	63g CARBOHYDRATE
4g PROTEIN	13g FAT	4.2g FIBER

¼ cup	(50 ml) sugar
1 tsp	(5 ml) vanilla
1 cup	(250 ml) water
4	large peaches, blanched, peeled and halved
1 cup	(250 ml) strawberries, hulled and halved
1 cup	(250 ml) raspberries
2 tbsp	(30 ml) fine sugar
2 tbsp	(30 ml) Cointreau
4	large scoops vanilla ice cream
	whipped cream

Place sugar, vanilla and water in saucepan; bring to boil. Continue cooking 2 to 3 minutes over medium heat.

Add peaches and cook 2 minutes over medium heat. Remove pan from heat and let fruit cool in syrup.

Purée strawberries and raspberries in food processor. Transfer to nonstick frying pan and stir in fine sugar. Cook 3 minutes over medium heat.

Add liqueur and cook 1 more minute over high heat. Force mixture through sieve into bowl.

Spoon a bit of berry sauce into bottom of glass dessert dishes. Add a half peach and follow with scoop of ice cream.

Cover with another peach half, top with berry sauce and decorate with whipped cream.

Berries and Broiled Cream

(serves 4)

1 SERVING	355 CALORIES	39g CARBOHYDRATE
1g PROTEIN	22g FAT	2.4g FIBER

1 cup	(250 ml) strawberries, hulled and halved
1 cup	(250 ml) raspberries
2	kiwi fruit, peeled and sliced
1 cup	(250 ml) heavy cream, whipped
½ cup	(125 ml) brown sugar
½ cup	(125 ml) hot rum

Divide fruit among 4 individual baking dishes.

Top fruit with whipped cream and sprinkle with brown sugar. Broil for 1 minute in oven.

Remove from oven, sprinkle with rum and flambé.

Cheese Fruitcup

(serves 4)

1 SERVING	348 CALORIES	31g CARBOHYDRATE
5g PROTEIN	23g FAT	2.1g FIBER

2	kiwis, peeled and diced
2	bananas, peeled and sliced
1	apple, cored, peeled and sliced
4 tbsp	(60 ml) yogurt, flavor of your choice
2 tbsp	(30 ml) your preferred liqueur
8 oz	(250 g) package cream cheese, softened
	juice 1 orange

Place kiwis and bananas in food processor and purée.

Add apple and orange juice; continue blending several seconds.

Add yogurt, liqueur and cream cheese; blend well until quite smooth.

Spoon into small cup-like glasses and refrigerate before serving.

Blueberries in Syrup

(serves 4)

1 SERVING	295 CALORIES	46g CARBOHYDRATE
5g PROTEIN	10g FAT	2.1g FIBER

4 tbsp	(60 ml) brown sugar
1 tsp	(5 ml) vanilla
1 tbsp	(15 ml) grated lemon rind
1 tbsp	(15 ml) grated orange rind
1 cup	(250 ml) water
2 cups	(500 ml) blueberries
4	large scoops ice cream

Place sugar, vanilla, fruit rinds and water in saucepan; mix well and bring to boil. Cook 2 to 3 minutes over low heat until syrup thickens.

Stir in blueberries, remove saucepan from heat and let fruit cool in syrup.

Spoon blueberries over ice cream and serve.

Wally's Watermelon Punch

(serves 10-12)

1 SERVING	129 CALORIES	21g CARBOHYDRATE
0g PROTEIN	0g FAT	0.5g FIBER

½	watermelon, seeded and cubed
½ cup	(125 ml) lime juice
1 cup	(250 ml) light rum
4 cups	(1 L) orange juice
1 cup	(250 ml) pineapple juice
½ cup	(125 ml) fine sugar
	plenty of ice

Purée watermelon in food processor. Pass through sieve into large punch bowl.

Add remaining ingredients, mix very well and refrigerate 3 to 4 hours.

If desired, decorate with slices of fruit and serve in a bowl with plenty of ice.

Watermelon Compote

(serves 4)

1 SERVING	129 CALORIES	31g CARBOHYDRATE
1g PROTEIN	0g FAT	1.5g FIBER

¼ cup	(50 ml) brown sugar
½ cup	(125 ml) water
1 tbsp	(15 ml) grated lemon rind
2 cups	(500 ml) diced watermelon
2	large peaches, blanched, peeled and thinly sliced
½ cup	(125 ml) seedless green grapes
	juice 2 limes

Place sugar, water, lemon rind and lime juice in small saucepan. Bring to boil.

Add fruit and mix well; cover and cook 3 to 4 minutes over low heat.

Remove pan from heat and let fruit cool in syrup. Serve over ice cream.

Cantaloupe Tarts *(serves 4)*

1 SERVING	605 CALORIES	71g CARBOHYDRATE
9g PROTEIN	32g FAT	1.4g FIBER

1 cup	(250 ml) milk
1 tbsp	(15 ml) water
1 tsp	(5 ml) Pernod
½ cup	(125 ml) sugar
3	egg yolks
¼ cup	(50 ml) all-purpose flour, sifted
1	small ripe cantaloupe
8	cooked pastry tarts
	green maraschino cherries

Pour milk and water into medium-size saucepan. Bring to boil over medium heat. Stir in Pernod, remove from heat and set aside.

Place sugar and egg yolks in stainless steel bowl. Beat together with electric beater for 3 to 4 minutes or until eggs become foamy and almost white in color.

Mix in flour with whisk until well incorporated.

Gradually pour half of hot milk into bowl containing egg mixture, stirring constantly with whisk. Incorporate well.

Incorporate remaining milk and immediately place bowl over saucepan half-filled with hot water.

Cook over medium heat while whisking constantly until very thick and cream coats the back of a spoon.

Pour cream into clean bowl and let cool. Cover with buttered waxed paper and chill before using.

To prepare tarts, remove all seeds from cantaloupe. Slice into quarters and thinly slice flesh on slight angle.

Spread pastry cream in bottom of cooked tarts and arrange cantaloupe slices decoratively on top.

Serve tarts immediately or glaze if desired. Decorate with green maraschino cherries.

Banana Mousse

(serves 4)

1 SERVING	369 CALORIES	39g CARBOHYDRATE
4g PROTEIN	22g FAT	2.4g FIBER

¼ cup	(50 ml) sugar
⅓ cup	(75 ml) water
4	ripe bananas, peeled and sliced
¼ tsp	(1 ml) cinnamon
3	egg whites, beaten stiff
1 cup	(250 ml) heavy cream, whipped

Cook sugar and water together in saucepan 1 minute over medium heat.

Add bananas and cinnamon; cook 3 minutes over medium-high heat.

Transfer bananas to food processor and blend until puréed. Chill.

Transfer puréed bananas to mixing bowl. Fold in stiff egg whites until well incorporated.

Have whipped cream ready in large bowl. Fold banana mixture into cream using spatula until well incorporated.

Spoon into dessert dishes and chill before serving.

Macaroon Bananas

(serves 4)

1 SERVING	574 CALORIES	73g CARBOHYDRATE
8g PROTEIN	28g FAT	4.9g FIBER

4	large bananas
¼ cup	(50 ml) bourbon
1 tsp	(5 ml) lime juice
2	beaten eggs
1½ cups	(375 ml) crushed macaroons
3 tbsp	(45 ml) butter

Peel bananas and place them on large platter. Add bourbon and lime juice; marinate 1 hour.

Dip bananas in beaten eggs and roll in crushed macaroons.

Heat butter in large frying pan. Add bananas and cook 2 to 3 minutes over medium heat, turning to brown all sides.

If desired, flambé with heated marinade before serving.

Banana Flip

(serves 4)

1 SERVING	224 CALORIES	25g CARBOHYDRATE
4g PROTEIN	12g FAT	1.2g FIBER

2	bananas, peeled
1½ cups	(375 ml) cold milk
1 cup	(250 ml) cold light cream
2 tbsp	(30 ml) maple syrup
¼ cup	(50 ml) dark rum
	few drops lime juice
	orange slices for decoration

Place bananas in blender and purée.

Add milk, cream, maple syrup, rum and lime juice; continue blending until well mixed and frothy.

Pour into tall-stemmed glasses and decorate with orange slices.

Passion Fruit Cream Dessert

(serves 4)

1 SERVING	333 CALORIES	49g CARBOHYDRATE
7g PROTEIN	12g FAT	—g FIBER

4	egg yolks
½ cup	(125 ml) sugar
1 cup	(250 ml) boiled milk, tepid
1 tbsp	(15 ml) rum
4	passion fruits
3 tbsp	(45 ml) heavy cream

Place egg yolks and sugar in stainless steel bowl; beat together with electric beater until mixture forms ribbons.

Mix in milk until well incorporated. Stir in rum and set bowl over saucepan half-filled with hot water. Cook over medium heat while stirring constantly with wooden spoon. Do not boil.

When cream coats the back of the spoon, remove bowl from saucepan and set aside to cool.

Slice passion fruits in half, widthwise. Using spoon, scoop out pulp and seeds and place in blender. Add heavy cream and blend at medium speed for 1 minute.

Pour blended fruit into custard cream and mix. Serve cold in dessert bowls.

Mango Sherbet

1 SERVING	174 CALORIES	40g CARBOHYDRATE
0g PROTEIN	0g FAT	0.9g FIBER

3½ lb	(1.6 kg) ripe mangoes
1 cup	(250 ml) granulated sugar
⅔ cup	(150 ml) water
3 tbsp	(45 ml) white rum
	juice 3 limes

Peel mangoes and slice off flesh from pits. Purée fruit in food processor and transfer to bowl.

Place sugar and water in small saucepan; cook 5 minutes over high heat.

Remove saucepan from heat and let syrup cool.

Add syrup, rum and lime juice to mangoes in bowl; mix well.

Freeze following the directions for your particular brand of ice cream maker.

Mango Salad

(serves 4)

1 SERVING	176 CALORIES	31g CARBOHYDRATE
8g PROTEIN	2g FAT	0.9g FIBER

2	large mangoes
3 tbsp	(45 ml) fine sugar
1-1½ cups	(250-375 ml) cottage cheese
1½ cups	(375 ml) raspberries
	juice 2 limes

Using sharp knife, run blade around mangoes against the large flat pit. Peel one half and slice flesh in wedges. Repeat for other side.

Place all wedges in bowl; add lime juice and sugar. Marinate 30 minutes.

Scoop cottage cheese onto dessert plates or in bowls. Surround with mangoes and top with raspberries. Serve.

Mango Mousse

(serves 4)

1 SERVING	260 CALORIES	35g CARBOHYDRATE
3g PROTEIN	12g FAT	1.4g FIBER

3	mangoes, peeled and sliced
3 cups	(750 ml) water
¼ cup	(50 ml) sugar
½ cup	(125 ml) heavy cream, whipped
3	egg whites, beaten stiff
	juice ½ lemon
	chocolate shavings

Place sliced mangoes in saucepan. Add water, sugar and lemon juice; cook 5 to 6 minutes over medium heat.

Force mixture through sieve into bowl; set aside to cool.

Incorporate whipped cream, then fold in beaten egg whites until well incorporated.

Chill before serving and decorate with chocolate shavings.

Mango and Prosciutto

(serves 4)

1 SERVING	138 CALORIES	23g CARBOHYDRATE
7g PROTEIN	2g FAT	1.4g FIBER

3	mangoes, peeled
¼ lb	(125 g) prosciutto slices
	lime slices
	ground pepper

Slice mangoes into 1 inch (2.5 cm) pieces.

Cut prosciutto slices into 3 and wrap around mango pieces; secure with toothpicks.

Serve with lime slices and season well with pepper.

Raspberry
Rice Pudding

(serves 4-6)

1 SERVING	355 CALORIES	72g CARBOHYDRATE
7g PROTEIN	4g FAT	1.7g FIBER

2½ cups	(625 ml) salted water
1 cup	(250 ml) long grain rice, rinsed
3 cups	(750 ml) milk
1 cup	(250 ml) sugar
1 tsp	(5 ml) vanilla
½ tsp	(2 ml) nutmeg
1½ cups	(375 ml) raspberries

Pour salted water into saucepan and bring to boil. Mix in rice, cover and cook 19 to 21 minutes over low heat.

Add milk, half of sugar, vanilla and nutmeg; bring to boil. Mix rice well and cover saucepan; cook 30 to 35 minutes over low heat. Stir 2 to 3 times.

Transfer cooked rice to 8 cup (2 L) soufflé mold; refrigerate to cool.

Meanwhile, place raspberries and remaining sugar in small saucepan. Partially cover and cook 4 to 5 minutes.

Purée in food processor and spread over rice pudding. Serve.

Chestnut
Parfait

(serves 4)

1 SERVING	395 CALORIES	47g CARBOHYDRATE
7g PROTEIN	20g FAT	0.8g FIBER

⅓ cup	(75 ml) granulated sugar
4	egg yolks
2 tbsp	(30 ml) rum
1 cup	(250 ml) hot milk
¼ cup	(50 ml) candied fruit
1 cup	(250 ml) canned puréed chestnuts
2 cups	(500 ml) whipped cream

Place sugar, egg yolks and rum in bowl. Mix together with electric beater until fluffy — about 2 minutes.

Pour in hot milk and whisk well. Cook cream in double-boiler until it coats the back of a spoon. Whisk constantly!

Stir in candied fruit.

Choose tall dessert glasses and spoon layer of puréed chestnuts in bottom. Follow with layer of custard cream and repeat until ingredients are used.

Top parfaits with whipped cream and if desired decorate with icing.

Place sugar, egg yolks and rum in bowl. **1**

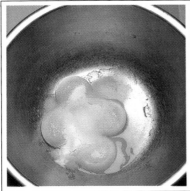

Mix together **2** with electric beater until fluffy — about 2 minutes.

3 Pour in hot milk and whisk well.

4 After cream has cooked, begin layering the puréed chestnuts and custard cream in tall dessert glasses.

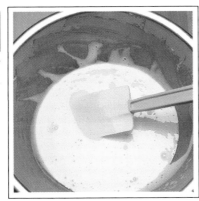

Place flour, ¾ cup (175 ml) butter and cinnamon in bowl.

Add granulated sugar.

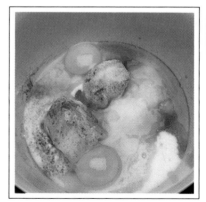 Add 2 eggs and vanilla.

 Incorporate with pastry blender.

Apple Galette

(serves 6-8)

1 SERVING	536 CALORIES	77g CARBOHYDRATE
5g PROTEIN	23g FAT	1.8g FIBER

2 cups	(500 ml) all-purpose flour
¾ cup	(175 ml) softened butter
1 tsp	(5 ml) cinnamon
¾ cup	(175 ml) granulated sugar
2	eggs
1 tsp	(5 ml) vanilla
2 tbsp	(30 ml) cold water
2 tbsp	(30 ml) butter
4	apples, cored, peeled and sliced
⅓ cup	(75 ml) brown sugar
1 tbsp	(15 ml) grated lemon rind
1 cup	(250 ml) icing sugar
2 tbsp	(30 ml) lemon juice
1 tbsp	(15 ml) hot water
	beaten egg

Place flour, ¾ cup (175 ml) butter and cinnamon in bowl. Add granulated sugar, 2 eggs and vanilla; incorporate with pastry blender.

Add cold water and pinch dough to incorporate. Shape into ball and cover with waxed paper; refrigerate 2 hours.

Preheat oven to 350°F (180°C).

When ready to prepare galette, cut dough in half. Roll both on floured surface until about ¼ inch (0.65 cm) thick. Dust with more flour if needed. Place 9 inch (23 cm) plate on dough and trace galettes. Cut away excess dough to form circles.

Place galettes on separate buttered and floured cookie sheets; brush lightly with beaten egg. Bake 10 minutes.

Set aside to cool while you prepare the filling.

Melt 2 tbsp (30 ml) butter in frying pan. Add apples and cook 15 minutes over high heat, stirring frequently.

Sprinkle in brown sugar and lemon rind; continue cooking 3 minutes.

Remove frying pan from heat and set aside to cool.

Meanwhile, prepare icing by placing icing sugar, lemon juice and hot water in small bowl. Mix together.

To assemble dessert, place one galette on bottom of serving platter. Cover with cooled apples and top with second galette. Generously spread lemon icing over top, letting it drip down sides. Decorate with additional colored icings if desired.

Slice (carefully) and serve.

Rhubarb and Raspberry Compote

(serves 4)

1 SERVING	319 CALORIES	64g CARBOHYDRATE
2g PROTEIN	6g FAT	5.3g FIBER

1 cup	(250 ml) sugar
1¼ cups	(300 ml) water
1½ lb	(750 g) diced rhubarb
1¼ cups	(300 ml) raspberries
3 tbsp	(45 ml) grated orange rind
	juice 1 lime
	heavy cream

Place sugar and water in large saucepan. Cook 4 to 5 minutes over medium-low heat or until sugar is melted.

Stir in rhubarb and lime juice; cook 10 minutes over low heat.

Add raspberries and orange rind; mix well. Continue cooking 3 minutes.

Spoon compote into dessert bowls and serve with heavy cream.

Super-Moist Cheesecake

(serves 10-12)

1 SERVING	410 CALORIES	32g CARBOHYDRATE
6g PROTEIN	29g FAT	0.1g FIBER

2	8 oz (250 g) packages cream cheese, softened
½ cup	(125 ml) granulated sugar
3 tbsp	(45 ml) Tia Maria liqueur
2 tbsp	(30 ml) cornstarch
4	egg yolks
1 cup	(250 ml) heavy cream, whipped
4	egg whites, beaten stiff
14 oz	(398 ml) can pitted Bing cherries
¼ cup	(50 ml) granulated sugar
1 tbsp	(15 ml) cornstarch
3 tbsp	(45 ml) cold water
	graham crumb bottom crust, cooked in 10 inch (25 cm) spring-form cake pan

Preheat oven to 300°F (150°C).

Place cheese and ½ cup (125 ml) sugar in bowl of electric mixer. Mix at medium speed until creamed.

Add liqueur and 2 tbsp (30 ml) cornstarch; continue mixing until completely incorporated and smooth.

Add egg yolks and mix very well — about 2 minutes.

Add whipped cream and continue mixing until incorporated.

Remove bowl from mixer and fold in beaten egg whites with spatula. Continue folding until well incorporated.

Pour batter into cake pan prepared with crumb crust and bake 1¼-1½ hours or until toothpick inserted comes out clean.

Remove cake from oven and let cool in pan.

Unmold and refrigerate 1 hour.

Meanwhile, begin preparing topping. Pour cherry juice (set cherries aside) and ¼ cup (50 ml) sugar in small saucepan. Bring to boil and continue cooking 2-3 minutes.

Mix 1 tbsp (15 ml) cornstarch with 3 tbsp (45 ml) cold water; stir into sauce and continue cooking 1 minute over medium heat.

When sauce has thickened enough, stir in cherries and set aside on counter to cool.

Spread cherries over cheesecake, slice and serve.

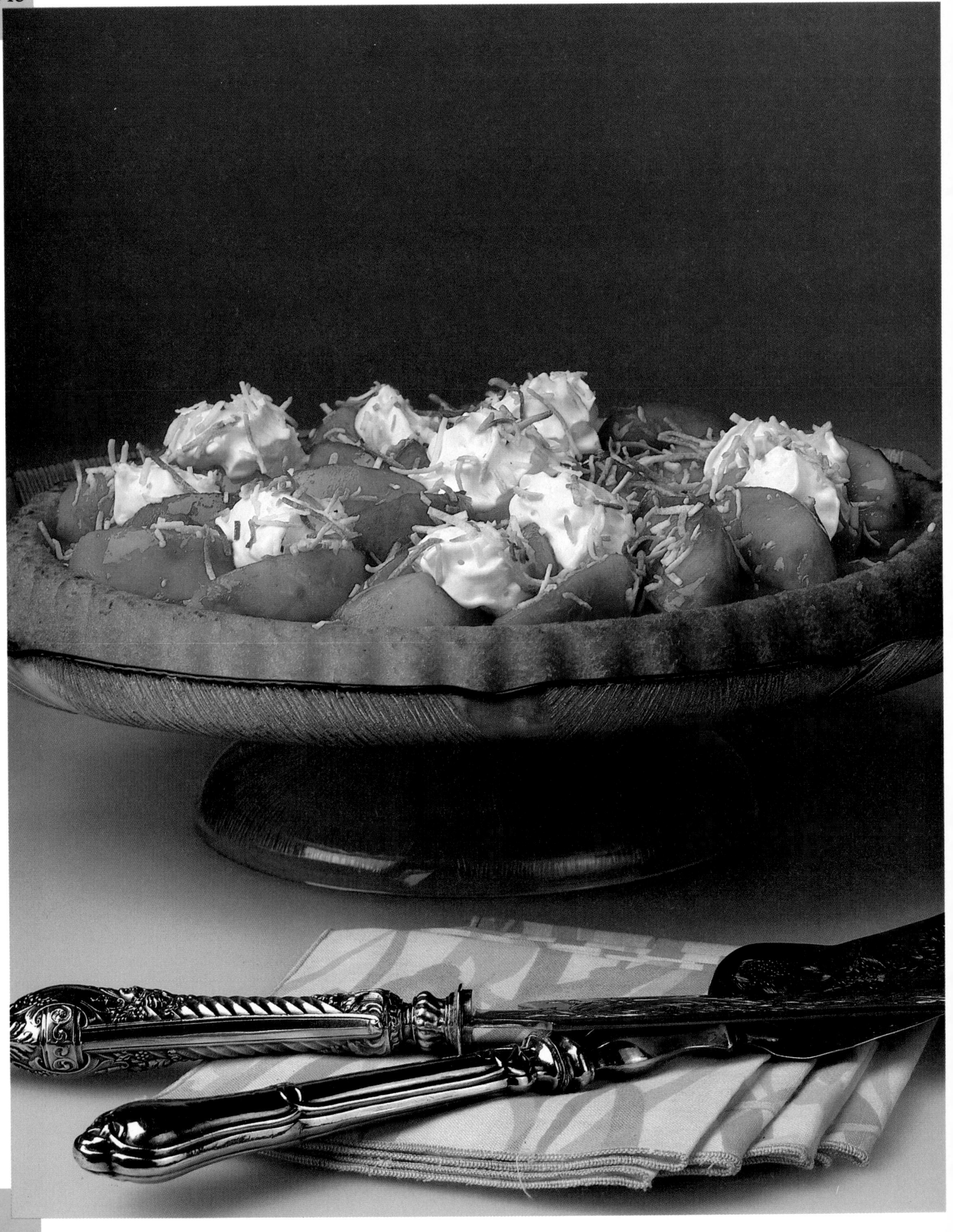

One Layer Fruit Cake

(serves 4-8)

1 SERVING	262 CALORIES	51g CARBOHYDRATE
3g PROTEIN	5g FAT	0.9g FIBER

4	ripe nectarines
2	ripe peaches
½ cup	(125 ml) sugar
1 cup	(250 ml) water
1	1.2 oz (34 g) package glaze mix, prepared
1	6 oz (169 g) short-cake layer
	juice 1 orange
	whipped cream for decoration

Cut fruit in half to remove pits — if they are not ripe this might be difficult.

Cut halves into quarters and set aside.

Place sugar, water and orange juice in saucepan; bring to boil. Continue cooking 3 to 4 minutes over high heat.

Add fruit to hot liquid in saucepan and bring to boiling point. Reduce heat to medium-low and continue cooking 2 minutes.

Remove fruit from liquid, peel and cut quarters in half; set aside on plate.

Replace saucepan containing syrup over heat and bring to boil.

Remove from heat and mix ⅓ cup (75 ml) of syrup into prepared glaze mix. Generously spread glaze over bottom of cake.

Arrange fruit on cake over glaze and brush with any remaining glaze.

Refrigerate before serving. Decorate with whipped cream and if desired, sprinkle with coconut.

Cut fruit in half to remove pits — if they are not ripe this might be difficult.

Add fruit to syrup mixture in saucepan and bring to boiling point. Reduce heat to medium-low and continue cooking 2 minutes.

Mix ⅓ cup (75 ml) of syrup into prepared glaze mix.

Generously spread glaze over bottom of cake and arrange fruit on top. Brush with leftover glaze.

Afternoon Rum Cake

(serves 8-10)

1 SERVING	524 CALORIES	51g CARBOHYDRATE
9g PROTEIN	32g FAT	0.3g FIBER

1¼ cups	(300 ml) softened butter
1 cup	(250 ml) granulated sugar
5	eggs
3 cups	(750 ml) all-purpose flour
1 tsp	(5 ml) cinnamon
2 tsp	(10 ml) baking powder
2 tbsp	(30 ml) dark rum
1 cup	(250 ml) milk
½ cup	(125 ml) slivered almonds
	grated rind 1 lemon
	pinch salt
	icing sugar

Preheat oven to 325°F (160°C). Generously butter 9 inch (23 cm) spring-form cake pan.

Place butter and lemon rind in large bowl; work butter until pliable.

Add sugar and cream together using spatula.

Add 1 egg and 3 tbsp (45 ml) flour and cinnamon; beat together with electric beater.

Add remaining eggs and beat until completely incorporated.

Place remaining flour with baking powder and salt in small bowl; mix together.

Sift half into egg batter and mix very well with spatula.

Pour in rum and incorporate with spatula.

Add remaining flour and continue incorporating.

Pour in milk and with spatula, mix until incorporated. Fold in almonds.

Pour batter into prepared cake pan and rap bottom against counter to settle mixture. Bake 40 minutes or until toothpick inserted comes out clean.

Remove pan from oven and cool 5-6 minutes.

Unmold onto wire rack and set aside until cold.

Place icing sugar in wire sieve and dust cake just before serving.

Place butter and lemon rind in bowl; work butter until pliable.

Add sugar and cream together using spatula.

Add 1 egg, 3 tbsp (45 ml) flour and cinnamon; beat together with electric beater.

After remaining eggs have been added, start adding the rest of the flour.

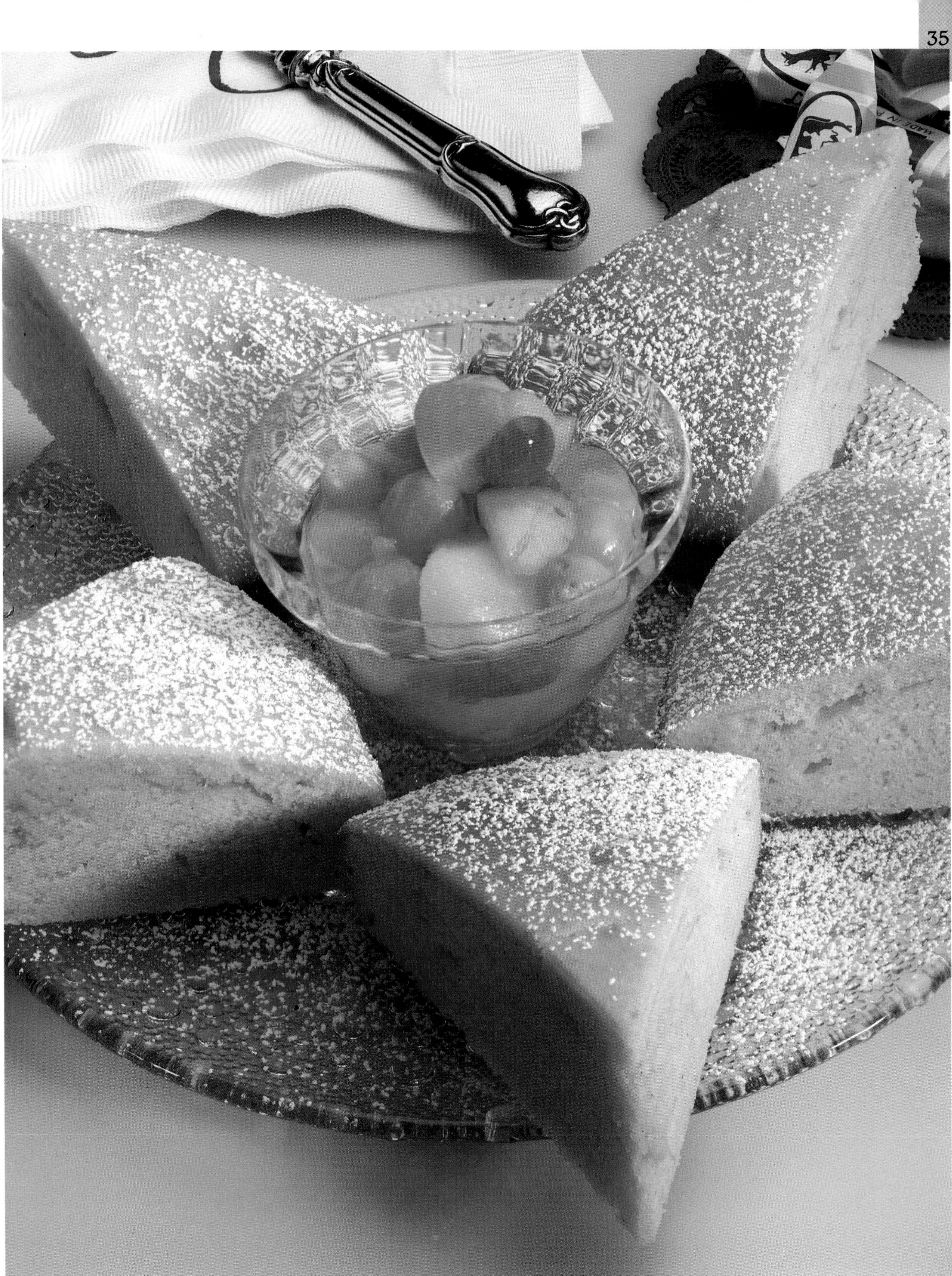

Midnight Snacking Cake

(serves 6-8)

1 SERVING	240 CALORIES	25g CARBOHYDRATE
4g PROTEIN	14g FAT	0g FIBER

½ cup	(125 ml) softened butter
½ cup	(125 ml) granulated sugar
1 tsp	(5 ml) cinnamon
3	eggs
4 tbsp	(60 ml) rum
1¼ cups	(300 ml) all-purpose flour
1 tsp	(5 ml) baking powder
	pinch salt

Preheat oven to 350°F (180°C). Butter 8½ inch (21 cm) spring-form cake pan.

Place butter, sugar and cinnamon in bowl; cream together.

Add first egg and beat well with electric beater.

Add remaining eggs, one at a time, beating well after each addition. Add rum during this time.

Mix flour with baking powder and salt; sift into batter and mix with spatula until smooth.

Pour batter into prepared cake pan and bake 30-35 minutes or until toothpick inserted comes out clean.

Cool in pan about 10-15 minutes before unmolding cake onto wire rack for continued cooling.

Ice with vanilla icing or another one of your favorites.

* Make recipe twice for two-layer cake.

Place butter, sugar and cinnamon in bowl; cream together.

Add eggs, one at a time, beating well after each addition. At some point during this time, add the rum too.

Mix flour with baking powder and salt; sift into batter and mix with spatula until smooth.

Pour batter into prepared cake pan.

Raisin Almond Fruit Cake

(serves 8-10)

1 SERVING	619 CALORIES	59g CARBOHYDRATE
9g PROTEIN	39g FAT	2.1g FIBER

1¾ cups	(425 ml) all-purpose flour
1 tbsp	(15 ml) baking powder
¾ cup	(175 ml) sultana raisins
1 cup	(250 ml) chopped walnuts
1 cup	(250 ml) slivered almonds
1 cup	(250 ml) all-vegetable shortening
½ cup	(125 ml) brown sugar
½ cup	(125 ml) granulated sugar
4	eggs
½ cup	(125 ml) chopped candied mixed fruit
¼ cup	(50 ml) Tia Maria
	pinch salt
	pinch powdered ginger

Preheat oven to 325°F (160°C). Butter 8 inch (20 cm) square cake pan.

Sift flour, baking powder, salt and ginger into bowl.

Place raisins, walnuts and almonds in another bowl; add ⅓ of flour mixture. Toss and set aside.

Place shortening, brown and granulated sugar in bowl containing just flour. Incorporate well with pastry blender.

Add eggs and blend well with wooden spoon.

Incorporate raisin/flour mixture along with candied fruit; mix very well with wooden spoon.

Pour in Tia Maria and blend well. Pour batter into prepared cake pan and bake 1 hour or until toothpick inserted comes out clean.

Cool cake in pan before unmolding onto wire rack.

Serve with tea, coffee, as a snack or in your children's lunches as a nutritious dessert.

Sift flour, baking powder, salt and ginger into bowl.

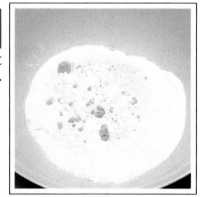

Place raisins, walnuts and almonds in another bowl; add ⅓ of flour mixture. Toss and set aside.

Place shortening, brown and granulated sugar in bowl containing just flour. Incorporate well with pastry blender.

Add eggs and blend well with wooden spoon.

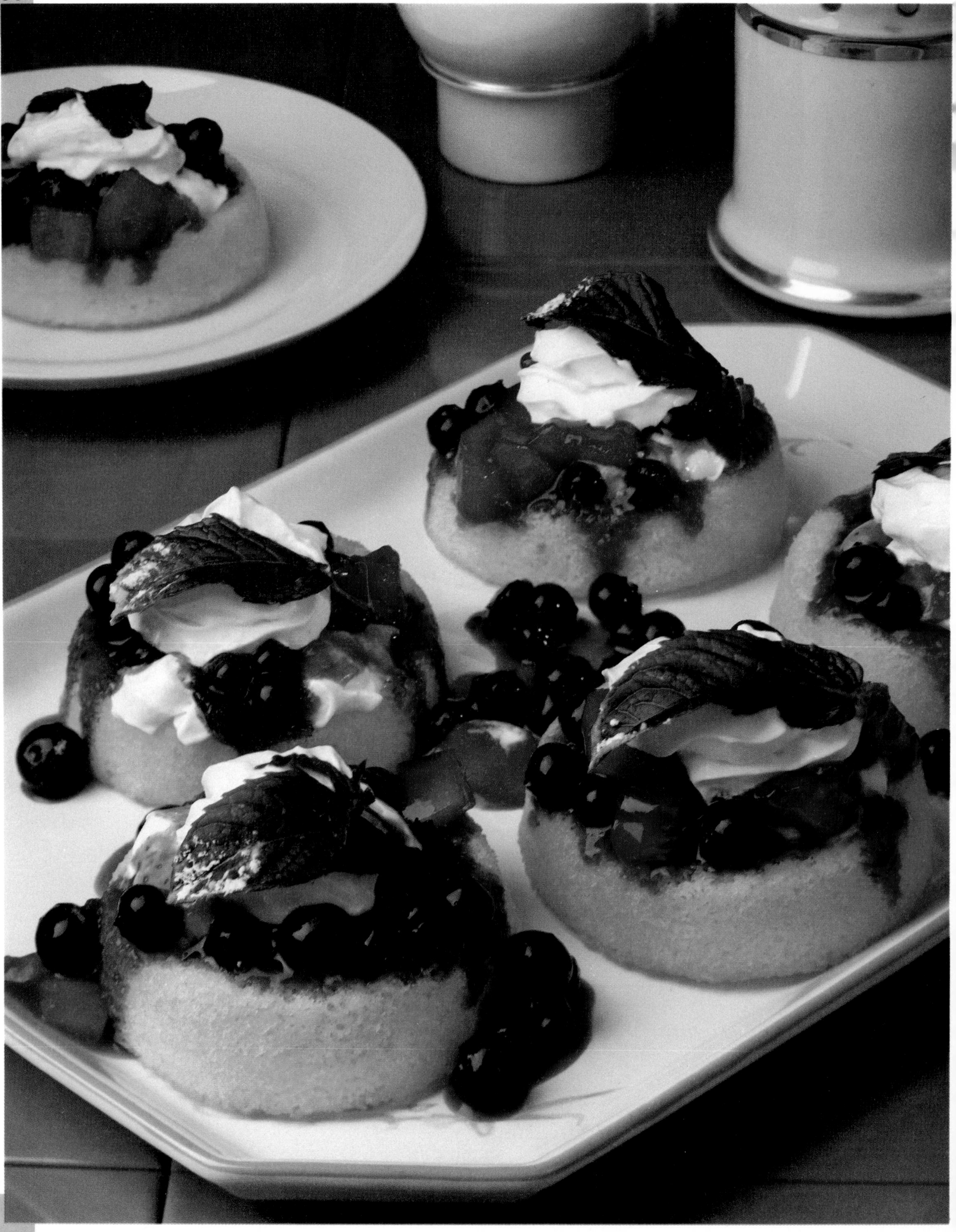

Blueberry and Papaya Cakes

(serves 6)

1 SERVING	233 CALORIES	43g CARBOHYDRATE
4g PROTEIN	5g FAT	1.3g FIBER

½	papaya
⅓ cup	(75 ml) sugar
¼ cup	(50 ml) water
1½ cups	(375 ml) blueberries
¼ cup	(50 ml) orange juice
2 tsp	(10 ml) cornstarch
3 tbsp	(45 ml) cold water
6	cake dessert shells
	dash grated lemon rind
	whipped cream to taste

Slice half papaya in half again, lengthwise. Seed, peel and dice flesh.

Place papaya in saucepan with sugar and ¼ cup (50 ml) water. Bring to boil over medium heat and continue cooking 3 minutes.

Stir in blueberries, orange juice and lemon rind; bring to boil again.

Mix cornstarch with 3 tbsp (45 ml) water; stir into cooking fruit and cook 1 more minute.

Pour into bowl and refrigerate until cold.

Fill cakes with whipped cream to taste; arrange on attractive serving platter.

Spoon fruit topping over cream, letting it drip down sides of cakes. Decorate with more whipped cream and serve.

Orange Cake Sauce

¼ cup (50 ml)	93 CALORIES	23g CARBOHYDRATE
0g PROTEIN	0g FAT	0.5g FIBER

1	small orange
1	lime
½	lemon
½ cup	(125 ml) strawberries, hulled
½ cup	(125 ml) brown sugar
½ cup	(125 ml) granulated sugar
⅔ cup	(150 ml) water
1 oz	(30 ml) rum

Slice orange and lime in half; remove seeds and dice with rind. Dice ½ seeded lemon with rind as well.

Place diced fruit in food processor and mix well. Add strawberries and blend 30 seconds; set aside.

Place both sugars and water in saucepan; bring to boil. Continue cooking until temperature reaches 260°F (125°C). If you do not have a candy thermometer, drop a bit of syrup in cold water — if it forms a soft ball, it has reached the correct temperature.

Remove saucepan from stove, cool 5 minutes, then add fruit and rum.

Cool sauce before serving over cake.

Almond Brownies

(serves 6-8)

1 SERVING	410 CALORIES	33g CARBOHYDRATE
7g PROTEIN	28g FAT	0.7g FIBER

2 oz	(60 g) unsweetened chocolate
½ cup	(125 ml) softened butter
¾ cup	(175 ml) granulated sugar
3 tbsp	(45 ml) honey
1 tsp	(5 ml) vanilla
2	eggs
½ cup	(125 ml) sifted all-purpose flour
1 cup	(250 ml) slivered almonds
1	egg white, beaten stiff
	pinch salt

Preheat oven to 350°F (180°C). Butter 8 inch (20 cm) square cake pan.

Place chocolate in stainless steel bowl. Melt over saucepan half-filled with boiling water.

Place butter, sugar and honey in large bowl. Add melted chocolate and mix well.

Add vanilla and eggs, one at a time, beating well after each addition. It is best to use electric beater.

Fold in flour and salt and mix until completely incorporated. Stir in almonds and incorporate stiff egg white.

Pour batter into prepared cake pan and bake 25-30 minutes or until toothpick inserted comes out clean.

Cool brownies in pan 10-15 minutes, then finish cooling on wire rack. Serve with cold milk if desired.

Add melted **1** chocolate to butter, sugar and honey placed in large bowl. Mix well.

Fold in flour **3** and salt and mix until completely incorporated.

Add vanilla **2** and first egg; beat well before adding second egg.

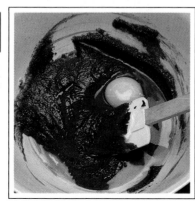

Stir in almonds **4** and incorporate stiff egg white.

Papaya Pie

(serves 6-8)

1 SERVING	336 CALORIES	47g CARBOHYDRATE
3g PROTEIN	15g FAT	1.0g FIBER

4	large ripe papayas, peeled
¾ cup	(175 ml) granulated sugar
1 tsp	(5 ml) nutmeg
1 tsp	(5 ml) cinnamon
2 tbsp	(30 ml) butter
2 tbsp	(30 ml) cornstarch
1	beaten egg
	enough dough for bottom and top crusts*

Preheat oven to 425°F (220°C).

Cut papayas in half, seed and slice ½ inch (1.2 cm) thick. Place in bowl with sugar, nutmeg, cinnamon, butter and cornstarch; mix well.

Line 10 inch (25 cm) pie plate with half of rolled dough.

Add papaya filling and brush edges of dough with a bit of water.

Cover with top crust and pinch edges shut. Score top several times and brush with beaten egg.

Bake 7 minutes.

Reduce heat to 350°F (180°C) and continue baking 35-40 minutes. Note: If upper crust browns too quickly, cover with small sheet of aluminum foil.

Let cool slightly before serving.

* If desired you can use the dough recipe from the Blueberry Pie.

Cold Lime Soufflé

(serves 4-6)

1 SERVING	326 CALORIES	32g CARBOHYDRATE
7g PROTEIN	19g FAT	0g FIBER

2	small envelopes unflavored gelatine
¼ cup	(50 ml) cold water
4	egg yolks
¾ cup	(175 ml) super-fine sugar
4	egg whites, beaten stiff
1 cup	(250 ml) heavy cream, whipped
	juice of 6 large limes

Sprinkle gelatine over water poured into small bowl; set aside.

Place egg yolks and sugar in large bowl; mix together with whisk.

If bowl is stainless steel, set over saucepan half-filled with boiling water. Otherwise, use double-boiler.

Reduce heat to low and cook while whisking constantly until mixture becomes thick enough to coat the back of a spoon.

Whisk in gelatine and cook 1 more minute.

Squeeze in lime juice, whisk quickly and remove from heat.

Set aside to cool.

When egg yolks are cool, incorporate beaten egg whites by folding in with spatula.

Fold in whipped cream, incorporating with spatula.

Attach a foil collar around the outside edge of 4 cup (1 L) soufflé mold. Tape to secure.

Pour in soufflé mixture and refrigerate 4 hours.

Remove collar and serve with a fruit sauce if desired.

Lime Pie

(serves 6)

1 SERVING	443 CALORIES	48g CARBOHYDRATE
9g PROTEIN	24g FAT	0g FIBER

9 inch	(23 cm) pie shell
1¼ cups	(300 ml) can sweetened condensed milk
3	egg yolks
2 tbsp	(30 ml) grated lime rind
½ cup	(125 ml) lime juice
2	egg whites, beaten stiff
½ cup	(125 ml) heavy cream, whipped stiff

Bake pie shell in oven preheated at 425°F (220°C) for 12 to 15 minutes. Remove and set aside to cool.

Place milk, egg yolks, lime rind and juice in stainless steel bowl. Set over saucepan half-filled with hot water on medium-low heat. Cook mixture until thickened, stirring constantly.

Transfer bowl to counter and let cool.

Fold in egg whites, then whipped cream, with spatula.

Pour filling into pie shell and refrigerate overnight. Garnish pie with roasted almonds or with slices of lime if desired.

Blueberry Pie

(serves 6-8)

1 SERVING	433 CALORIES	65g CARBOHYDRATE
3g PROTEIN	18g FAT	2.1g FIBER

2 cups	(500 ml) all-purpose flour
⅔ cup	(150 ml) all-vegetable shortening
5-6 tbsp	(75-90 ml) cold water
1¼ cups	(300 ml) granulated sugar
3 tbsp	(45 ml) cornstarch
4 cups	(1 L) thawed blueberries
1 tbsp	(15 ml) melted butter
1 tbsp	(15 ml) grated lemon rind
	several pinches salt
	light cream

Sift flour with one pinch salt into large bowl. Add shortening and incorporate with pastry blender.

Knead in enough cold water to form a ball. Wrap in waxed paper and refrigerate 2-3 hours.

Preheat oven to 425°F (220°C).

Cut dough in half. Roll out on floured surface and line 10 inch (25 cm) pie plate. Set aside.

Place sugar, cornstarch and remaining ingredients in saucepan; mix well. Cook 15 minutes over low heat.

Pour cooled berry mixture into pie shell. Cover with top crust and pinch edges shut. Score top several times and brush with light cream.

Bake 10 minutes.

Reduce heat to 375°F (190°C) and continue baking 45 minutes.

Let cool slightly before serving.

Sift flour and salt into large bowl.

1 Sift flour and salt into large bowl.

2 Add shortening and incorporate with pastry blender — the dough will begin to take shape.

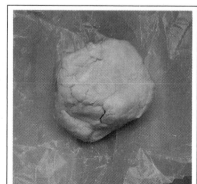

3 Add water as required and knead dough to form ball. The dough should be pliable and all ingredients completely combined.

4 Wrap dough in waxed paper and refrigerate 2-3 hours.

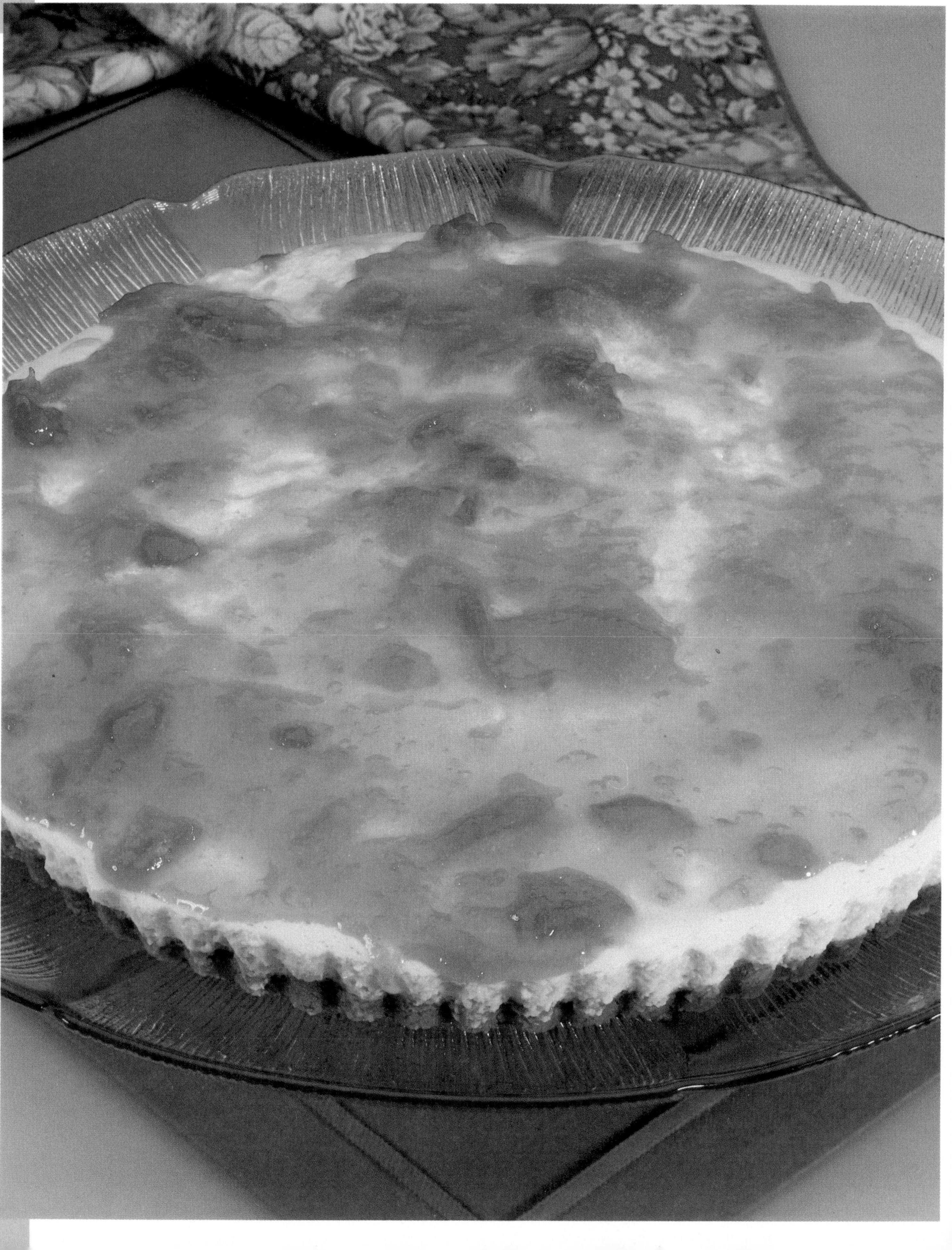

Rum Graham Pie

(serves 6-8)

1 SERVING	419 CALORIES	43g CARBOHYDRATE
7g PROTEIN	23g FAT	0.5g FIBER

1½ cups	(375 ml) graham crumbs
½ cup	(125 ml) brown sugar
¼ cup	(50 ml) softened butter
¼ cup	(50 ml) cold water
1	small envelope unflavored gelatine
3	egg yolks
¼ cup	(50 ml) granulated sugar
¼ cup	(50 ml) rum
¼ cup	(50 ml) light cream
3	egg whites, beaten stiff
1 cup	(250 ml) heavy cream, whipped
	grated rind 1 orange

Preheat oven to 375°F (190°C).

Place graham crumbs and half of brown sugar in bowl; mix together.

Add butter and incorporate well. Press mixture into 10 inch (25 cm) spring-form cake pan. Bake 8 minutes. Remove from oven and set aside.

Pour cold water into small bowl. Sprinkle in gelatine and let stand without stirring.

Place egg yolks in large bowl. Add remaining brown sugar and all of granulated sugar; beat well with electric beater.

Mix in orange rind. Pour in rum and light cream; mix well.

Cook pastry cream in double-boiler until it coats the back of a spoon. Whisk constantly!

Incorporate gelatine and whisk 30 seconds. Remove from heat and refrigerate.

When custard cream is cold and almost settled, incorporate egg whites and whipped cream with whisk.

Make a collar from double sheets of foil that can be placed around the cake pan to help keep the cream mixture in position during chilling. Tape securely to pan.

Once the collar is positioned correctly, pour in the rum cream mixture and refrigerate overnight.

Unmold. Serve plain or with a variety of fruit toppings.

Place egg yolks in large bowl with remaining brown sugar and all of granulated sugar; beat well.

Mix in orange rind. Pour in rum and light cream; mix well.

Be sure to beat the egg whites until stiff. Notice how they form peaks.

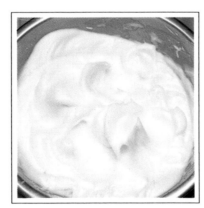

When custard cream is cold and almost settled, incorporate egg whites and whipped cream.

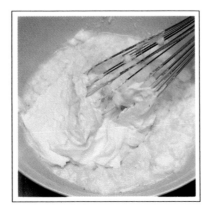

Rhubarb Pie

(serves 6)

1 SERVING	476 CALORIES	71g CARBOHYDRATE
5g PROTEIN	19g FAT	2.4g FIBER

1½ lb	(750 g) cubed rhubarb
¾ cup	(175 ml) granulated sugar
¾ cup	(175 ml) brown sugar
2 tbsp	(30 ml) grated lemon rind
2½ tbsp	(40 ml) cornstarch
2	large eggs
2 tbsp	(30 ml) heavy cream
	pastry dough for pie shell and top crust

Preheat oven to 425°F (220°C).

Mix rhubarb with sugars, lemon rind and cornstarch; toss to evenly coat.

Beat eggs with cream; pour half over rhubarb and mix.

Spoon rhubarb into uncooked pie shell. Cover with top crust, crimp edges and prick with fork or knife. Brush with remaining beaten eggs.

Bake 25 minutes in oven.

Reduce heat to 350°F (180°C) and continue baking 15 minutes.

Cool before serving.

Rum Cream Pie

(serves 6-8)

1 SERVING	260 CALORIES	23g CARBOHYDRATE
2g PROTEIN	16g FAT	0g FIBER

3	egg yolks
½ cup	(125 ml) granulated sugar
1 tbsp	(15 ml) grated lemon rind
1 cup	(250 ml) hot milk
4 tbsp	(60 ml) rum
1	small envelope unflavored gelatine
½ cup	(125 ml) heavy cream, whipped
3	egg whites, beaten stiff
9 inch	(23 cm) pie shell, precooked
	grated sweet chocolate

Place egg yolks and sugar in large bowl and mix with electric beater until color changes to nearly white.

Stir in lemon rind. Pour in hot milk and whisk very well.

Pour rum into small bowl and sprinkle in gelatine; set aside.

Cook milk mixture in double-boiler until cream coats the back of a spoon. It is essential to whisk constantly.

Add gelatine and continue cooking 1 more minute, whisking constantly.

Refrigerate cream until it settles and starts to cling to the sides of the bowl.

Remove cream from refrigerator and fold in whipped cream. Incorporate with whisk.

Fold in beaten egg whites and gently whisk to finish incorporating. Refrigerate 5-6 minutes.

Whisk mixture again and pour into prepared pie shell. Refrigerate 6 hours.

Dust with grated chocolate just before serving.

Place egg 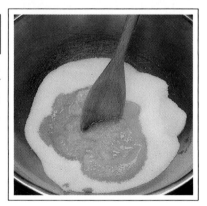 yolks and sugar in large bowl, preferably stainless steel for use later as double-boiler.

Mix with  electric beater until color changes to nearly white. Stir in lemon rind.

 Pour in hot milk and whisk very well.

 After cream has been cooked and chilled, fold in whipped cream and incorporate with whisk.

Honey Walnut Clusters

(yield: 24-36)

2 CLUSTERS	140 CALORIES	13g CARBOHYDRATE
2g PROTEIN	9g FAT	0.2g FIBER

⅓ cup	(75 ml) granulated sugar
½ cup	(125 ml) softened butter
1 tsp	(5 ml) vanilla
1¼ cups	(300 ml) all-purpose flour
¾ cup	(175 ml) chopped walnuts
¼ cup	(50 ml) light cream
¼ cup	(50 ml) liquid honey

Prepare cookie sheet by lining it with sheet of lightly buttered aluminum foil; set aside.

Place sugar and butter in large bowl; cream together.

Add vanilla and flour; combine with pastry blender.

Mix in walnuts. Add cream and blend everything together (best to use your hands) until well incorporated.

Knead with heel of your hand and shape into ball. Cover with waxed paper and refrigerate 30 minutes.

Preheat oven to 350°F (180°C).

Drop about 1 tbsp (15 ml) of cookie dough onto prepared sheet. Flatten slightly with fork, brush tops with honey and bake 18-20 minutes.

Cool cookies on wire racks.

Place sugar and butter in large bowl; cream together.

Mix in walnuts. Add cream and blend everything together.

Add vanilla and flour; combine with pastry blender.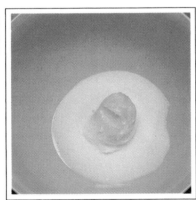

Knead dough with the heel of your hand and shape into ball for chilling.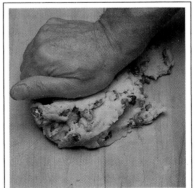

Lemon Glazed Cookies

(yield: 24-36)

2 COOKIES	145 CALORIES	16g CARBOHYDRATE
0g PROTEIN	9g FAT	0g FIBER

2 cups	(500 ml) all-purpose flour
½ cup	(125 ml) all-vegetable shortening
1 tsp	(5 ml) nutmeg
½ cup	(125 ml) granulated sugar
2	egg yolks
¼ cup	(50 ml) softened butter
⅓ cup	(75 ml) light cream
1 cup	(250 ml) icing sugar
2 tbsp	(30 ml) lemon juice
1 tbsp	(15 ml) hot water
	pinch salt
	grated rind 1 orange

Preheat oven to 350°F (180°C).

Place flour, salt, shortening, nutmeg, granulated sugar and orange rind in bowl.

Add egg yolks and butter; incorporate well with pastry blender.

Add cream and pinch dough to incorporate. Roll on floured surface until about ¼ inch (0.65 cm) thick. Dust with more flour if needed.

Using assorted cookie cutters, cut shapes and place on buttered cookie sheet. Bake 12 minutes.

Meanwhile, mix remaining ingredients together for glaze.

As soon as cookies are done, brush tops with lemon glaze.

Cool cookies on wire racks.

Place flour, salt, shortening and nutmeg in bowl.

Add granulated sugar and orange rind.

Add egg yolks.

Add butter and incorporate well with pastry blender.

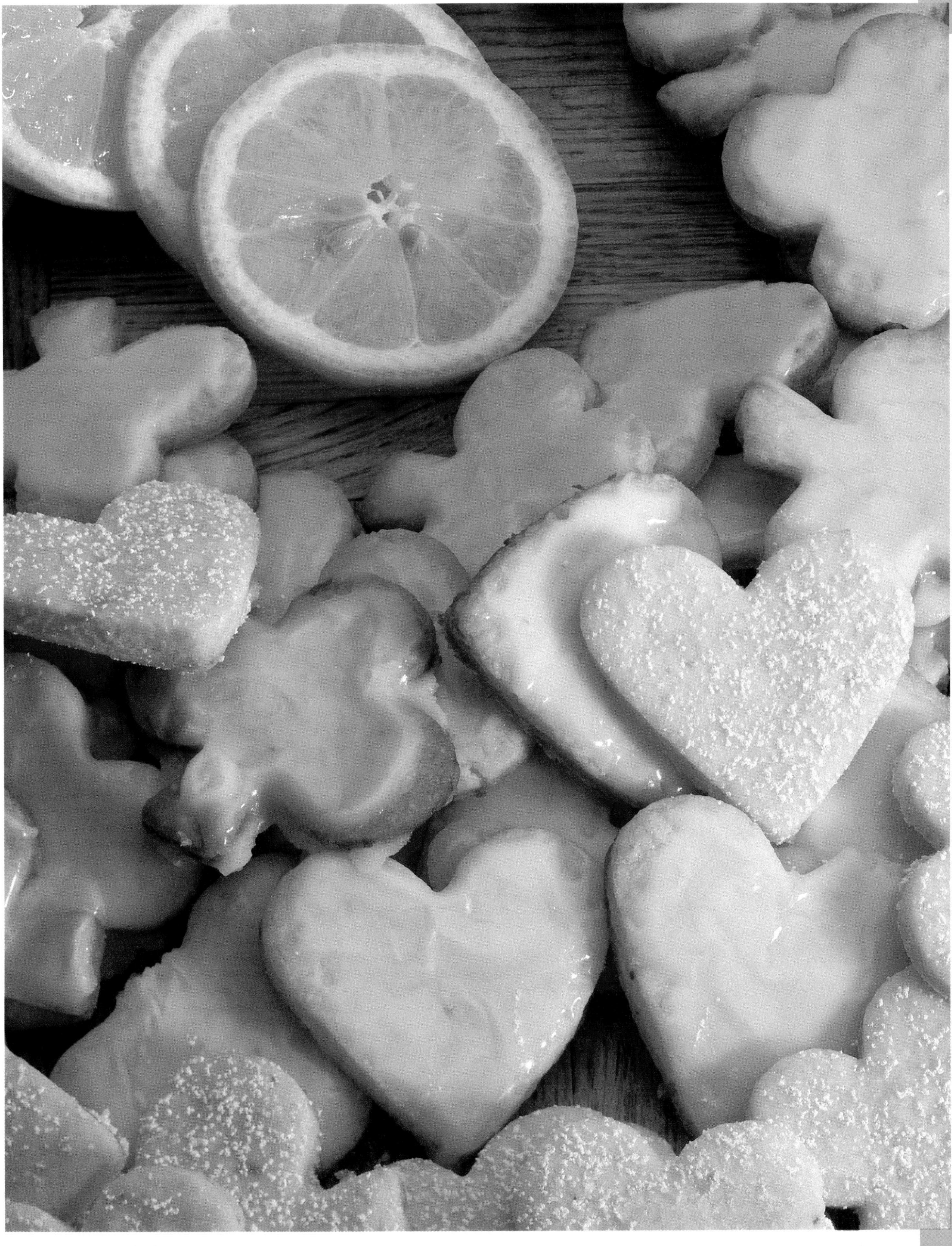

Almond Cookies

(yield: 24-36)

2 COOKIES	152 CALORIES	15g CARBOHYDRATE
3g PROTEIN	9g FAT	0.1g FIBER

¾ cup	(175 ml) softened butter
½ cup	(125 ml) granulated sugar
¾ cup	(175 ml) ground almonds
1¾ cups	(425 ml) all-purpose flour
¼ cup	(50 ml) light cream
2 tbsp	(30 ml) cold water

Place butter, sugar and almonds in bowl; cream together.

Add flour and incorporate with pastry blender.

Pour in cream and pinch dough with fingers.

Add water, incorporate and shape dough into ball. Cover with waxed paper and refrigerate 1 hour.

Preheat oven to 350°F (180°C).

Place dough on floured surface and roll until about ¼ inch (0.65 cm) thick. Dust with more flour if needed.

Using assorted cookie cutters, form shapes and place on buttered cookie sheet. Bake 10-12 minutes.

Cool cookies on wire racks.

Anise Cookies

(yield: 24-36)

2 COOKIES	102 CALORIES	21g CARBOHYDRATE
2g PROTEIN	1g FAT	0.1g FIBER

3	eggs
1 cup	(250 ml) granulated sugar
2 cups	(500 ml) all-purpose flour
1 tsp	(5 ml) baking powder
1 tbsp	(15 ml) anise seeds

Place eggs in large bowl and add sugar; mix together.

In separate bowl, sift flour with baking powder. Drop in anise seeds and mix.

Incorporate flour into wet batter. Cover with waxed paper and refrigerate dough overnight.

Preheat oven to 350°F (180°C).

Place cookie dough on floured surface and roll dough until about ¼ inch (0.65 cm) thick. Sprinkle with additional flour to avoid sticking.

Using cookie cutters (of different shapes if desired), form shapes and place cookies on buttered cookie sheet. Bake 10 minutes.

Cool cookies on wire racks.

Party Cookies

(yield: 24-36)

2 COOKIES	119 CALORIES	13g CARBOHYDRATE
1g PROTEIN	7g FAT	0g FIBER

½ cup	(125 ml) softened butter
¾ cup	(175 ml) granulated sugar
1 oz	(30 g) grated semi-sweet chocolate
1	egg
¼ cup	(50 ml) shredded coconut
1¼ cups	(300 ml) all-purpose flour
1 tsp	(5 ml) baking powder
	pinch salt
	green sprinkles

Place butter, sugar and chocolate in bowl; cream together with electric beater.

Add egg and continue beating.

Mix in coconut. Sift flour with baking powder and salt; incorporate into wet batter. Cover with waxed paper and refrigerate 3 hours. Preheat oven to 350°F (180 °C).

Place cookie dough on floured surface and roll dough until about ¼ inch (0.65 cm) thick. Sprinkle with additional flour to avoid sticking.

Shower dough with green sprinkles and cut into shapes with cookie cutters.

Place cookies on buttered cookie sheet and bake 10 minutes. Cool on wire racks.

Place butter, sugar and chocolate in bowl; cream together with electric beater.

Add egg and continue beating.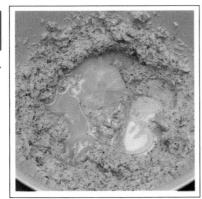

 Mix in coconut. Sift flour with baking powder and salt; incorporate into wet batter. Cover with waxed paper and refrigerate 3 hours.

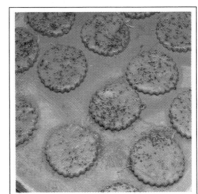 Place prepared cookies on buttered sheet and bake 10 minutes.

Chocolate Tube Cake   *(serves 8-10)*

1 SERVING	424 CALORIES	27g CARBOHYDRATE
10g PROTEIN	31g FAT	0.2g FIBER

8 oz	(250 g) sweet chocolate
½ cup	(125 ml) strong black coffee
2 tbsp	(30 ml) Tia Maria liqueur
10	egg yolks
½ cup	(125 ml) granulated sugar
10	egg whites
1½ cups	(375 ml) heavy cream, whipped with dash vanilla
½ cup	(125 ml) slivered almonds

Preheat oven to 350°F (180°C). Butter 2 cookie sheets and cover each with sheet of buttered waxed paper.

Place chocolate, coffee and liqueur in stainless steel bowl (or double-boiler) and place over saucepan half-filled with boiling water. Allow chocolate to melt, then remove and set aside to cool.

Place egg yolks in bowl and add granulated sugar; beat with electric beater about 3-4 minutes.

Stir in melted chocolate and continue beating 2-3 minutes. Place bowl in refrigerator 5-6 minutes.

Beat egg whites until stiff. Incorporate ⅓ into cooled chocolate mixture, mixing with spatula.

Add remaining egg whites and fold in with spatula, scraping bottom of bowl to incorporate. Turn bowl during this procedure and be careful not to overmix!

Pour batter onto prepared cookie sheets and spread evenly with spatula. Bake 15 minutes.

Turn off oven. With door ajar, let cakes stand 10 minutes.

Remove from oven and let cool 5-6 minutes.

Spread whipped cream over cakes and sprinkle with almonds. Delicately detach cake from waxed paper while rolling it onto itself.

Completely rid of old waxed paper, wrap chocolate tubes in new waxed paper and refrigerate 12 hours before serving.

Place egg yolks in bowl and add granulated sugar; beat with electric beater about 3-4 minutes.

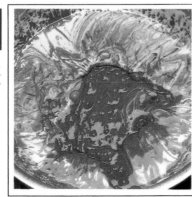

Stir in melted chocolate and continue beating 2-3 minutes.

Incorporate ⅓ of beaten egg whites into cooled chocolate mixture. Mix with spatula.

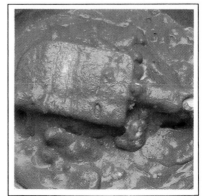

Add remaining egg whites and fold with spatula, scraping bottom of bowl, to incorporate.

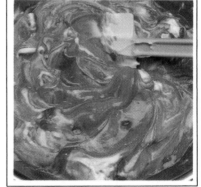

Shortbread Cookies

(yield: 24-36)

2 COOKIES	179 CALORIES	19g CARBOHYDRATE
1g PROTEIN	11g FAT	0.1g FIBER

½ lb	(250 g) softened, unsalted butter
½ cup	(125 ml) icing sugar
½ cup	(125 ml) cornstarch
1½ cups	(375 ml) all-purpose flour
1 tsp	(5 ml) cinnamon
	pinch salt
	candied cherries, halved

Preheat oven to 325°F (160°C).

Place butter in food processor. Add sugar and mix 2-3 minutes.

Add cornstarch, flour, cinnamon and salt; continue mixing until well blended.

Roll dough between the palms of your hands into small balls. Place on buttered and floured cookie sheet and flatten with tines of fork. Top with candied cherries.

Bake 14 minutes. Cool cookies on wire racks.

Place softened, unsalted butter in bowl of food processor.

Mix 2-3 minutes.
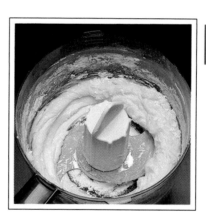

Add icing sugar.

Add remaining ingredients, except cherries, and continue mixing until well blended.

Royal Biscuits

(yield: 24-36)

2 COOKIES	155 CALORIES	21g CARBOHYDRATE
2g PROTEIN	7g FAT	0.3g FIBER

1 cup	(250 ml) all-purpose flour
¾ tsp	(3 ml) baking soda
1 tsp	(5 ml) baking powder
½ tsp	(2 ml) ground cloves
1 cup	(250 ml) brown sugar
½ cup	(125 ml) softened butter
1	beaten egg
1 tsp	(5 ml) vanilla
1 cup	(250 ml) quick-cooking rolled oats
½ cup	(125 ml) shredded coconut
	pinch salt

Place flour, baking soda, baking powder, cloves and salt in bowl; stir and set aside.

Cream brown sugar and butter in another bowl using spatula.

Stir in egg and vanilla; mix with electric beater.

Add rolled oats and coconut; incorporate well with spatula.

Fold in flour mixture and mix until completely incorporated. Cover with sheet of waxed paper and refrigerate 2-3 hours.

Preheat oven to 350°F (180°C).

When ready to bake cookies, roll dough on floured surface until about ¼ inch (0.65 cm) thick.

Using assorted cookie cutters, form shapes and place on buttered cookie sheet. Bake 10 minutes.

Cool cookies on wire racks.

These wholesome biscuits are a perfect companion for afternoon breaks.

Cream brown sugar and butter together using spatula.

Stir in egg and vanilla; then mix with electric beater.

Add rolled oats and coconut; incorporate well with spatula.

Fold in flour mixture and mix until completely incorporated.

Cheese Parfait

(serves 2-4)

1 SERVING	505 CALORIES	19g CARBOHYDRATE
6g PROTEIN	45g FAT	3.1g FIBER

8 oz	(250 g) package cream cheese, softened
3 tbsp	(45 ml) brown sugar
2 tbsp	(30 ml) Tia Maria liqueur
½ cup	(125 ml) heavy cream, whipped
1 cup	(250 ml) chopped fresh strawberries
	whole fresh strawberries for decoration

Place cheese in bowl of electric mixer. Add sugar and mix well for 2 minutes.

Add Tia Maria and continue mixing 30 seconds.

Add whipped cream and chopped strawberries; incorporate using spatula until well blended.

Spoon mixture into parfait glasses and refrigerate 3-4 hours before serving.

Decorate with fresh strawberries.

Walnut Chocolate Chewies

(serves 6-8)

1 SERVING	298 CALORIES	24g CARBOHYDRATE
6g PROTEIN	20g FAT	1.0g FIBER

1 cup	(250 ml) chopped walnuts
1 cup	(250 ml) slivered almonds
½ cup	(125 ml) liquid honey
2 tbsp	(30 ml) strong black coffee
	sweet cocoa to taste

Place walnuts and almonds in small bowl and toss together. Transfer to food processor and blend several minutes.

Replace nuts in small bowl and add honey; mix together.

Transfer nuts back to food processor and add coffee; blend about 1 minute.

Spread mixture on large plate and cover with sheet waxed paper, pressed against surface. Refrigerate 2-3 hours.

Remove and shape into small balls with hands. Roll in cocoa and continue to chill another hour before serving.

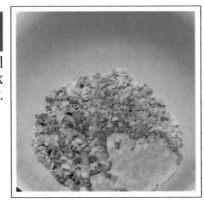

Place walnuts **1**
and almonds in small
bowl and toss
together.

Replace **2**
blended nuts in bowl
and add honey; mix
together.

3 Transfer nuts
back to food
processor and add
coffee.

4 Blend
about 1 minute.

Coffee Custard Pudding

(serves 6)

1 SERVING	174 CALORIES	12g CARBOHYDRATE
5g PROTEIN	12g FAT	0g FIBER

1 cup	(250 ml) hot milk
1 cup	(250 ml) hot, light cream
2 tbsp	(30 ml) hot expresso coffee or very strong coffee
1 tbsp	(15 ml) rum
⅓ cup	(75 ml) granulated sugar
4	eggs
	whipped cream

Preheat oven to 350°F (180°C).

Pour milk, cream and coffee into bowl; whisk together.

Add rum and beat with electric beater.

Add sugar and continue beating to incorporate.

Lightly beat eggs with fork. Pour into bowl containing custard mixture and whisk well until incorporated.

Place 6 individual custard dishes in roasting pan and pour in 1 inch (2.5 cm) hot water.

Fill custard dishes with mixture and bake 40 minutes.

Cool before unmolding and refrigerate. Before serving decorate with whipped cream.

Molasses Custard

(serves 6)

1 SERVING	183 CALORIES	14g CARBOHYDRATE
5g PROTEIN	12g FAT	0g FIBER

1 cup	(250 ml) hot milk
1 cup	(250 ml) hot, light cream
4	eggs
⅓ cup	(75 ml) molasses
½ tsp	(2 ml) vanilla
	pinch salt
	whipped cream

Preheat oven to 350°F (180°C).

Pour milk and cream into bowl; whisk well.

Lightly beat eggs with fork. Add to bowl along with molasses, salt and vanilla; whisk very well.

Place 6 individual custard dishes in roasting pan and pour in 1 inch (2.5 cm) hot water.

Fill custard dishes with mixture and bake 40 minutes.

Cool before unmolding and refrigerate. Before serving decorate with whipped cream.

Eggnog

(serves 4-6)

1 SERVING	257 CALORIES	21g CARBOHYDRATE
8g PROTEIN	12g FAT	0g FIBER

4	eggs, separated
½ cup	(125 ml) fine sugar
¼ cup	(50 ml) rum
2 tbsp	(30 ml) cognac
2 cups	(500 ml) cold milk
1 cup	(250 ml) cold, light cream
2	egg whites
	pinch nutmeg

Beat egg yolks with electric beater. Add half of sugar and continue beating until thick.

Pour in rum and cognac; beat 1 minute.

Add milk and cream; continue beating 30 seconds.

Place all egg whites in bowl. Beat with electric beater until they peak. Add remaining sugar and continue beating 1 minute.

Using spatula, fold in egg whites until well incorporated.

Serve in glasses with dash of nutmeg.

MICROWAVE

Microwave Notes:

Understanding how your microwave works is easy — just think of it as a chain reaction. As microwaves penetrate the food, they cause the food molecules to vibrate. This in turn causes heat which cooks the food; the cooking process spreads from the outside towards the center.

Because food cooks from the outside in, there are some techniques you should use to avoid uneven cooking:

— position the thickest portion of irregularly shaped food toward the walls of the microwave where it will receive more microwave energy.

— when stirring foods, move the food from the outside of the dish towards the center and vice-versa.

— rotating is a technique used with such foods as cakes or puddings which cannot be stirred. If a recipe calls for this procedure, simply rotate the dish a quarter or half turn (depending on the size of the mold).

You can cover food with the matching casserole top or in some cases with sheets of paper towel, plastic wrap or waxed paper. When you use plastic wrap be sure to pierce the wrap or tuck up one corner to allow excess steam an escape.

Although it is not essential to have a cupboard stacked with special microwave utensils, it is advisable to invest in at least several casserole dishes, plus perhaps a serving platter and a rectangular glass dish. Some dessert recipes call for particular cake molds; refer to the recipe for a description.

Because microwave ovens vary in terms of maximum power and power settings, you should study the following chart before you begin any recipes. Our test microwave was 650 watts.

Setting	Approximate wattage	Percent of power
HIGH	650	100
MEDIUM-HIGH	485	75
MEDIUM	325	50
LOW	160	25

Please consult your manufacturer's guide booklet if you are not already familiar with your microwave's controls and settings.

Mozza Sticks

(serves 2)

1 SERVING	352 CALORIES	17g CARBOHYDRATE
30g PROTEIN	22g FAT	0.5g FIBER

Setting: HIGH

Cooking Time: 14 minutes

Utensil: Roasting Rack
8 cups (2 L) casserole with cover

8	slices bacon
8	2 in (5 cm) carrot sticks
8	2 in (5 cm) mozzarella sticks
	salt and pepper

Arrange bacon on roasting rack; microwave 7 minutes. Cover with paper towel to prevent spattering.

Remove bacon from rack and set aside. Clean rack for later use.

Place carrot sticks in casserole; pour in about 1 cup (250 ml) water. Cover and microwave 6 minutes.

Drain carrots and rinse under cold water for several seconds.

Team carrot sticks with cheese sticks; carefully wrap with bacon. Secure with toothpicks.

Place bundles on roasting rack and season generously. Microwave 1 minute uncovered.

Snacking Eggs

(serves 4)

1 SERVING	594 CALORIES	20g CARBOHYDRATE
34g PROTEIN	42g FAT	trace FIBER

Setting: HIGH

Cooking Time: 6½ minutes

Utensil: 8 cups (2 L) casserole with cover

1 tbsp	(15 ml) butter
1	onion, diced
1	garlic clove, smashed and chopped
1	green pepper, diced
¾ lb	(375 g) piece Italian sausage, sliced
4	large eggs, beaten
1 cup	(250 ml) cubed mozzarella
4	large hot buns
	salt and pepper

Place butter, onion, garlic and green pepper in casserole. Cover and microwave 2 minutes.

Add sausage slices and microwave 1 minute covered.

Pour in beaten eggs and season well; mix with wooden spoon. Microwave 1½ minutes uncovered.

Stir eggs well and add cheese. Microwave 1 minute uncovered. Stir again; microwave 1 minute uncovered.

Serve on hot buns.

Stuffed Mushrooms

(serves 4)

1 SERVING	211 CALORIES	5g CARBOHYDRATE
5g PROTEIN	15g FAT	1.0g FIBER

Setting: MEDIUM

Cooking Time: 3 minutes

Utensil: Stoneware serving platter

1	bunch fresh watercress
3 tbsp	(45 ml) walnuts
1	tomato, cut in chunks
1	garlic clove, smashed and chopped
¼ cup	(50 ml) olive oil
4 tbsp	(60 ml) grated Parmesan cheese
16	large mushroom caps
	few drops Tabasco sauce
	few drops Worcestershire sauce
	salt and pepper

Wash watercress well and dry. Place in food processor and blend until almost puréed.

Add walnuts and tomato; blend until puréed.

Add garlic and oil; blend several seconds. Add cheese, Tabasco, Worcestershire, salt and pepper; blend again for several seconds.

Stuff mushroom caps with mixture and arrange on stoneware plate. Microwave 3 minutes.

Serve as an appetizer.

Place washed dried watercress in bowl of food processor. Blend until almost puréed.

Add walnuts and tomato; blend until puréed.

After oil and garlic have been incorporated, add cheese and remaining ingredients; blend for several seconds.

Stuff mushroom caps with mixture. Microwave 3 minutes.

Artichoke Appetizer

(serves 4)

1 SERVING	166 CALORIES	13g CARBOHYDRATE
9g PROTEIN	10g FAT	1.0g FIBER

Setting: HIGH and MEDIUM-HIGH

Cooking Time: 5 minutes

Utensil: 8 cups (2 L) casserole with cover
Stoneware serving platter

14 oz	(398 ml) can artichoke bottoms, drained and rinsed
2 tbsp	(30 ml) butter
½ lb	(250 g) mushrooms, sliced
½	celery stalk, very finely chopped
1	small onion, finely chopped
2	slices crisp bacon, chopped
1	garlic clove, smashed and chopped
3 tbsp	(45 ml) ricotta cheese
	salt and pepper

Arrange artichoke bottoms on stoneware platter; set aside.

Place butter, mushrooms, celery and onion in casserole. Cover and microwave 3 minutes at HIGH.

Mix in bacon, garlic and cheese; season well.

Fill artichoke bottoms with mixture. Microwave 2 minutes at MEDIUM-HIGH uncovered.

Sausage Sloppy Joes

(serves 4)

1 SERVING	376 CALORIES	35g CARBOHYDRATE
16g PROTEIN	21g FAT	2.0g FIBER

Setting: HIGH

Cooking Time: 10 minutes

Utensil: 12 cups (2.8 L) casserole with cover

1 tbsp	(15 ml) butter
1	onion, sliced
1	green pepper, thinly sliced
28 oz	(796 ml) can tomatoes, drained and chopped
½ cup	(125 ml) stuffed green olives, chopped
2	small pepperoni sausages, sliced
1 tbsp	(15 ml) cornstarch
2 tbsp	(30 ml) cold water
4	hamburger buns, toasted open
1¼ cups	(300 ml) grated mozzarella cheese
	salt and pepper

Place butter, onion and green pepper in casserole. Cover and microwave 5 minutes.

Stir in tomatoes and season to taste. Add olives and pepperoni; microwave 4 minutes covered.

Mix cornstarch with water; stir into casserole and microwave 1 minute uncovered.

Separate hamburger buns and place tops over bottoms. Set on cookie sheet and spoon sausage mixture over bread. Top with cheese and broil in conventional oven until melted.

Serve immediately.

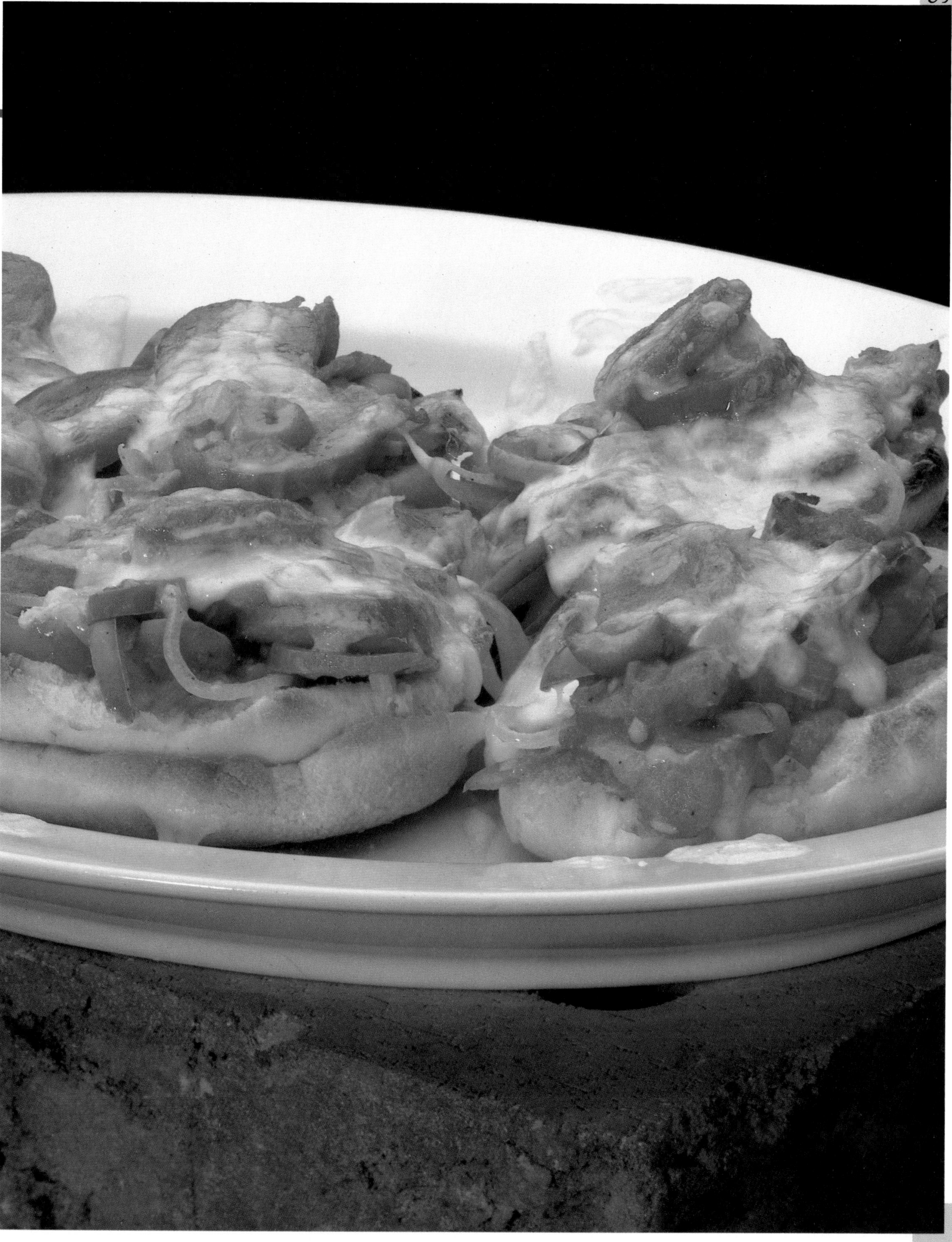

Meatloaf Muffins

(serves 4)

1 SERVING	293 CALORIES	55g CARBOHYDRATE
41g PROTEIN	6g FAT	1.0g FIBER

Setting: HIGH

Cooking Time: 5 minutes

Utensil: Muffin Ring

2	small potatoes, peeled and grated fine
2	carrots, pared and grated
1 lb	(500 g) lean ground beef
1	egg
2	medium onions, chopped and cooked
¼ tsp	(1 ml) allspice
½ tsp	(2 ml) chili powder
	salt and pepper

Combine potatoes and carrots in large bowl. Add beef and mix together well.

Add remaining ingredients and mix until thoroughly incorporated.

Press mixture into cups of muffin ring. Microwave 5 minutes uncovered.

Remove and let cool slightly before serving. These are ideal for after-school snacks and are handy to have on weekends.

Combine potatoes and carrots in large bowl.

Add beef and mix together well.

Add egg and remaining ingredients and mix until thoroughly incorporated.

Press mixture into cups of muffin ring.

Shrimp on Muffins

(serves 4)

1 SERVING	472 CALORIES	40g CARBOHYDRATE
23g PROTEIN	23g FAT	1.0g FIBER

Setting: HIGH

Cooking Time: 8 minutes

Utensil: 12 cups (2.8 L) casserole with cover

3 tbsp	(45 ml) butter
1 lb	(500 g) mushrooms, diced
1	shallot, chopped
4 tbsp	(60 ml) flour
1½ cups	(375 ml) hot milk
4 oz	(113 g) can shrimp, drained and rinsed
¼ tsp	(1 ml) nutmeg
4	English muffins, lightly toasted whole
1 cup	(250 ml) grated cheddar cheese
	salt and pepper

Place butter, mushrooms and shallot in casserole. Cover and microwave 4 minutes.

Mix in flour. Pour in milk and season; mix again. Microwave 4 minutes uncovered.

Add shrimp and nutmeg; mix well.

Using small knife pare away some of bread in the middle of each muffin. Place on cookie sheet and fill holes with shrimp mixture. Top with grated cheese and broil in conventional oven until melted.

Serve as a light lunch.

Bacon Bite

(serves 4)

1 SERVING	131 CALORIES	7g CARBOHYDRATE
37g PROTEIN	8g FAT	1.0g FIBER

Setting: HIGH

Cooking Time: 5 minutes

Utensil: 8 cups (2 L) rectangular dish

4	slices fast-fry back bacon
4	rings yellow pepper
4	thick slices tomato
4	slices Camembert or Brie cheese

Arrange bacon in rectangular dish; top each with ring of yellow pepper.

Cover loosely with plastic wrap and microwave 3 minutes.

Add tomato slices and cheese; finish microwaving 2 minutes covered.

Serve as snack or for breakfast.

Bacon Potato Treats

(serves 4)

1 SERVING	379 CALORIES	28g CARBOHYDRATE
26g PROTEIN	25g FAT	1.0g FIBER

Setting: HIGH

Cooking Time: 10 minutes

Utensil: 8 cups (2 L) rectangular dish

5	potatoes, unpeeled, sliced ½ in (1.2 cm) thick
1	onion, grated and cooked
24	stuffed green olives, chopped
½ tsp	(2 ml) chopped jalapeno
6	slices crisp bacon, chopped
1½ cups	(375 ml) grated Gruyère cheese
	salt and pepper

Arrange slices of potato in rectangular dish — this may require a couple of layers depending on the size of potatoes. Cover dish with plastic wrap and microwave 4 minutes. Rotate and microwave another 4 minutes.

When potatoes are cooked, top with grated onion. Mix olives with jalapeno and sprinkle over; add bacon and cheese.

Season very well and microwave 2 minutes uncovered. Serve as an afternoon snack or at lunchtime.

Watercress and Leek Soup

(serves 4)

1 SERVING	202 CALORIES	22g CARBOHYDRATE
8g PROTEIN	8g FAT	trace FIBER

Setting: HIGH

Cooking Time: 23 minutes

Utensil: 12 cups (2.8 L) casserole with cover

2 tbsp	(30 ml) butter
2	green onions, chopped
1	large leek, white part only, chopped
3 tbsp	(45 ml) flour
4	medium potatoes, peeled and sliced
4 cups	(1 L) hot chicken stock
¼ tsp	(1 ml) thyme
¼ tsp	(1 ml) anise
1	bunch fresh watercress, chopped
	salt and pepper

Place butter, onions and leek in casserole. Cover and microwave 4 minutes.

Mix in flour, salt and pepper. Microwave 4 minutes uncovered.

Add potatoes, chicken stock and seasonings; cover and microwave 7 minutes.

Stir well. Add watercress, season, and microwave 5 minutes covered.

Remove cover; finish microwaving 3 minutes.

Open leek by cutting it in 4 lengthwise. Do not, however, cut through the base. Wash well in cold water.

Depending on the recipe you can use the entire leek or as in this recipe, discard the green portion and use only the white part. In either case check that sand has all been washed away.

After the onions and leek have been microwaved 4 minutes, sprinkle in flour, salt and pepper. Mix well and continue microwaving 4 minutes uncovered.

Add potatoes, chicken stock and seasonings; cover and microwave 7 minutes.

Green Soup

(serves 4)

1 SERVING	260 CALORIES	24g CARBOHYDRATE
12g PROTEIN	14g FAT	2.0g FIBER

Setting: HIGH

Cooking Time: 19 minutes

Utensil: 12 cups (2.8 L) casserole with cover

3 tbsp	(45 ml) butter
1	small onion, chopped
2	small stalks broccoli, pared and diced
5 tbsp	(75 ml) flour
2 cups	(500 ml) hot chicken stock
1 tsp	(5 ml) basil
2 tbsp	(30 ml) tomato paste
2 cups	(500 ml) hot milk
1	large head broccoli, in flowerets
	salt and pepper
	dash paprika

Place butter, onion and diced broccoli stalks in casserole. Cover and microwave 3 minutes.

Mix in flour and season with salt, pepper and paprika; mix very well with wooden spoon. Cover and microwave 3 minutes.

Stir in chicken stock and basil; correct seasoning. Add tomato paste and mix well. Cover and continue microwaving 4 minutes.

Pour in milk and mix well; cover and microwave another 4 minutes.

Add broccoli flowerets, cover and finish microwaving 5 minutes.

After 3 minutes of microwaving, add flour to vegetables. Sprinkle in paprika and season to taste.

Mix well with wooden spoon. Cover and microwave 3 minutes.

Stir in chicken stock and basil; correct seasoning. Add tomato paste and mix well. Continue microwaving 4 minutes.

Pour in milk. Add broccoli flowerets. Cover and finish microwaving 5 minutes.

Squash and Macaroni Soup

(serves 4)

1 SERVING	136 CALORIES	15g CARBOHYDRATE
8g PROTEIN	5g FAT	2.0g FIBER

Setting: HIGH

Cooking Time: 18 minutes

Utensil: 12 cups (2.8 L) casserole with cover

1 tbsp	(15 ml) butter
1	leek, washed and thinly sliced
½	squash, seeded and diced small
1	carrot, pared and thinly sliced
1	zucchini, peeled and sliced
5 cups	(1.2 L) hot chicken stock
1	bay leaf
¼ tsp	(1 ml) thyme
½ tsp	(2 ml) basil
½ cup	(125 ml) elbow macaroni
	salt and pepper

Place butter, leek and squash in casserole. Cover and microwave 6 minutes.

Add remaining ingredients; cover and microwave 12 minutes.

Serve hot.

Red Pepper Soup

(serves 4)

1 SERVING	141 CALORIES	16g CARBOHYDRATE
5g PROTEIN	7g FAT	1.0g FIBER

Setting: HIGH

Cooking Time: 20 minutes

Utensil: 12 cups (2.8 L) casserole with cover

2 tbsp	(30 ml) butter
1	celery stalk, diced
2	green onions, diced
4 tbsp	(60 ml) flour
2	large red peppers, seeded and sliced
2 cups	(500 ml) tomato clam juice, heated
2 cups	(500 ml) chicken stock, heated
¼ tsp	(1 ml) celery seed
1 tsp	(5 ml) sugar
	salt and pepper

Place butter, celery and onions in casserole; microwave 4 minutes covered.

Mix in flour; microwave 4 minutes covered.

Add red peppers and remaining ingredients; mix well. Cover and finish microwaving 12 minutes.

Transfer soup to food processor and purée.

Country Soup

(serves 4)

1 SERVING	289 CALORIES	11g CARBOHYDRATE
32g PROTEIN	12g FAT	1.0g FIBER

Setting: HIGH

Cooking Time: 48 minutes

Utensil: 12 cups (2.8 L) casserole with cover

2 tbsp	(30 ml) butter
1	celery stalk, diced
1	carrot, pared and diced
1	medium onion, diced
1	garlic clove, smashed and chopped
½ tsp	(2 ml) chervil
1	bay leaf
½ cup	(125 ml) yellow split peas
½ lb	(250 g) flank steak, thinly sliced and seared in oil
5 cups	(1.2 L) light beef stock, heated
6	large mushrooms, diced
	salt and pepper

Place butter, celery, carrot, onion, garlic, seasonings and bay leaf in casserole; cover and microwave 5 minutes.

Mix in peas, meat and beef stock; correct seasoning. Cover and continue microwaving 40 minutes.

Stir in mushrooms and finish microwaving 3 minutes uncovered.

Fennel Soup

(serves 4)

1 SERVING	246 CALORIES	11g CARBOHYDRATE
7g PROTEIN	20g FAT	trace FIBER

Setting: HIGH

Cooking Time: 22 minutes

Utensil: 12 cups (2.8 L) casserole with cover

4 tbsp	(60 ml) butter
1	leek, slit lengthwise in 4, washed and thinly sliced
1	medium fennel bulb, leaves and bulb thinly sliced
5 tbsp	(75 ml) flour
4 cups	(1 L) hot light chicken stock
½ cup	(125 ml) hot light cream
	pinch chervil
	salt and pepper
	lemon juice

Place butter, leek and fennel in casserole. Cover and microwave 10 minutes.

Mix well and add remaining ingredients, except cream. Continue microwaving 10 minutes covered.

Force mixture through fine sieve or food mill; stir in cream and replace in casserole. Microwave 2 minutes uncovered.

Serve hot.

Potato Onion Cream

(serves 4)

| 1 SERVING | 313 CALORIES | 42g CARBOHYDRATE |
| 15g PROTEIN | 11g FAT | 1.0g FIBER |

Setting: MEDIUM-HIGH and MEDIUM

Cooking Time: 31 minutes

Utensil: 12 cups (2.8 L) casserole with cover

2	slices bacon, diced
3	medium onions, diced
4 tbsp	(60 ml) flour
4 cups	(1 L) hot milk
3	large potatoes, peeled and thinly sliced
1 tsp	(5 ml) tarragon
	salt and white pepper
	dash paprika

Place bacon and onions in casserole; cover and microwave 6 minutes at MEDIUM-HIGH.

Mix in flour. Pour in milk, stir, and add tarragon, salt, pepper and paprika.

Add potatoes and cover. Microwave 14 minutes at MEDIUM-HIGH.

Stir mixture well and microwave 11 minutes at MEDIUM, covered.

Serve hot.

Thick Leftover Vegetable Soup

(serves 4)

| 1 SERVING | 289 CALORIES | 27g CARBOHYDRATE |
| 20g PROTEIN | 11g FAT | 1.0g FIBER |

Setting: HIGH

Cooking Time: 23 minutes

Utensil: 12 cups (2.8 L) casserole with cover

2 tbsp	(30 ml) butter
2	leeks, white part only, thinly sliced
1	garlic clove, smashed and chopped
1	green pepper, diced
2	potatoes, peeled, quartered and thinly sliced
1	large sweet potato, peeled, quartered and thinly sliced
½ tsp	(2 ml) basil
¼ tsp	(1 ml) celery seed
¼ tsp	(1 ml) anise
5 cups	(1.2 L) hot chicken stock
1 cup	(250 ml) diced cooked chicken
	salt and pepper

Place butter in casserole; cover and microwave 1 minute. Add leeks and continue microwaving 5 minutes covered.

Stir in garlic and green pepper; season well. Cover and microwave 3 minutes.

Stir and add potatoes, sweet potato and seasonings; cover and microwave 3 minutes.

Pour in chicken stock; mix well and microwave 10 minutes uncovered.

Add diced chicken and correct seasoning. Finish microwaving 1 minute with cover.

Perch Soup

(serves 4)

1 SERVING	209 CALORIES	23g CARBOHYDRATE
21g PROTEIN	4g FAT	2.0g FIBER

Setting: MEDIUM-HIGH and MEDIUM

Cooking Time: 31 minutes

Utensil: 12 cups (2.8 L) casserole with cover

2	slices bacon, diced
1	celery stalk, diced
1	garlic clove, smashed and chopped
4 tbsp	(60 ml) flour
4 cups	(1 L) light chicken stock, heated
2	large potatoes, peeled and diced
¼ tsp	(1 ml) fennel
1 tsp	(5 ml) chopped parsley
1	bay leaf
½ tsp	(2 ml) thyme
2	perch filets, cubed
1	red pepper, diced
	salt and pepper

Place bacon, celery and garlic in casserole. Cover and microwave 5 minutes at MEDIUM-HIGH.

Mix in flour, pour in chicken stock and mix again. Add potatoes, fennel, parsley, bay leaf and thyme. Cover and microwave 20 minutes at MEDIUM-HIGH; stir once during this time.

Mix in fish and red pepper; correct seasoning. Microwave 6 minutes at MEDIUM uncovered.

Serve hot.

Chicken Casserole

(serves 4)

1 SERVING	361 CALORIES	22g CARBOHYDRATE
31g PROTEIN	16g FAT	1.0g FIBER

Setting: HIGH
Cooking Time: 16 minutes
Utensil: 12 cups (2.8 L) casserole with cover

4 tbsp	(60 ml) butter
2	potatoes, peeled and cubed
2	carrots, pared and cubed
2	celery stalks, pared and cubed
1 tbsp	(15 ml) chopped fresh parsley
2	chicken breasts, skinned, halved and boned
¼ tsp	(1 ml) anise
3 tbsp	(45 ml) flour
1½ cups	(375 ml) hot chicken stock
1 cup	(250 ml) cooked pearl onions
	salt and pepper

Place butter, potatoes, carrots, celery and parsley in casserole. Cover and microwave 8 minutes.

Add chicken breasts and anise; season generously.

Mix in flour until well incorporated. Pour in chicken stock, cover and microwave 6 minutes.

Stir in onions and microwave 2 minutes uncovered.

Place butter, potatoes, carrots, celery and parsley in casserole. Cover and microwave 8 minutes.

Check if vegetables are cooked by piercing with knife.

Add chicken breasts and anise; season generously.

Mix in flour until well incorporated.

Chicken and Shrimp Casserole

(serves 4)

1 SERVING	644 CALORIES	35g CARBOHYDRATE
84g PROTEIN	13g FAT	1.0g FIBER

Setting: MEDIUM-HIGH

Cooking Time: 10 minutes

Utensil: 12 cups (2.8 L) casserole with cover

2 tbsp	(30 ml) butter
1 tbsp	(15 ml) chopped shallot
1 lb	(500 g) mushrooms, diced
24	large shrimp, shelled and deveined
2	chicken breasts, skinned, halved, boned, meat cut in 1 in (2.5 cm) chunks
2 cups	(500 ml) cooked elbow macaroni
1 cup	(250 ml) grated mozzarella cheese
½ cup	(125 ml) tomato sauce, heated
1 cup	(250 ml) brown sauce, heated
	salt and pepper

Place butter, shallot, mushrooms, shrimp and chicken in casserole. Cover and microwave 5 minutes.

Season well and mix. Add remaining ingredients and finish microwaving 5 minutes covered.

Serve with green salad.

Chicken and Melon Casserole

(serves 4)

1 SERVING	334 CALORIES	14g CARBOHYDRATE
30g PROTEIN	13g FAT	1.0g FIBER

Setting: HIGH

Cooking Time: 13 minutes

Utensil: 12 cups (2.8 L) casserole with cover

3 tbsp	(45 ml) butter
2	chicken breasts, skinned, halved, boned, and cut in large pieces
1 tbsp	(15 ml) chopped parsley
1 tsp	(5 ml) tarragon
1	celery stalk, sliced
20	mushrooms, halved
3 tbsp	(45 ml) flour
1¼ cups	(300 ml) beer
1	cantaloupe melon, cut in half
	salt and pepper

Place butter and chicken in casserole. Add parsley, tarragon, celery, salt and pepper. Cover and microwave 6 minutes.

Add mushrooms and mix in flour; pour in beer. Microwave 6 minutes uncovered.

Using melon-ball cutter, scoop out melon flesh and add to casserole. Mix very well and finish microwaving 1 minute uncovered.

Chicken Chili

(serves 4)

1 SERVING	387 CALORIES	37g CARBOHYDRATE
31g PROTEIN	13g FAT	2.0g FIBER

Setting: HIGH

Cooking Time: 95 minutes

Utensil: 12 cups (2.8 L) casserole with cover

1 tbsp	(15 ml) butter
1	onion, chopped
2	celery stalks, chopped
1	small leek, washed and chopped
1½ cups	(375 ml) diced raw chicken, dark meat preferably
3 cups	(750 ml) white beans, soaked in water overnight
¼ tsp	(1 ml) crushed chillies
½ tsp	(2 ml) oregano
½ tsp	(2 ml) cumin
½ tsp	(2 ml) allspice
2	hot banana peppers
	hot chicken stock
	salt and pepper
	grated mozzarella cheese

Place butter, onion, celery, leek, salt and pepper in casserole. Cover and microwave 5 minutes.

Mix well and add raw chicken, beans (with liquid), seasonings and banana peppers. Pour in enough hot chicken stock to cover by 2 in (5 cm). Cover casserole and microwave 75 minutes. Stir at least 2 or 3 times.

Note: At some point during this cooking time the banana peppers must be removed. The exact time will depend on how spicy you desire the chili — leaving them in 15 minutes will produce a medium-hot flavor.

Also, if at any time the chicken stock reduces considerably, add more.

Stir in mozzarella cheese to taste and correct seasoning. Cover and finish microwaving beans 15 minutes.

Meat and Potato Casserole

(serves 4)

1 SERVING	473 CALORIES	33g CARBOHYDRATE
61g PROTEIN	11g FAT	2.0g FIBER

Setting: HIGH

Cooking Time: 25 minutes

Utensil: 12 cups (2.8 L) casserole with cover

1 tbsp	(15 ml) butter
½	red onion, finely chopped
1½ lb	(750 g) lean ground beef
¼ tsp	(1 ml) chili powder
¼ tsp	(1 ml) allspice
½ tsp	(2 ml) thyme
3	potatoes, peeled and thinly sliced
¼ tsp	(1 ml) paprika
28 oz	(796 ml) can tomatoes, drained and chopped
1 cup	(250 ml) tomato sauce, heated
	salt and pepper
	chopped parsley to taste

Place butter, onion and meat in casserole. Season well with chili powder, allspice and thyme. Cover and microwave 6 minutes.

Mix well and cover with ½ of sliced potatoes; sprinkle with paprika.

Add tomatoes, tomato sauce and chopped parsley. Cover with remaining potatoes and season well.

Cover and microwave 12 minutes.

Mix well and continue microwaving 7 minutes covered.

Place butter, onion and meat in casserole. Season well with chili powder, allspice and thyme. Cover and microwave 6 minutes.

3 Add tomatoes, tomato sauce and parsley.

Mix well and cover with ½ of sliced potatoes; sprinkle with paprika.

4 Cover with remaining potatoes and season well. Cover and microwave 12 minutes. Stir and finish microwaving 7 minutes.

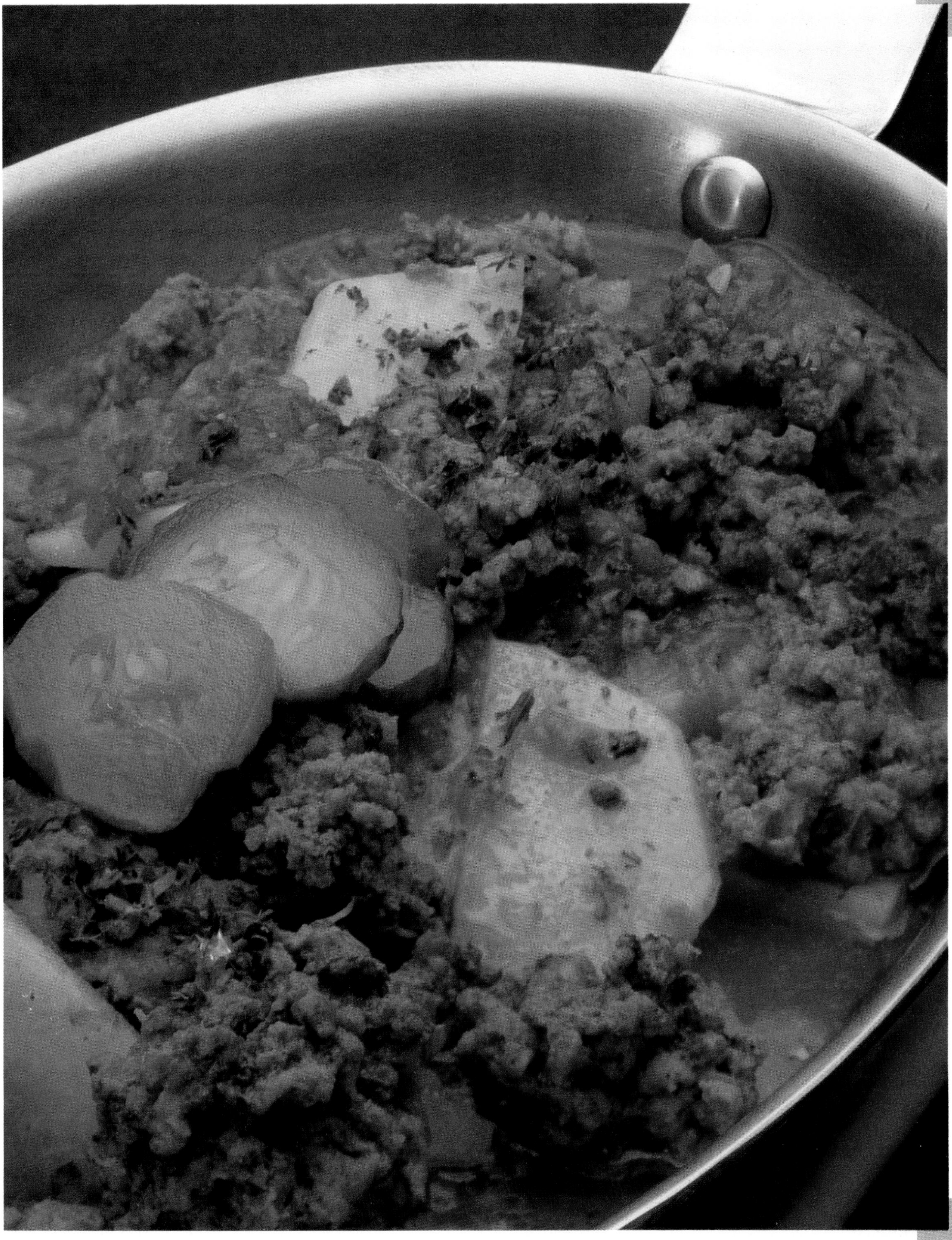

Ground Veal Casserole

(serves 4)

1 SERVING	498 CALORIES	15g CARBOHYDRATE
55g PROTEIN	24g FAT	2.0g FIBER

Setting: HIGH

Cooking Time: 10 minutes

Utensil: 12 cups (2.8 L) casserole with cover

2 tbsp	(30 ml) butter
1	medium onion, chopped
1	green pepper, diced
1	yellow pepper, diced
1 tsp	(5 ml) oregano
1½ lb	(750 g) lean ground veal
28 oz	(796 ml) can tomatoes, chopped with juice
2 tbsp	(30 ml) tomato paste
1 cup	(250 ml) diced cheddar cheese
	salt and pepper

Place butter, onion, peppers and oregano in casserole. Cover and microwave 3 minutes.

Add veal, mix and season. Continue microwaving 3 minutes covered.

Add remaining ingredients and mix well. Correct seasoning and microwave 4 minutes covered.

Serve with fresh bread.

Meaty Tomato Casserole

(serves 4)

1 SERVING	446 CALORIES	13g CARBOHYDRATE
60g PROTEIN	17g FAT	1.0g FIBER

Setting: HIGH

Cooking Time: 10 minutes

Utensil: 12 cups (2.8 L) casserole with cover

2 tbsp	(30 ml) butter
1	small onion, finely chopped
2	garlic cloves, smashed and chopped
½ lb	(250 g) mushrooms, diced
1 tbsp	(15 ml) chopped chives
½ tsp	(2 ml) chili powder
1½ lb	(750 g) lean ground beef
1½ cups	(375 ml) tomato sauce, heated
¼ cup	(50 ml) sour cream
	salt and pepper

Place butter, onion, garlic, mushrooms, chives and chili powder in casserole. Cover and microwave 4 minutes.

Season well and mix in ground beef; cover and continue microwaving 3 minutes.

Stir and pour in tomato sauce; microwave 3 minutes covered.

Remove from microwave, mix in sour cream and serve over noodles.

Leftover Casserole

(serves 4)

1 SERVING	681 CALORIES	50g CARBOHYDRATE
63g PROTEIN	24g FAT	1.0g FIBER

Setting: HIGH

Cooking Time: 7 minutes

Utensil: 12 cups (2.8 L) casserole with cover

1 lb	(500 g) leftover cooked ham, in strips
½	onion, thinly sliced
2 tbsp	(30 ml) garlic butter
2	garlic cloves, smashed and chopped
1 tbsp	(15 ml) chopped parsley
28 oz	(796 ml) can tomatoes, chopped, with ½ of juice
3 cups	(750 ml) leftover cooked macaroni
½	green pepper, thinly sliced
1 tbsp	(15 ml) tomato paste
1 cup	(250 ml) grated cheddar or other leftover cheese
	salt and pepper

Place ham, onion, garlic butter, garlic, parsley, salt and pepper in casserole. Cover and microwave 3 minutes.

Mix in tomatoes, macaroni and green pepper; season generously.

Add tomato paste and cheese; stir well. Cover and microwave 4 minutes.

Lima Bean Dinner

(serves 4)

1 SERVING	261 CALORIES	42g CARBOHYDRATE
15g PROTEIN	8g FAT	2.0g FIBER

Setting: HIGH

Cooking Time: 56½ minutes

Utensil: 12 cups (2.8 L) casserole with cover

1 tbsp	(15 ml) butter
1	medium onion, chopped
½ tsp	(2 ml) marjoram
½ tsp	(2 ml) chervil
4	slices bacon, diced
3	celery stalks, diced
14 oz	(400 g) dried lima beans, soaked in water overnight
2 tbsp	(30 ml) brown sugar
2 tbsp	(30 ml) molasses
1 tsp	(5 ml) dry mustard
1 tbsp	(15 ml) cornstarch
2 tbsp	(30 ml) cold water
	salt and pepper
	dash paprika
	hot chicken stock

Microwave butter ½ minute in casserole uncovered.

Add onion, marjoram and chervil. Cover and microwave 2 minutes.

Stir in bacon and microwave 4 minutes uncovered. Mix well; microwave another 3 minutes.

Spread celery over bacon. Cover with beans (including liquid). Sprinkle in brown sugar and molasses.

Mix in mustard and season with salt, pepper and paprika; mix again.

Pour in enough hot chicken stock to cover. Cover casserole and microwave 30 minutes.

Mix well; continue microwaving 17 minutes covered.

Mix cornstarch with water; stir into bean mixture, let stand ½ minute and serve.

Microwave onion, marjoram and chervil for 2 minutes covered.

Microwave bacon a total of 7 minutes but be sure to stir about halfway through.

Add celery, beans, brown sugar and molasses.

Mix in mustard, salt, pepper and paprika. Pour in enough chicken stock to cover. Microwave a total of 47 minutes covered, stirring once.

Watercress Rice

(serves 4)

1 SERVING	124 CALORIES	18g CARBOHYDRATE
4g PROTEIN	5g FAT	trace FIBER

Setting: HIGH

Cooking Time: 20½ minutes

Utensil: 12 cups (2.8 L) casserole with cover

1 tbsp	(15 ml) butter
2	green onions, chopped
½	medium white onion, chopped
1 cup	(250 ml) long grain rice, rinsed
2 cups	(500 ml) hot chicken stock
3 tbsp	(45 ml) finely chopped watercress
1 tbsp	(15 ml) chopped parsley
1 tbsp	(15 ml) chopped chives
	salt, pepper, paprika
	pinch tarragon
	butter to taste

Microwave butter ½ minute in casserole uncovered.

Add both onions; cover and microwave 2 minutes.

Stir in rice, salt, pepper and paprika. Pour in chicken stock and mix again. Cover and microwave 18 minutes, mixing halfway through.

Stir in remaining ingredients and serve.

After onions have microwaved 2 minutes, stir in rice, salt, pepper and paprika.

Pour in chicken stock and mix again. Cover and microwave 18 minutes.

Cooked rice should be moist and fluffy.

Stir in remaining ingredients and serve.

Vegetable Pasta Casserole

(serves 4)

1 SERVING	407 CALORIES	56g CARBOHYDRATE
17g PROTEIN	14g FAT	2.0g FIBER

Setting: HIGH

Cooking Time: 14 minutes

Utensil: 12 cups (2.8 L) casserole with cover

1 tbsp	(15 ml) butter
½	yellow pepper, diced large
½	red pepper, diced large
½	green pepper, diced large
1	very small eggplant, diced
3 tbsp	(45 ml) flour
1½ cups	(375 ml) hot milk
2	celery stalks, sliced
½	cucumber, peeled, seeded and sliced
8	lichees
3 cups	(750 ml) cooked medium conch shells
1 cup	(250 ml) grated mozzarella cheese
¼ tsp	(1 ml) nutmeg
¼ tsp	(1 ml) celery salt
1 cup	(250 ml) tomato sauce, heated
	salt and pepper

Place butter, peppers, eggplant, salt and pepper in casserole. Cover and microwave 4 minutes.

Mix in flour, pour in hot milk and stir well.

Mix in remaining ingredients and correct seasoning. Cover and microwave 10 minutes.

If desired decorate servings with sliced tomatoes.

Macaroni and Eggs

(serves 4)

1 SERVING	818 CALORIES	59g CARBOHYDRATE
54g PROTEIN	41g FAT	1.0g FIBER

Setting: HIGH and MEDIUM-HIGH

Cooking Time: 10 minutes

Utensil: 12 cups (2.8 L) casserole with cover

2 tbsp	(30 ml) butter
⅓ lb	(150 g) mushrooms, diced
1 tsp	(5 ml) chopped parsley
1	shallot, chopped
4 cups	(1 L) leftover cooked macaroni
5	hard-boiled eggs, sliced
1½ cups	(375 ml) diced cooked ham
1 cup	(250 ml) grated Gruyère cheese
2½ cups	(625 ml) hot light white sauce
	salt and pepper
	few drops lemon juice

Place butter, mushrooms, parsley, shallot, salt, pepper and lemon juice in casserole. Cover and microwave 4 minutes at HIGH.

Drain mushrooms, reserving liquid, and set aside.

Spread ½ of macaroni in bottom of casserole. Top with all sliced eggs.

Cover with ham and drained mushrooms; top with ½ of cheese. Add remaining macaroni.

Mix reserved cooking liquid from mushrooms with white sauce. Pour this over macaroni and finish with grated cheese.

Cover casserole and microwave 6 minutes at MEDIUM-HIGH.

Scallop Salad

(serves 4)

1 SERVING	395 CALORIES	8g CARBOHYDRATE
20g PROTEIN	31g FAT	1.0g FIBER

Setting: MEDIUM-HIGH

Cooking Time: 3 minutes

Utensil: 12 cups (2.8 L) casserole with cover

1 lb	(500 g) sea scallops
2 tbsp	(30 ml) lime juice
1 tbsp	(15 ml) butter
¼ tsp	(1 ml) anise seed
¼ cup	(50 ml) dry white wine
1	celery stalk, sliced
½ cup	(125 ml) radishes, thinly sliced
2	green onions, chopped
1 tbsp	(15 ml) Dijon mustard
3 tbsp	(45 ml) raspberry wine vinegar
½ cup	(125 ml) olive oil
	salt and fresh ground pepper
	lemon juice
	few drops Tabasco sauce

Place scallops, lime juice, butter, anise seed, wine and pepper in casserole. Cover and microwave 3 minutes.

Drain scallops and transfer to bowl. Mix in celery, radishes and onions; set aside.

In second bowl, whisk mustard, vinegar, salt and pepper together.

Incorporate oil in thin stream while whisking constantly. Correct seasoning, add lemon juice and Tabasco sauce and pour vinaigrette over salad to taste.

Toss and serve.

Haddock Casserole

(serves 4)

1 SERVING	414 CALORIES	45g CARBOHYDRATE
25g PROTEIN	15g FAT	2.0g FIBER

Setting: HIGH

Cooking Time: 21 minutes

Utensil: 12 cups (2.8 L) casserole with cover

4 tbsp	(60 ml) butter
2	celery stalks, sliced thick
1	onion, in chunks
1	fennel bulb, cut in ½ and cubed
5 tbsp	(75 ml) flour
3 cups	(750 ml) hot chicken stock
10 oz	(300 g) haddock filets, cut in 1 in (2.5 cm) wide strips
8	small round potatoes, peeled and cooked*
1	sweet potato, peeled, cooked and cubed*
	salt and pepper

Place butter, celery, onion and fennel in casserole; season well. Cover and microwave 5 minutes.

Mix in flour. Cover and microwave 2 minutes.

Pour in chicken stock, mix and microwave 5 minutes uncovered. Stir well; continue microwaving 5 minutes uncovered.

Correct seasoning and add fish, potatoes and sweet potato. Microwave 4 minutes uncovered.

* The canned variety serves as an excellent substitute for fresh produce.

Place butter, celery, onion and fennel in casserole; season well. Cover and microwave 5 minutes.

Mix in flour. Cover and microwave 2 minutes.

Pour in chicken stock, mix and microwave 5 minutes uncovered. Stir well; continue microwaving 5 minutes uncovered.

Correct seasoning and add fish, potatoes and sweet potatoes. Microwave 4 minutes uncovered.

Boston Bluefish with Vegetables

(serves 4)

1 SERVING	169 CALORIES	8g CARBOHYDRATE
19g PROTEIN	6g FAT	1.0g FIBER

Setting: HIGH and MEDIUM-HIGH

Cooking Time: 12 minutes

Utensil: 12 cups (2.8 L) casserole with cover

1	leek, cut in 4 lengthwise, washed and chopped
1 tbsp	(15 ml) chopped parsley
1 tbsp	(15 ml) butter
¼ tsp	(1 ml) fennel
12 oz	(350 g) Boston Bluefish filets
8	lichees nuts
2	tomatoes, sliced
	salt and pepper

Place leek, parsley, butter and fennel in casserole. Cover and microwave 4 minutes at HIGH.

Lay filets in casserole; add lichees and tomato slices. Cover and microwave 5 minutes at MEDIUM-HIGH.

Turn filets over and correct seasoning. Cover and microwave 3 minutes at MEDIUM-HIGH.

Shrimp Bisque

(serves 4)

1 SERVING	315 CALORIES	13g CARBOHYDRATE
24g PROTEIN	20g FAT	trace FIBER

Setting: HIGH

Cooking Time: 25 minutes

Utensil: 12 cups (2.8 L) casserole with cover

4 tbsp	(60 ml) butter
1	carrot, pared and diced small
1	celery stalk, diced small
1	shallot, chopped
12	large shrimp, unpeeled
¼ tsp	(1 ml) fennel
1 tsp	(5 ml) chopped chives
5 tbsp	(75 ml) flour
4 cups	(1 L) hot fish stock
½ cup	(125 ml) hot light cream
	salt and pepper

Place butter, vegetables, shallot, shrimp, salt and pepper in casserole. Cover and microwave 8 minutes.

Remove shrimp from casserole and shell. Set shrimp and shells aside.

Add seasonings and flour to vegetables in casserole; mix well. Place shrimp shells and fish stock in casserole. Cover and microwave 15 minutes.

Pass mixture through sieve using pestle and pour back into casserole.

Chop shrimp and stir into soup. Add cream and season to taste. Microwave 2 minutes uncovered.

Grilled Rainbow Trout

(serves 2)

1 SERVING	370 CALORIES	1g CARBOHYDRATE
28g PROTEIN	27g FAT	--g FIBER

Setting: HIGH

Cooking Time: 5½ minutes

Utensil: 12 cups (2.8 L) casserole with cover

1 tbsp	(15 ml) butter
2	rainbow trout, gutted and cleaned
	lime juice
	salt and pepper
	melted butter
	toasted slivered almonds

Place butter in casserole and microwave ½ minute uncovered.

Season insides of trout with lime juice, salt and pepper. Place in casserole, cover and microwave 3 minutes.

Turn trout over; continue microwaving 2 minutes covered.

Serve with melted butter and garnish with slivered almonds.

Vermouth Scallops

(serves 4)

1 SERVING	336 CALORIES	14g CARBOHYDRATE
28g PROTEIN	17g FAT	1.0g FIBER

Setting: MEDIUM-HIGH and HIGH

Cooking Time: 11 minutes

Utensil: 12 cups (2.8 L) casserole with cover
4 individual microwave coquille dishes

1 lb	(500 g) fresh scallops
3 tbsp	(45 ml) butter
1 tbsp	(15 ml) chopped parsley
½ lb	(250 g) mushrooms, quartered
1 tbsp	(15 ml) lime juice

3 tbsp	(45 ml) dry vermouth
3 tbsp	(45 ml) flour
½ cup	(125 ml) hot milk
¼ tsp	(1 ml) fennel seed
1 cup	(250 ml) grated mozzarella cheese
	salt and pepper
	dash paprika
	few drops lemon juice

Place scallops, butter, parsley, mushrooms and lime juice in casserole.

Pour in vermouth, cover and microwave 3 minutes at MEDIUM-HIGH.

Mix in flour. Continue microwaving 3 minutes, covered, at MEDIUM-HIGH.

Remove scallops and set aside.

Add hot milk, fennel, salt, pepper and paprika to casserole; mix well and sprinkle in lemon juice to taste. Microwave 4 minutes at HIGH uncovered.

Replace scallops in casserole and mix well. Spoon mixture into coquille dishes and top with cheese; microwave 1 minute at HIGH uncovered.

Place scallops, butter, parsley, mushrooms and lime juice in casserole.

Mix in flour. Continue microwaving 3 minutes covered at MEDIUM-HIGH.

Pour in vermouth, cover and microwave 3 minutes at MEDIUM-HIGH.

Remove scallops and set aside.

Haddock Topped with Cheese

(serves 4)

1 SERVING	166 CALORIES	2g CARBOHYDRATE
21g PROTEIN	7g FAT	trace FIBER

Setting: MEDIUM-HIGH

Cooking Time: 8 minutes

Utensil: 12 cups (2.8 L) casserole with cover Microwave serving platter

12.3 oz	(350 g) package frozen haddock filets
1 tbsp	(15 ml) lime or lemon juice
3	green onions, chopped
1 tbsp	(15 ml) butter
¼ tsp	(1 ml) fennel seed
¼ tsp	(1 ml) tarragon
½ cup	(125 ml) grated mozzarella cheese
	salt and pepper
	paprika to taste

Grease casserole and add frozen fish, lime juice and onions.

Sprinkle in butter, fennel seed and tarragon; season well. Cover and microwave 5 minutes.

Turn filets over; cover and continue microwaving 2 minutes.

Transfer fish to serving platter, season with paprika and top with cheese. Finish microwaving 1 minute uncovered.

Serve with small salad and vegetables.

Use fish straight from the freezer.

 Turn filets over; cover and continue microwaving 2 minutes.

Place frozen fish, lime juice and onions in greased casserole. Add butter, fennel seed and tarragon; season well. Cover and microwave 5 minutes.

 Transfer fish to serving platter, season with paprika and top with cheese. Finish microwaving 1 minute uncovered.

Oyster Bake

(serves 4)

1 SERVING	390 CALORIES	10g CARBOHYDRATE
48g PROTEIN	16g FAT	trace FIBER

Setting: HIGH

Cooking Time: 13 minutes

Utensil: 8 cups (2 L) rectangular dish

2 tbsp	(30 ml) butter
4	large sole filets
1 tbsp	(15 ml) chopped shallot
1 tbsp	(15 ml) chopped parsley
24	shrimp, shelled and deveined
1 cup	(250 ml) halved mushrooms
1 cup	(250 ml) shucked oysters
½ cup	(125 ml) dry white wine
½ cup	(125 ml) hot light cream
	pinch fennel
	salt and pepper
	lemon juice

Place half of butter and all filets in rectangular dish. Season well and cover with pierced plastic wrap; microwave 3 minutes.

Turn filets over and continue microwaving 4 minutes covered.

Remove fish and transfer to serving platter; set aside.

Add remaining butter, shallot, parsley, shrimp and mushrooms to rectangular dish; cover with plastic wrap and microwave 4 minutes.

Season well with fennel, salt, pepper and lemon juice. Add oysters and wine; mix well. Cover and continue microwaving 2 minutes.

Stir in cream and correct seasoning.

Pour over fish and serve.

Scampi Parisienne

(serves 4)

1 SERVING	494 CALORIES	23g CARBOHYDRATE
66g PROTEIN	15g FAT	1.0g FIBER

Setting: HIGH

Cooking Time: 5½ minutes

Utensil: 12 cups (2.8 L) casserole with cover

4 tbsp	(60 ml) butter
32	scampi, shelled
2	garlic cloves, smashed and chopped
1 cup	(250 ml) water chestnuts
1 cup	(250 ml) cooked Parisienne potatoes
2	tomatoes, peeled and diced
1 tbsp	(15 ml) chopped parsley or chives
1 tsp	(5 ml) soya sauce
1 tsp	(5 ml) chopped pickled banana pepper
	salt and pepper

Place butter in casserole and microwave ½ minute uncovered.

Add scampi and garlic; season well. Cover and microwave 2 minutes.

Mix in remaining ingredients and correct seasoning. Finish microwaving 3 minutes covered.

Ocean Perch and Cabbage

(serves 4)

1 SERVING	228 CALORIES	11g CARBOHYDRATE
31g PROTEIN	6g FAT	1.0g FIBER

Setting: MEDIUM-HIGH

Cooking Time: 12 minutes

Utensil: 12 cups (2.8 L) casserole with cover

½	cabbage, thinly sliced, cooked
4 tbsp	(60 ml) grated Parmesan cheese
4	ocean perch filets
2 tsp	(10 ml) butter
½ tsp	(2 ml) fennel seeds
¼ tsp	(1 ml) anise
¼ tsp	(1 ml) paprika
14 oz	(398 ml) tomato sauce, heated
	salt and pepper

Lightly grease casserole. Add half of cabbage and top with half of cheese.

Add filets flat and dot with butter. Sprinkle in seasonings followed by remaining cheese and cabbage.

Season again with salt and pepper and pour in tomato sauce. Cover and microwave 12 minutes.

Serve with spaghetti squash.

Baked Apples

(serves 4)

1 SERVING	87 CALORIES	11g CARBOHYDRATE
trace PROTEIN	2g FAT	1.0g FIBER

Setting: HIGH

Cooking Time: 9 minutes

Utensil: 8 cups (2 L) casserole with cover

2	apples, hollowed
2 tsp	(10 ml) butter
½ tsp	(2 ml) cinnamon
	lemon juice

Using small knife score apples around middle to prevent skin from splitting during cooking.

Place apples in casserole and sprinkle remaining ingredients over. Cover and microwave 9 minutes.

When apples are cooked, cut each into half and serve as garnish with flounder filets.

Pineapple Flounder Filets

(serves 4)

1 SERVING	163 CALORIES	8g CARBOHYDRATE
15g PROTEIN	4g FAT	1.0g FIBER

Setting: HIGH and MEDIUM-HIGH

Cooking Time: 6 minutes

Utensil: 8 cups (2 L) rectangular dish

1 tbsp	(15 ml) butter
4	flounder filets
1 tbsp	(15 ml) chopped parsley
1	yellow pepper, thinly sliced
4	fresh pineapple rings
	salt and pepper
	dash paprika
	lemon juice

Arrange all ingredients in rectangular dish and cover with pierced plastic wrap; microwave 4 minutes at HIGH.

Turn filets over and continue microwaving 2 minutes at MEDIUM-HIGH, covered with plastic wrap.

Serve with baked apples.

Sweet, Sweet Potatoes

(serves 4)

1 SERVING	173 CALORIES	41g CARBOHYDRATE
2g PROTEIN	trace FAT	1.0g FIBER

Setting: HIGH

Cooking Time: 23 minutes

Utensil: Stoneware serving platter

2	large sweet potatoes
1 tbsp	(15 ml) brown sugar
1 tsp	(5 ml) cinnamon
¼ cup	(50 ml) orange juice
2 tbsp	(30 ml) molasses

Wrap each potato in plastic wrap, prick several times and place in microwave. Microwave 20 minutes depending on size, turning 3 to 4 times.

Remove and slice with skin about ½ in (1.2 cm) thick. Arrange pieces on stoneware plate and top with remaining ingredients. Microwave 1½ minutes uncovered.

Turn pieces over; continue microwaving another 1½ minutes uncovered.

Garlicky Sweet Potatoes

(serves 4)

1 SERVING	349 CALORIES	62g CARBOHYDRATE
12g PROTEIN	6g FAT	2.0g FIBER

Setting: HIGH

Cooking Time: 23 minutes

Utensil: None

4	large sweet potatoes
3	slices crisp bacon, chopped
2	garlic cloves, smashed and chopped
1 tbsp	(15 ml) chopped parsley
½ cup	(125 ml) cooked shrimp, chopped
4 tbsp	(60 ml) sour cream
	salt and pepper

Wrap each potato in plastic wrap; prick each several times with knife. Place in microwave for 8 minutes.

Turn potatoes over; continue microwaving 15 minutes. Remove and unwrap.

Mix remaining ingredients together; season to taste.

Slit potatoes open and top with mixture. Serve.

Endive Ham Bake

(serves 4)

1 SERVING	350 CALORIES	11g CARBOHYDRATE
26g PROTEIN	11g FAT	1.0g FIBER

Setting: HIGH

Cooking Time: 23 minutes

Utensil: 12 cups (2.8 L) casserole with cover

4	endives
2 tbsp	(30 ml) butter
1 tbsp	(15 ml) lemon juice
1 tbsp	(15 ml) chopped parsley
½ tsp	(2 ml) tarragon
½ cup	(125 ml) light chicken stock
4	large slices Black Forest ham, fat removed
1½ cups	(375 ml) light white sauce, heated
1 cup	(250 ml) grated mozzarella cheese
	salt and pepper

Slit endives in four lengthwise without cutting through the base. Wash well in cold water and shake off excess.

Place endives, butter, lemon juice, parsley, tarragon and chicken stock in casserole; season well. Cover and microwave 20 minutes; turn endives over halfway through.

Remove endives from casserole and discard ½ of cooking liquid.

Wrap endives in slices of ham and secure with toothpicks; replace in casserole. Pour in white sauce, season and top with cheese. Microwave 3 minutes uncovered.

Quick Vegetable Mix

(serves 4)

1 SERVING	182 CALORIES	22g CARBOHYDRATE
10g PROTEIN	8g FAT	3.0g FIBER

Setting: HIGH

Cooking Time: 24 minutes

Utensil: 12 cups (2.8 L) casserole with cover

1 tbsp	(15 ml) butter
1	medium onion, chopped
1	garlic clove, smashed and chopped
3	slices bacon, diced
1 lb	(500 g) fresh okra, ends snipped
4	tomatoes, peeled, seeded and chopped
1	green pepper, diced
1 tsp	(5 ml) chopped jalapeno pepper
1 tbsp	(15 ml) curry powder
1 tbsp	(15 ml) cumin powder
1 tsp	(5 ml) olive oil
	salt and pepper

Microwave butter 1 minute in casserole uncovered.

Add onion, garlic and bacon; cover and microwave 6 minutes.

Add okra and mix; microwave 2 minutes covered.

Stir in tomatoes, green pepper, jalapeno, seasonings and oil; cover and microwave 7 minutes.

Mix well; finish microwaving 8 minutes covered.

Sprinkle with cheese if desired.

Trim ends from fresh okra.

An easy way to peel fresh tomatoes is to blanch them in boiling water for 2 to 3 minutes. The skin should separate quite easily from the flesh.

Microwave onion, garlic and bacon 6 minutes covered. Then, add okra and microwave 2 minutes.

Stir in tomatoes, green pepper, jalapeno, seasonings and oil; cover and microwave 7 minutes.

434

Spaghetti Squash

(serves 4)

1 SERVING	57 CALORIES	2g CARBOHYDRATE
1g PROTEIN	6g FAT	trace FIBER

Setting: HIGH
Cooking Time: 25 minutes
Utensil: none

1	spaghetti squash
2 tbsp	(30 ml) butter
	salt and pepper
	butter to taste

Cut squash in half lengthwise; remove all seeds and hair-like fibers.

Divide butter between halves and season very generously. Wrap loosely in pierced plastic wrap and place in microwave.

Microwave 25 minutes.

Remove from oven, scoop out squash and place in bowl. Add more butter to taste and serve as garnish with ocean perch.

Creamy Cauliflower

(serves 4)

1 SERVING	213 CALORIES	17g CARBOHYDRATE
5g PROTEIN	11g FAT	2.0g FIBER

Setting: HIGH
Cooking Time: 9 minutes
Utensil: 12 cups (2.8 L) casserole with cover

1 tbsp	(15 ml) butter
1	small cauliflower, in flowerets
2	large potatoes, peeled, cooked and diced
1	cucumber, peeled, seeded and diced
2	garlic cloves, smashed and chopped
1 tbsp	(15 ml) chopped parsley
2 tbsp	(30 ml) chopped pimento
1 cup	(250 ml) hot light cream
	salt and pepper
	few drops lemon juice

Place butter and cauliflower in casserole; season with salt, pepper and lemon juice. Cover and microwave 5 minutes.

Add potatoes, cucumber, garlic, parsley and pimento; mix well. Continue microwaving 2 minutes covered.

Mix again and stir in cream; finish microwaving 2 minutes uncovered.

Layered Asparagus Dish

(serves 4)

1 SERVING	174 CALORIES	14g CARBOHYDRATE
16g PROTEIN	15g FAT	1.0g FIBER

Setting: HIGH
Cooking Time: 15 minutes
Utensil: 12 cups (2.8 L) casserole with cover

1 lb	(500 g) fresh asparagus, pared
½ cup	(125 ml) water
1 cup	(250 ml) tomato sauce, heated
1 cup	(250 ml) white sauce, heated
¼ tsp	(1 ml) nutmeg
1 cup	(250 ml) grated Gruyère cheese
	salt and pepper

Place asparagus and water in casserole. Season with salt, cover and microwave 6 minutes.

Using tongs bring asparagus at bottom of casserole towards top; replace cover and microwave 6 more minutes. (If asparagus are very large continue microwaving an extra minute.)

Discard liquid from casserole and remove half of asparagus.

Add half of each: tomato sauce, white sauce, nutmeg and cheese.

Cover with remaining asparagus and repeat above layers. Cover and microwave 3 minutes.

Broccoli and Asparagus

(serves 4)

1 SERVING	79 CALORIES	6g CARBOHYDRATE
3g PROTEIN	5g FAT	1.0g FIBER

Setting: HIGH

Cooking Time: 9 minutes

Utensil: 12 cups (2.8 L) casserole with cover

1	bunch fresh asparagus, tips only
1 tbsp	(15 ml) butter
1	head broccoli, in flowerets
1 tbsp	(15 ml) chopped fresh ginger
3 tbsp	(45 ml) toasted slivered almonds
	salt and pepper

Slice asparagus tips in half lengthwise. Cut each half into 2 pieces. Place in casserole with butter, salt and pepper. Cover and microwave 4 minutes.

Add broccoli, ginger and almonds; mix well. Cover and microwave 5 minutes.

Serve.

Almond Cake

(serves 10-12)

1 SERVING	298 CALORIES	35g CARBOHYDRATE
5g PROTEIN	16g FAT	trace FIBER

Setting: MEDIUM

Cooking Time: 19 minutes

Utensil: 12 cups (3 L) bundt mold

1⅔ cups	(400 ml) all-purpose flour
1 cup	(250 ml) granulated sugar
¼ cup	(50 ml) powdered almonds
1 tsp	(5 ml) baking soda
¼ tsp	(1 ml) salt
¼ tsp	(1 ml) nutmeg
1 cup	(250 ml) milk

½ cup	(125 ml) vegetable oil
1	egg
1 tsp	(5 ml) vanilla
¼ cup	(50 ml) slivered almonds
½ cup	(125 ml) crushed pineapple
2	egg whites, beaten stiff

Lightly oil bundt mold and set aside.

Sift flour, sugar, powdered almonds, baking soda, salt and nutmeg into bowl of mixer. Using whisk attachment, mix at low speed for 2 minutes.

Add milk, oil, whole egg and vanilla; beat 2 minutes or until well incorporated.

Add almonds and pineapple; blend 2 minutes at low speed.

Using spatula fold in stiff egg whites until thoroughly incorporated.

Pour batter into mold and rap bottom on counter to settle mixture. Microwave 19 minutes, rotating 4 times.

Let cake stand in mold to cool. When ready to serve, ice with your favorite frosting.

Sift flour, sugar, powdered almonds, baking soda, salt and nutmeg into bowl of mixer.

Beat milk, oil, egg and vanilla for 2 minutes or until well incorporated.

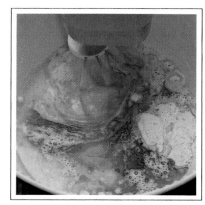

Using whisk attachment, mix at low speed for 2 minutes.

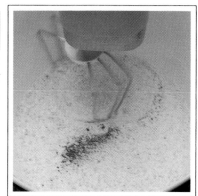

Add almonds and pineapple; blend 2 minutes at low speed.

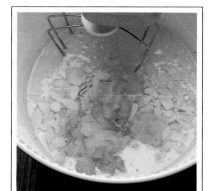

Almond Brownies

(serves 8)

1 SERVING	445 CALORIES	42g CARBOHYDRATE
8g PROTEIN	28g FAT	trace FIBER

Setting: HIGH
Cooking Time: 5½ minutes
Utensil: 8 cups (2 L) square plastic mold

½ cup	(125 ml) butter
¾ cup	(175 ml) granulated sugar
¼ cup	(50 ml) brown sugar
3	beaten eggs
1 tbsp	(15 ml) rum
4 tbsp	(60 ml) heavy cream
1 cup	(250 ml) sifted all-purpose flour
½ cup	(125 ml) cocoa
1 tsp	(5 ml) baking powder
1	egg white, beaten stiff
½ cup	(125 ml) slivered almonds

Grease plastic mold and set aside.

Place butter in glass bowl and microwave 1 minute uncovered or until melted.

Pour butter in large mixing bowl. Incorporate both sugars using electric hand beater.

Add beaten whole eggs, rum and cream; continue beating until well combined.

Sift dry ingredients into bowl; incorporate very well.

Using spatula fold in egg white and almonds. Pour batter into plastic mold and rap bottom on counter to settle mixture.

Microwave 4½ minutes uncovered. Rotate twice.

Remove from microwave and set aside to cool before serving.

Crêpes Stuffed with Bananas

(serves 4)

1 SERVING	313 CALORIES	53g CARBOHYDRATE
6g PROTEIN	13g FAT	1.0g FIBER

Setting: MEDIUM-HIGH
Cooking Time: 4 minutes
Utensil: 8 cups (2 L) casserole

1 tbsp	(15 ml) butter
1 tbsp	(15 ml) maple syrup
4	bananas, sliced 1 in (2.5 cm) thick
2 tbsp	(30 ml) Caribbean Cream liqueur
3	egg whites
2 tbsp	(30 ml) granulated sugar
4	crêpes
	juice 1½ oranges

Place butter and maple syrup in casserole; microwave 1 minute uncovered.

Add bananas, liqueur and orange juice; mix and microwave 3 minutes uncovered.

Meanwhile, beat egg whites until stiff. Add sugar slowly and continue beating 1 minute.

Spread banana mixture on crêpes, roll and place on platter. Top with dollops of meringue and brown in conventional oven set at broil.

Chocolate Cake

(serves 10-12)

1 SERVING	396 CALORIES	38g CARBOHYDRATE
6g PROTEIN	24g FAT	trace FIBER

Setting: MEDIUM

Cooking Time: 29 minutes

Utensil: 12 cups (3 L) bundt mold

1 cup	(250 ml) granulated sugar
1½ cups	(375 ml) all-purpose flour
½ cup	(125 ml) cocoa
1½ tbsp	(25 ml) baking powder
¼ tsp	(1 ml) salt
¼ cup	(50 ml) powdered almonds
1 cup	(250 ml) soft unsalted butter
1 cup	(250 ml) milk
2 tbsp	(30 ml) Tia Maria
2	egg yolks
2	whole eggs
3	egg whites, beaten stiff
	oil

Lightly oil bundt mold and set aside.

Sift granulated sugar, flour, cocoa, baking powder, salt and powdered almonds into bowl of mixer. Using dough hook, mix at low speed for 2 minutes.

Add butter to bowl; continue mixing at medium speed until well incorporated. If necessary use spatula occasionally to prevent mixture from riding up sides.

Reduce mixer speed to low. Add milk and Tia Maria; blend for 1 minute.

Replace dough hook with whisk attachment. Increase speed to medium and add yolks and whole eggs; beat about 4 to 5 minutes.

Using spatula, fold in stiff egg whites until thoroughly incorporated.

Pour batter into mold and rap bottom on counter to settle mixture. Microwave 29 minutes, rotating 4 times.

Let cake stand in mold to cool. When ready to serve, ice with your favorite frosting.

Tasty Strawberry Sauce

1 RECIPE	800 CALORIES	187g CARBOHYDRATE
7g PROTEIN	.5g FAT	2.5g FIBER

Setting: HIGH

Cooking Time: 7 minutes

Utensil: 8 cups (2 L) casserole

15 oz	(425 g) package frozen strawberries
4 tbsp	(60 ml) black currant jelly
2 tbsp	(30 ml) orange liqueur
2 tbsp	(30 ml) cornstarch
4 tbsp	(60 ml) cold water

Thaw strawberries according to directions on package.

Place strawberries, jelly and liqueur in casserole. Microwave 4 minutes uncovered.

Mix cornstarch with water; stir into sauce and continue microwaving 3 minutes.

Cool and pour over ice cream or drizzle over sponge cake.

Rhubarb Sauce

1 RECIPE	1661 CALORIES	344g CARBOHYDRATE
4g PROTEIN	27g FAT	trace FIBER

Setting: HIGH

Cooking Time: 31 minutes

Utensil: 12 cups (2.8 L) casserole with cover

4 cups	(1 L) frozen rhubarb
3 tbsp	(45 ml) light rum
1 cup	(250 ml) granulated sugar
½ cup	(125 ml) brown sugar
¼ cup	(50 ml) freshly squeezed orange juice
2 tbsp	(30 ml) butter
2 tbsp	(30 ml) cornstarch
5 tbsp	(75 ml) cold water
	chopped rind 1 lemon
	chopped rind 1 orange

Place rhubarb in casserole and pour in rum.

Add both sugars, orange juice, butter and chopped rinds.

Mix slightly and cover; microwave 30 minutes.

Mix rhubarb sauce well. Mix cornstarch with water; stir into sauce. Microwave 1 minute uncovered.

Serve with cake or over ice cream.

Place rhubarb in casserole and pour in rum.

It is not necessary to defrost the rhubarb before microwaving.

Add both sugars.

Add orange juice, butter and chopped rinds.

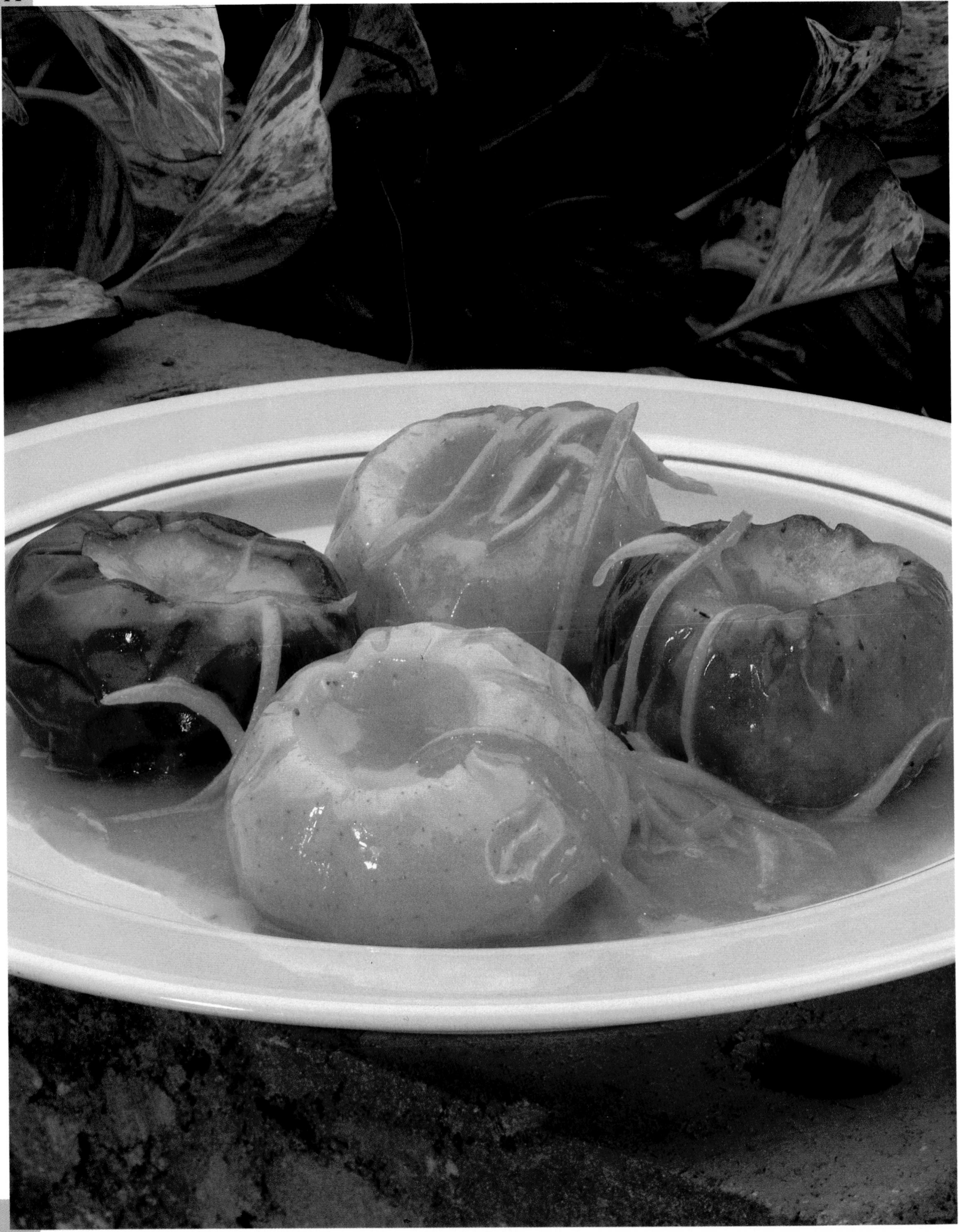

Baked Apples

(serves 4)

1 SERVING	298 CALORIES	39g CARBOHYDRATE
1g PROTEIN	10g FAT	1.0g FIBER

Setting: HIGH

Cooking Time: 12 minutes

Utensil: 8 cups (2 L) casserole with cover

4	large baking apples
3 tbsp	(45 ml) brown sugar
2 tbsp	(30 ml) butter
2 tbsp	(30 ml) heavy cream
¼ tsp	(1 ml) nutmeg
½ cup	(125 ml) light rum
1 tbsp	(15 ml) cornstarch
2 tbsp	(30 ml) cold water
	rind 1 orange in julienne

Core apples and using small knife score around middle. This will prevent skin from cracking during cooking.

Cut away a bit of apple flesh at one end to make hole wider for filling. Place apples in casserole.

Mix brown sugar with butter in small bowl. Stir in cream and nutmeg.

Pour rum into bottom of casserole and fill apple cavities with cream mixture.

Cover and microwave 11 minutes. Remove apples from casserole and set aside.

Add orange rind to juices in casserole. Mix cornstarch with water; stir into sauce to thicken. Microwave 1 minute uncovered.

Pour sauce over apples and serve.

Core apples. **1**

Using small knife **2** score apples around middle to prevent skin from cracking during cooking.

3 Cut away a bit of apple flesh at one end to make hole wider for filling. Place apples in casserole and pour in rum.

4 Fill apple cavities with cream mixture.

Dessert Drink

(serves 4)

1 SERVING	248 CALORIES	19g CARBOHYDRATE
1g PROTEIN	17g FAT	trace FIBER

Setting: HIGH

Cooking Time: 2 minutes

Utensil: 12 cups (2.8 L) casserole

4	lemon slices
3	cinnamon sticks
1 tbsp	(15 ml) grated orange rind
2	cloves
3 tbsp	(45 ml) dark rum
3 tbsp	(45 ml) brown sugar
1 tbsp	(15 ml) honey
4 cups	(1 L) strong black coffee, hot
¾ cup	(175 ml) heavy cream, whipped
	granulated sugar
	dash cinnamon

Coat rims of 4 tall-stemmed glasses with lemon. Dip in granulated sugar and set aside.

Place remaining ingredients, except cream and cinnamon, in casserole. Microwave 2 minutes uncovered.

Pour into glasses and top with dollops of whipped cream. Sprinkle with dash of cinnamon and serve immediately.

Creamy Rice Pudding

(serves 4-6)

1 SERVING	345 CALORIES	53g CARBOHYDRATE
9g PROTEIN	7g FAT	1.0g FIBER

Setting: MEDIUM-HIGH and LOW

Cooking Time: 39 minutes

Utensil: 12 cups (2.8 L) casserole with cover

1 cup	(250 ml) long grain rice, rinsed
½ cup	(125 ml) brown sugar
3½ cups	(875 ml) hot milk
1 tbsp	(15 ml) grated lemon rind
¼ cup	(50 ml) sultana raisins
½ cup	(125 ml) light cream
2 tbsp	(30 ml) mixed candied fruit
1 tbsp	(15 ml) cinnamon
1	beaten egg

Place rice in casserole and sprinkle in sugar. Mix in milk and lemon rind. Cover and microwave 18 minutes at MEDIUM-HIGH, stirring twice.

Add raisins, cream, fruit and cinnamon; incorporate well. Continue microwaving 19 minutes covered, stirring occasionally.

Add egg, mix well and finish microwaving 2 minutes at LOW uncovered.

Serve plain or drizzled with maple syrup.

Creamy Cheesecake

(serves 8-10)

1 SERVING	403 CALORIES	28g CARBOHYDRATE
7g PROTEIN	30g FAT	--g FIBER

Setting: HIGH

Cooking Time: 8¾ minutes

Utensil: 6 cups (1.5 L) glass pie plate

¾ cup	(175 ml) crushed chocolate wafers
¼ cup	(50 ml) fine granulated sugar
¼ cup	(50 ml) soft butter
2	8 oz (227 g) packages cream cheese, soft
½ cup	(125 ml) fine granulated sugar
3 tbsp	(45 ml) orange liqueur
1 tbsp	(15 ml) grated lemon rind
1 tbsp	(15 ml) grated orange rind
1 tbsp	(15 ml) cornstarch
3	large eggs
½ cup	(125 ml) heavy cream, whipped
1	egg white, beaten stiff

First, prepare crust by combining wafers, ¼ cup (50 ml) sugar and butter until thoroughly blended. Press into pie plate and microwave ¾ minute uncovered. Set aside to cool while filling is being prepared.

Place cheese and second measure of sugar in bowl of mixer; blend until smooth.

Add liqueur, rinds and cornstarch; mix to incorporate.

Add eggs one at a time, mixing well between additions.

Fold in whipped cream and egg white with spatula.

Pour filling into cooled crust and smooth with spatula. Microwave 8 minutes uncovered. Rotate every 2 minutes.

Remove from microwave and set aside to cool. Refrigerate 2 hours before serving.